ALL THE WORLD

Universalism, Particularism and the High Holy Days

Other Jewish Lights Books by
Rabbi Lawrence A. Hoffman, PhD

My People's Prayer Book:
Traditional Prayers, Modern Commentaries, Vols. 1–10

My People's Passover Haggadah:
Traditional Texts, Modern Commentaries, Vols. 1 & 2
(coedited with David Arnow, PhD)

The Art of Public Prayer, 2nd Ed.:
Not for Clergy Only
(A book from SkyLight Paths, Jewish Lights' sister imprint)

Rethinking Synagogues:
A New Vocabulary for Congregational Life

Israel—A Spiritual Travel Guide:
A Compoanion for the Modern Jewish Pilgrim

The Way Into Jewish Prayer

What You Will See Inside a Synagogue
(coauthored with Dr. Ron Wolfson)

Also in the Prayers of Awe Series

Who by Fire, Who by Water—Un'taneh Tokef

All These Vows—Kol Nidre

We Have Sinned: Sin and Confession in Judaism—Ashamnu *and* Al Chet

May God Remember: Memory and Memorializing in Judaism—Yizkor

PRAYERS OF AWE

ALL THE WORLD

Universalism, Particularism and the High Holy Days

Edited by
Rabbi Lawrence A. Hoffman, PhD

JEWISH LIGHTS Publishing

All the World: Universalism, Particularism and the High Holy Days

Library of Congress Cataloging-in-Publication Data
All the world : universalism, particularism and the High Holy Days / edited by Rabbi Lawrence A. Hoffman, PhD.
     pages cm
  Includes bibliographical references.
   ISBN 978-1-58023-783-3 (hardcover) — ISBN 978-1-58023-811-3 (ebook)   1. High Holidays. 2. Universalism. 3. Particularism (Theology) I. Hoffman, Lawrence A., 1942– editor.
  BM693.H5A64 2014
  296.4'31—dc23

                              2014020089

ISBN: 978-1-68162-974-2 (paperback)

Manufactured in the United States of America
Cover Design: Jeff Miller
Cover Mechanical Design: Grace Cavalier

Published by Jewish Lights Publishing
An imprint of Turner Publishing Company
4507 Charlotte Avenue, Suite 100
Nashville, TN 37209
Tel: (615) 255-2665
www.jewishlights.com

Contents

Acknowledgments

I wish to begin by thanking the many readers of this series and of the prior set of volumes, *My People's Prayer Book*, who write to thank me for them. To these worshipers in general, I add the many colleagues, artists, composers, poets, philosophers, theologians, and critics who advise me with regularity. Many of them are included here. To them—to all the contributors whose commentaries found their way into this volume—I am grateful.

I continue to be blessed with support from my extraordinary publisher, Stuart M. Matlins, founder of Jewish Lights, and from Emily Wichland, vice president of Editorial and Production there. It was Stuart who first approached me with the idea for the Prayers of Awe series, as suggested to him by Dan Adler in response to a High Holy Day program developed by Rob Eshman, editor in chief of the *Jewish Journal of Greater Los Angeles*, and David Suissa. Their program sprang from an idea first conceived by Rabbi Elazar Muskin of Young Israel of Century City, California. Emily continues to amaze me in all she does: her abundant wisdom, skill, patience, and perseverance are precisely what an author most desires. For her copyediting, my thanks go again to Debra Corman. I happily include as well all the others at Jewish Lights, especially Tim Holtz, director of Production, who designed the cover for this book and typeset the English text.

The very act of compiling an anthology such as this is enormously challenging. Beyond the editing of each article, sometimes more than once, an enormous number of e-mails go back and forth with each and every contributor, on such matters as titles, style, and content. Contributions thus move slowly along the path toward completion, eventually to be classified as "ready for the publisher" and assembled in their final form. In this entire process, I have been aided immeasurably by Dr. Gayle Hoover, who has overseen the inclusion of contributions at every stage along the way.

Dr. Joel M. Hoffman worked assiduously to translate the liturgy as a whole, but also the citations from prayers cited by Rabbi Dalia Marx, PhD, from Israel.

We should be enormously grateful to all the authors mentioned. Theirs is genuinely a work of commitment and love for the tradition of Jewish worship that this book represents.

❦

Introduction

In General and in Particular, the Moral and Theological Dilemma of Our Time

Rabbi Lawrence A. Hoffman, PhD

"No man is an island, entire of itself," wrote the English poet John Donne, famously; "every man is a piece of the continent, a part of the main." Yes, but what continent and what main? Are we "involved in mankind," as Donne proposed; part of the long evolution of our

---

Rabbi Lawrence A. Hoffman, PhD, has served for more than three decades as professor of liturgy at Hebrew Union College–Jewish Institute of Religion in New York. He is a world-renowned liturgist and holder of the Stephen and Barbara Friedman Chair in Liturgy, Worship and Ritual. He has written and edited many books, including the *My People's Prayer Book: Traditional Prayers, Modern Commentaries* series, winner of the National Jewish Book Award; and the Prayers of Awe series; and he is coeditor of *My People's Passover Haggadah: Traditional Texts, Modern Commentaries*, a finalist for the National Jewish Book Award. He cofounded and developed Synagogue 3000, a transdenominational project designed to envision and implement the ideal synagogue of the spirit for the twenty-first century.

species? Or are we answerable only to our family, our tribe, our people, our nation—or some other localized "something or other" that, whatever we name it, is less than humanity writ large.

To be human is to know firsthand these two perspectives, universalism and particularism: the first, an extended feeling of kinship with all humanity; and the second, the natural tendency to feel most at home with our own kind. They derive from the same source: the basic human need to reach beyond ourselves and affirm relationships with others. But they need not go together, and they may even be in conflict. There can hardly be a more important issue for our time than the need to balance the two.

In the evolution of human societies, particularism came first: the solidarity of small groups that arose in prehistoric times and, eventually, matured into tribal societies, each with its own culture, language, religion, and categories of thought. They are what anthropologists traditionally study in their fieldwork, but not, on that account, limited to so-called primitives. When the anthropologists return to their own communities, they experience the same sense of knowing they are home—the way even the most intrepid traveler does when the plane hits familiar tarmac and you feel once again that you are on familiar ground. In its rawest form, it is the sense of knowing you are among "us" rather than "them."

Eventually, all but the most isolated tribal units become aware of their neighbors and discover that, to some degree at least, these strangers are not just "them" but an extension of "us," an expression of humanity at large. In Western culture, the high point in this turn to universalism occurred in the eighteenth-century phenomenon that we call the Enlightenment, an extension of the prior century's turn to science. Scientific principles are, by definition, universal: they hold everywhere, among all people; they play no favorites. The language of mathematics holds everywhere in the universe, no matter where we live upon it; we all can read it.

Part and parcel of the scientific method is an emphasis on reason, which, again, is universal, the means by which thoughtful people who speak different languages at home solve universal equations together. The age of science, therefore, is similarly characterized by what we call the Age of Reason, a period when educated men and women were intoxicated by the heady possibility of a common human family united in reasoning together. Think of Isaac Newton (1642–1727), Gottfried Wilhelm

Leibniz (1646–1716), and Baruch (Benedict) Spinoza (1632–77), three representative minds of the era. We call them "minds" precisely because it was a mental capacity, "reason," that made them memorable.

On the surface, they seem quite different: a British Anglican (Newton), a German Lutheran (Leibniz), and a Dutch Jew (Spinoza)—a telling reminder of the chasms of consciousness that the Age of Reason had to bridge. From 1618 to 1648, the Thirty Years' War had pitted Protestants and Catholics against each other in murderous, ongoing, and continent-wide conflict; and the Spanish Inquisition had sent Spinoza's ancestors into hiding. Now these three geniuses could see themselves as allies in the enterprise of plotting the world philosophically, mathematically, and scientifically—evidence of the new era that emphasized the shared faculty of reason rather than peculiarities of nation, tribe, and religion.

This infatuation with universalism ground to a halt, however, in the wake of Napoleon, who had been formed by the universalist sentiment of the French Revolution and who sought, therefore, to eradicate all signs of medieval differences among peoples and nations. For most Jews, Napoleon was a hero, because his universalism entailed seeing Jews as human beings like everyone else and granting them citizenship and opportunity. For the privileged classes of Europe, however, Napoleon was the archenemy, intent on destroying the old order of monarchy, church, and heritage.

By the nineteenth century, then, Europe reacted with what we call the Romantic Era, a period that reemphasized the importance of peoplehood and particularism. The Age of Reason (it was said) had ignited the revolutionary excesses of the Reign of Terror; perhaps (it was said, as well) reason was not so universal after all; perhaps (it then followed) reason should be tempered by the forces of tradition and heritage. The stage was set for a return to the national and religious particularisms that divide us, not the universal qualities that make us all the same.

The rest, as they say, is history. Evolution suggested an upward spiral of human development, from which was derived the lesson that some of the world's peoples and cultures were more advanced than others. From here, it was but a short step to justifying political colonialism allied to religious imperialism, in a race for territory and power that produced World War I—exactly one hundred years prior to the publication of this volume. World War II was, similarly, an expression of particularistic pride and prejudice.

For quite some time, tribal loyalties were submerged by the Soviet Union in Eastern Europe and by local authorities left in place by the colonial powers elsewhere: the Arab states, for example, and parts of post-colonial Africa. With the fall of the Soviet system, however, tribalism reemerged and still operates with surprising vitality—even as I write this, Crimea is threatening independence from Ukraine. Elsewhere, too—in the Balkans, Africa, and the Mediterranean, to name just the most obvious instances—tribal/nationalist warfare has become the norm. Renewed tribalism has become endemic to the twenty-first century, as have local wars that evoke the worst of medieval atrocity.

At the same time, there is much to be said for particularism. Where would we be, after all, without the historic cultures that the world's peoples have created over time as both symptoms and symbols of ethnic pride and consciousness? Jews, of all people, can testify to that. The opposite of all particularism is assimilation, precisely what Jewish particularists have most feared. Without Jewish particularism, there would be no State of Israel, no revival of Hebrew, no celebration of Jewish history and culture. In the grand scheme of things, the pleasure one takes in being French, Jewish, Irish, Roman Catholic, or Japanese—all of them, particularisms—is what most prompts human cultural achievement.

We sorely require an end to the ever-growing animosity, cruelty, and war that human particularity can fuel. But equally important is the appropriate particularistic solidarity of family and home, the realization that we may all be alike in some ways but not necessarily in others. We require both the comfort of particularism and the commonality of universalism.

The potential conflict between universalism and particularism arose for ancient Israel when it first became aware of its neighbors, especially when those neighbors became powerful enough to overcome it. Jews who were carried away captive to Babylonia in the sixth century BCE necessarily wondered about the place of Jews in the grander scheme of things. The importation of Hellenism under Alexander the Great two centuries later further challenged assumptions about Jewish particularity. And the Rabbis formulated the Judaism we now have against a similar backdrop of the Greek and Roman world. The result was an ever-stronger affirmation of Jewish particularism balanced by the conviction of the universal God who had created everything and then planted the Jewish People with a mission to the larger world in which it found itself. Balancing Jewish universalism and particularism has remained a tricky business, especially in our time, when a commitment to our planet and its peoples has only grown in importance, even as Jewish continuity has become ever more contested.

In our current context, two separate but related issues stand out, one of them ethical, the other theological. The ethical issue is the extent to which responsibility for others, not just Jews, is central to Judaism. "If I am not for myself, who will be for me?" Hillel inquired, as if anticipating our own era, when (having passed through the Holocaust), we now ask with particular poignancy, "If we Jews do not care for ourselves, who else will care for us?" But Hillel also said, "Being for myself, what am I?" If we care only for ourselves, what are we? Are we not here to serve God's purposes? And don't those purposes include our being a "light to the nations"? The particularist mentality stresses the inherent good of Jewish continuity in and of itself. The universalist perspective links Jewish continuity to the larger mission of working toward the good of the world entire. No doubt, both are necessary. But what is to be the balance?

The theological issue arises from that very term "light to the nations," a phrase borrowed from Isaiah 49:6. To be a light to the nations implies the mandate to bring prosperity, freedom, and harmony to all of humanity—universalism at its ethical finest. But theologically, it raises the question of whether the light we bring must be the single solitary Jewish truth alone, in which case the nations must eventually come around to our way of viewing things or remain lost in their own darkness. Are religions other than Judaism valid, or is Judaism the sole truth?

The High Holy Day liturgy has much to say about both these dilemmas.

Ethically speaking, these Days of Awe picture us standing in the full light of God's scrutiny and wondering if we have remained true to the purpose for which we were created: have we taken proper responsibility for the world, or has our selfishness overcome our altruism?

Theologically, the Days of Awe picture the ultimate state of messianic harmony, when all the world will bask in the light of God's presence. Thus, the question: is the Jewish light the one true light for everyone?

The ethical question arises regularly, if only as the obvious question for a pluralistic age, "Why be Jewish?" The theological question, by contrast, receives little public discussion because it is tied to uncomfortable theological metaphors like salvation, deliverance, a world to come, a messiah, a messianic age, and other promises having to do with an afterlife for individuals or a better time to come for all the world. Many people feel no compunction to address the consequences of doctrines they are not entirely sure they believe in anyway. But even hypothetically, Jews need to know what they think about this basic theological question: "Who gets saved at the end of time—only Jews? Or adherents of other religions, too?" The answer matters because it implies a relationship between Jews and non-Jews that impacts the way we treat one another. Theology implies ethics; they go together.

The old canard, at least—though that is all it is—is that Judaism is shot through and through with particularism, whereas Christianity is universal in its appeal. On this reading, Judaism is tribal—one is a Jew by birth alone; while Christianity, as a matter of faith, is open to all thoughtful and believing human beings. Actually, if anything, things may be the other way around. Classical Christianity requires conversion for salvation—anyone who rejects the Christian truth is damned to eternity. By contrast, Judaism is not just for those born into it. In addition, the Rabbis recognized divine covenants made not with Jews alone but with others as well. Perhaps, then, Judaism is (theologically speaking) more universal than Christianity is.

But how universal is it? That is the theological question here. Do Jews believe that all the world can be saved without its inhabitants first adopting Judaism? Or must those who are not Jewish come round to the Jewish perspective, at least to some extent, in order to be saved? It seems clear that Judaism demands no prior conversion to Judaism. But it does assume a commitment to God and to monotheism, as well as to some basic human decencies that are thought to be part and parcel of the covenants God makes with peoples everywhere. What, however, counts as that commitment?

This book handles both these questions and does so from the perspective of the High Holy Days, which are a reminder of the universal mission for which the particular People of Israel exists.

If religion ought properly to deal with the big issues of our time, this book surely counts as religious. It treats the Days of Awe as what they are, awesome, not just because they are the annual Jewish call for individual penitence—although they surely are that—but also because they raise important issues for the Jewish People in its entirety, the most important being precisely this: what will be our commitment to the universal task for which God intends us?

The book looks carefully at that question in several stages. We begin with part 1, "Universalism and Particularism: Speaking Generally," a set of essays that establish the parameters of this important topic in general, especially as it is explored in the prayers of the High Holy Days that this book features. Part 2, "Views from Philosophy and Literature," provides more specialized treatment of the topic from the twin perspectives of philosophy and literature—the pioneering universalistic thought of nineteenth-century Jewish theologian Hermann Cohen, for example, and the appearance of the relevant High Holy Day liturgy in the literary work of Israel Zangwill and Jewish Nobel Prize winner S. Y. Agnon. Included here also are literary analyses of the liturgy, the poetic and stylistic features that go into giving the prayers their shape and message.

The title of this volume is derived from its central prayer, *V'ye'etayu*, literally, "Everyone will arrive ..."—a poem celebrating the ultimate messianic age when everyone will arrive to worship God. The prayer is better known to many through its loose translation by Israel Zangwill, "All the world will come to serve Thee." Zangwill's English was set to music and used extensively in Reform and Liberal congregations worldwide. Part 3, "'All the World' Remembered: Its Impact on Generations," provides two retrospectives on that poetic piece as it appeared in earlier prayer books and practices in America and in England. The music itself is analyzed in part 1.

We turn next to part 4, a translation of "The Liturgy," along with a running commentary by the translator, Dr. Joel M. Hoffman. As with other volumes in this series, Hoffman provides a true translation using a thorough knowledge of Hebrew in particular and linguistics in general.

Part 5 comprises a set of miscellaneous essays prompted by the prayers in question. Its authors span a gamut of perspectives, coming from various countries, denominations, and institutional points of view. We therefore label it "Interpretations from the Field."

This entire series is dedicated to exploring the spiritual depth of the liturgy that constitutes Rosh Hashanah and Yom Kippur, the Jewish Days of Awe, or High Holy Days. They are meant to raise questions of ultimate human consequence: matters of sin, repentance, and pardon; ethical obligation and default; human worth and promise; and the vision of a world suffused with meaning, purpose, and possibility. This volume presumes to do its share in raising such questions as part of the series, overall, so that readers can experience the Days of Awe in all their fullness.

᠎᠎᠎᠎

PART I
Universalism and Particularism
Speaking Generally

Why Be Jewish?

THE UNIVERSALIST MESSAGE OF THE HIGH HOLY DAYS

Rabbi Lawrence A. Hoffman, PhD

A relative newcomer to prayer once complained that the problem with services is not just their length but also their uniformity. All the pages of the prayer book look pretty much the same, she observed. There are a few highlights here and there, but in between, the drudgery goes on endlessly, page after page after page with no apparent rhyme or reason.

As I reflected on her complaint, I thought back to my childhood in southern Ontario and the automobile trips that my family frequently took along country roads that meandered through its endless rolling farmland. As my father and mother conversed in the front seat ahead of me, I would stare vacantly out the window at endless fields of grain interspersed with fenced-off meadows for grazing listless cows.

For the uninitiated, day trips through the countryside ramble over territory that is hardly worth noticing. Eventually, perhaps, you turn the corner to be surprised by a waterfall, gorge, or bird sanctuary, but for the most part you busy yourself with vacant stares into a horizon of sameness: winding roads and rolling hills; endless cornfields, clumps of trees, and bush-like secondary growth that is far from thrilling. Much of the liturgy is like that as well. To get to the *Un'taneh Tokef,* for instance, you must first wade through much of an ordinary *Amidah,* not to mention the proliferation of poems that two thousand years of accretion have added to the liturgical terrain—the secondary prayer-growth that seems sometimes to be endless and shapeless, just pages and pages of verbiage that one simply gets through. Only here and there do you arrive at the landmark passages that draw us all to this annual pilgrimage through the liturgy.

Yet there are always surprises, even in the most ordinary journey through the most familiar countryside. From time to time, you say to the driver, "Wait; stop here for a minute. I never noticed how the sun shines through this particular clump of trees, how that old familiar barn stands out against the horizon, and the way the corn bends with the breeze this time of year." And once you have noticed that particular old barn with its sunlit corn, it becomes a landmark, no longer just backdrop for the more obvious standouts along the journey.

What we observe is partly dependent on the keenness of our observation—everyone who has taken a course in art or music appreciation knows that. Even sleeping children bolt upright when the cannon goes off at the end of Tchaikovsky's *1812 Overture*. Eventually, perhaps, they learn to appreciate the rest of the piece. The same children stand similarly transfixed upon hearing the shofar. As adults, they may learn to watch for other contours to the liturgical day.

Some of the highlights come naturally: the cantorial moments of grandeur; the times we stand or beat our breasts; or *Kol Nidre,* where all eyes are focused on the Torah scrolls that have been removed from the ark and you can hear a pin drop. Other moments approximate the ordinary sameness of liturgical countryside, just pages upon pages that practically turn themselves, while you think about other things and watch the time go by. And some moments give you something you never noticed before, a place of hidden beauty suddenly revealed and a moment of meaning that you will never want to miss again.

This volume of our Prayers of Awe series provides just such a moment of meaning. It differs from its predecessors in that the prayers around which it is organized are generally part of the undifferentiated liturgical countryside; they are passed over, rushed through, barely recognized. This book should convince you ever after to stop and appreciate them. Taken together, they are the very soul of what the High Holy Days are all about: a very good reason for Judaism to go on existing and for Jews to go on being Jewish. At stake is the very large question of why be Jewish anyway.

"Why Be Jewish?"—A Question Newly Asked

"Why be Jewish?" is a relatively new question. For most of Jewish history, it would never have been asked. Jews were just Jews the way they were men or women, old or young, boys or girls. Being Jewish was part of one's general standing in the world, confirmed at birth, for better and for worse. Along with it came a certain kind of community, a particular sort of calendar, and specific customs, foods, beliefs, and habits—most of them hardwired into existence as just the way things were. From time to time, it may have occurred to a very few that they could exchange the Jewish part of themselves for something else, but that was hardly the norm and it came at quite a cost. Conversion out of Judaism meant conversion into something else, generally Christianity or Islam, and that meant, in turn, being cut off from family, friends, and all that mattered most.

In addition, most Jews were proud and happy being what they were, even if it meant, as it usually did, living in second-class status as individuals without full standing in the officially Christian or Muslim worlds. To begin with, Jewish life brought its own spectacular joys of the everyday: the holiday cycle, a community of friends and family, and such welcome and familiar ways of life as making *Kiddush* and eating Shabbat challah. Every people has such pleasures, but Jews were convinced that being a Jew was more: it was a privilege. Jews alone went back to Abraham and Sarah; they were God's chosen People, gifted with Torah and with life after death—a reward that would richly make up for whatever disabilities Jewishness might entail in this worldly life, which was just an anteroom (a *prozdor*, as the Rabbis put it) to the ultimate destination, the house of everlasting life. One was Jewish not just because that was the way it was, but because being a Jew was a blessing.

The onset of modernity in the nineteenth century changed much of that. Among other things, religion in general was displaced from its centrality, allowing people to change religions or even to drop religion completely as a determining factor in their day-to-day life. No longer a matter of consequential truth, religion became a matter of convenience (or inconvenience), leading some Jews to ask not just "Why be Jewish?" but "Why not be Christian?"—a more convenient way to get ahead in society, after all. Familiarity with modern versions of Christianity relativized the certainty of Judaism being the sole religious truth. And scientific study revealed the Bible to be the work of human editors, thereby raising questions about traditional theological verities: Are Jews really chosen? Is there really such a thing as reward and punishment or life after death? Is the Bible even true altogether? Modern forms of Judaism emerged specifically to respond to these newfound suspicions that were corroding old-time certainties.

A sophisticated recasting of old medievalisms so as to harmonize tradition with modernity was true not just of German Reform (where it all began), but also modern Orthodoxy; and, eventually, all the contemporary movements of today: Reform, Liberal, Conservative, Reconstructionist; and all the rest—each of them a scenario for remaining true to the Jewish past without renouncing the modern present. The result was an ever-expanding set of denominational options that sought to set to rest the question of "Why not leave" the Judaism of one's heritage.

With the late twentieth and the twenty-first centuries, however, the question changed from "Why not leave?" to "Why bother staying?" The lure to abandoning Judaism had hitherto been driven by a "push" factor: Jews had felt pushed out by a Judaism that seemed too medieval to take seriously or by anti-Semitic prejudice that prevented Jews from getting ahead in life without becoming Christian first. Modern Jewish denominations addressed the first issue, the secularization of society; and the horrified reaction to the Hitler years addressed the second. By the 1940s and '50s Jews could increasingly make their way in business and society without denying their Jewish past, and there was little point in converting to Christianity when Christianity itself was on the defensive against increasing secularization, and even atheism, as an acceptable option.

With modern movements available and upward mobility possible, even marginal Jews saw no good reason to leave Judaism—neither on principled nor on utilitarian grounds. But missing a reason to leave was not the same as having a reason to remain. That question would probably have emerged sooner than it did had it not been for the Six-Day War of June 1967.

The most compelling reason for Jewish pride in the years immediately following World War II was the miraculous existence of a Jewish state, just the third Jewish commonwealth in history, and a haven for Jewish victims worldwide. Jews around the world watched with amazement as swamps were cleared, cities built on sand dunes, and democracy established in a modern Hebrew tongue. With the Six-Day War, the specter of that state being wiped off the face of the earth reawakened the image from the Holocaust that still haunted Jewish minds and hearts. It now seemed self-evident that Jews should go on being Jewish as a simple matter of faithfulness to the recent Jewish past—identification with Israel became in and of itself sufficient symbolic reason to do so. As the decades proceeded, a similar cause arose: the "Refuseniks"—Jews in the Soviet Union who were unable to practice Judaism but who were, simultaneously, forbidden to leave it. Once again Jews in a happier situation elsewhere in the world took the lead in saving Jewish lives and preventing the demise of Judaism—making sure, that is (in the words of theologian Emil Fackenheim), not to give Hitler a posthumous victory.

The pride in saving Jews wherever they were threatened and seeing Jewish life established in an independent Jewish state was a profound response to the near demise of Jewish life under Hitler and then Stalin and the Communist state. It did not, however, address the underlying issue of what Judaism had to offer beyond its own continuity. The question "Why be Jewish?" raises that issue. Jews firmly committed to their heritage may find the question irrelevant. But increasing numbers of young Jews, especially, do not. Nor do spiritual seekers from other faiths or from no faith at all who look to Judaism as a potential spiritual home. For some, it is enough simply to point to the Jewish way of life as humanly fulfilling, spiritually satisfying, and personally engaging: synagogue life, the experience of community, study of Torah, and such cultural standbys as klezmer music and Jewish film festivals may be sufficient reason for Jewish identity. But less and less is that enough. Is there no transcendent reason, no theological reality, no profoundly compelling rationale for younger generations (and for generations yet to come) to choose Judaism as their way of expressing their fondest human aspirations here on earth?

As it happens, the High Holy Days present just such a transcendent message: a universal mission to which Jews as a particular people have been called. Before turning to it, however, we should pause to see why the ritual we call liturgy is so crucial in providing it. At stake is not just the ideas themselves, but also a mode of presenting the ideas that can prove convincing. As it happens, ritual is that mode.

Three Modes of Being Present: Believing, Behaving, and Ritualizing

Even those untrained in theological discourse will find this message of the High Holy Days easy enough to understand, but it may seem like relatively new ground, since for several decades now we have been more apt to discuss the saving of Jewish lives than the reality of Jewish ideas. We love Jewish community but have relatively few conversations to justify that love or to deepen it by affirming something theologically resonant about it. Jews have just not been a theological community.

God-talk, for example, is commonplace in churches and even in popular culture, but not among Jews, who are reticent to discuss God altogether. With some notable exceptions—largely among the Orthodox—Jews are similarly uncomfortable discussing other theological issues: being a chosen people, the authority of Torah, an ongoing Jewish covenant from Sinai, life after death, and so on. The absence of an ongoing conversation on these age-old Jewish ideas raises the question of whether Jews believe anything at all about Jewish Peoplehood, other than the obvious fact that it exists, the pride in being part of it, and the inchoate desire that it not disappear.

Such public discussion of theology and the consequent affirmation of truths beyond, or just other than, what science is prepared to confirm are part of what has been called "the believing mode" of making ourselves present in the world.

At issue is the evolution of human beings as the sole species to attain self-consciousness and, as a result, our propensity to spend our lives making ourselves present (to ourselves and to others) in ways that prompt thoughtfulness about who and what we are. Roosters crow, peacocks strut, and dogs howl at the moon. Each of these animals, and others too, makes its presence felt for its own specific ends. But those ends do not include thoughtfulness about what they believe, the morality that should drive their behavior, and the entire issue of identity: who and what they are or how (and how deeply) they wish to be known. Human beings are otherwise. We make ourselves present in three profound ways—believing, behaving, and ritualizing—each of them a separate mode of human self-consciousness.[1]

The first of these, the *believing* mode, is the human propensity to speak the deepest truths that we hold about existence, the ultimacies on which we stake our lives: what we believe about God (theology), human nature (religious anthropology), and the universe at large (cosmology). Is there a God? If so, does God care about what we do? And is God real in our lives? Do we think people are genuinely good at heart? Or are they untrustworthy? Are they perfectible or, at least, able to change for the better? Is the world a good place into which to be born, or would it have been better not to have been born at all? Is progress possible? If so, does God have anything to do with it? Is the universe designed so that moral improvement naturally occurs over time? If not, is it the human condition to struggle against all odds to make the world better anyway?

These three sets of issues (God, human nature, and the nature of the universe) are not mere matters of theory, luxuries for philosophers to ponder. Human nature drives us all toward curiosity about them. We cannot know them with scientific certainty, of course (they are, by definition, beyond the realm of scientific investigation), but we also cannot avoid acting as if we have the answers: we awaken each day with optimism or pessimism; we either trust or distrust those we meet; we feel alone in the universe or we do not; we freely sacrifice for others or we treat life like a jungle—dog eat dog, and survival of the fittest. Think of the three areas as vectors of identity, intersecting in the virtual space of our imagination: the point at which they meet—what we ultimately think about God, people, and the world—defines our deepest sense of who we are, our "moral space."[2]

Part of this deeply intuited moral terrain is the particularist/universalist dilemma. On the one hand, we are all *particularists*: members of some group, tribe, nation, or religion that we call our own. The other members are "like us"; we understand each other; support one another; if need be, fight for each other. On the other hand, we are all human beings who share a foreign and sometimes frightening world that we try to tame for our own ends. We all get born, we all get sick, and we all die. In between, we all laugh and grieve, work and play, build homes and, possibly, have children. Insofar as we are all individuals of the world, not just members of our own people, we are *universalists*.

Contrary to popular opinion, the ethical challenge of our time is not the conflict between reckless individualism and responsibility to others. Human beings cannot and do not live as unbridled individualists. Except for relatively rare cases of extreme pathology, even rampant individualists find at least some friends, some neighborhood group or online community that they call their own and to which they hold themselves accountable. The need for even the most unsavory among us to have such a reference group is behind our sense that there is loyalty even among thieves. What threatens our world today is not unmitigated individualism, then, so much as it is the burning question of the extent to which individuals throughout the world choose particularistic allegiance to their tribe alone rather than universalistic responsibility to the rest of humankind.

This may well be the most essential moral dilemma of our time. The *Oxford English Dictionary* defines particularism as "exclusive attachment to one's own party, sect, nation, etc." such that, in the extreme case, one acts entirely for the welfare of one's own group without regard for others. The opposite, universalism, implies loyalty to the larger whole of humanity, potentially (the ultimate example) turning one's back on one's own people. The dichotomy is well known elsewhere, too—in Christian theology, for instance, where particularism entails salvation only for one's own, as opposed to universalism, which promises salvation for everyone. Jewish theology has engaged in a similar debate—a matter discussed by several commentators in this volume.

Here, however, I wish to bracket the theological concern and focus on the ethical one: not salvation at the end of time but responsibility now, to one's own people (particularism) and also to the world (universalism). The issue, moreover, is not merely that *as Jews* we owe allegiance to the Jewish People, and *as human beings* we take responsibility for others; it is the question of what *Judaism* demands of us on both counts. The point to be made is that Judaism itself mandates universalist, not just particularist, sentiment. Indeed, it may be that the purpose of our particularist commitment to Jewish continuity is that the Jewish People whose continuity we guarantee can then turn to its universalistic task of effecting God's will for justice and goodness throughout all of God's world.

Particularism is a Jew's primary attachment to and concern for other Jews. Universalism is our parallel attachment to the causes of humanity in general. Both are part of Judaism. There need be no conflict between the two positions.

Some cultures encourage conversation about such weighty matters as a natural part of the ongoing discussion on what to believe and why to believe it. As we saw, however, that is less the case with Jewish culture, at least in our time. Jews are probably aware of the two poles that define the particularist/universalist debate—how can they not be? But Jewish organizations institute little ongoing opportunity for Jews to address the issue in any deeply thoughtful way, because the believing mode is poorly represented in Jewish organizational or social life.

By contrast, Jews are quite comfortable with the second of the three ways we make ourselves present to others: what we can call *the behavioral mode*. Behavior, not belief, has traditionally been the most comfortable means of Jewish self-expression. To begin with, Judaism is halakhic— and halakhah is concerned, first and foremost, with behavior. Unlike Christianity, that is, Judaism is not *essentially* a religion of belief. Not that Christians have nothing they must do, while Jews have nothing they must believe; but on balance, Christianity emphasizes belief, while Judaism emphasizes action. Over the course of centuries, for example, Christians have excommunicated one another on matters of faith, while Jews have shown enormous latitude about it. Jews, too, have excommunicated each other, but over issues of halakhah—how one keeps Shabbat, for instance, rather than whether one believes in it altogether. If you want to know whether people are Jewish and if so, what kind of Jews they are, watch what calendar they keep, what food they eat, and whether they say blessings before and after eating it. In an earlier era, when Jewish identity was a given and no rationale regarding "why be Jewish" was required, the internal Jewish debate over halakhah and Jewish behavior was quite sufficient to mark an individual's existential space within the Jewish community. Similarly, it was all one needed to chart the way one went about one's life in the larger human community roundabout.

The problem, and the challenge, of our time is that the behavioral mode of making ourselves present—the dialogue over how Jews ought to behave in the world—is relevant only after a prior decision to affirm Jewish identity in the first place. Without some predetermined rationale for sustaining Jewish commitment, the specifically Jewish guides to behavior are not likely to be consulted. More and more, therefore, Jews require some prior belief about the profundity of Jewish tradition and its desirability in their lives. That seems to return us to the believing mode, however—precisely the area of human engagement that Jews are least comfortable in.

Fortunately, there is a third mode by which we human beings make ourselves known in the world, and it is this third mode that poses the greatest possibility for affirming the transcendent Jewish purpose that contemporary seekers require. I mean the *ritual* mode of self-expression, the sacred dramas of synagogue and home by which we act out who we are. Some obvious Jewish examples are lighting Hanukkah candles, holding a seder at Passover time, a bar or bat mitzvah, affixing a mezuzah to our door, or marking Shabbat with a festive meal and prayers. All of these are ritualized demonstrations of identity. They are also matters of behavior, but they differ from the behavioral mode of presentation in that they follow ritualized scripts that are public and symbolic. They symbolize the fact that we choose to be Jewish; but simultaneously, they symbolize an underlying reason for so choosing.

As in the believing mode, they allude to certain beliefs that underlie the behavior in question. But because they are rituals, they are scripted, not matters of open-ended conversation. They come, as well, with multiple channels of communication: not just talking (as in conversation) but also music and chant, redundant recitation, poetry, and a mix of languages. They are more like theater or a concert, in that once begun, they proceed relentlessly to their end—no one interrupts the flow to debate what they are saying.

For all these reasons, we grant rituals latitude to say things we might otherwise question—we are able, that is, to engage in rituals without running up against the problem of our reticence to talk about what we believe.

Ritual thus becomes that peculiar mode of human self-expression that combines behavior and belief, but does so in a manner that stretches our potential for believing. A Passover seder, for example, can be any number of things: family time, fun for the children, and a happy reminder of springtime in the air. Theologically, however, it is the affirmation that we were once slaves in the land of Egypt and that God took us out (as the Bible puts it) "with a mighty hand and an outstretched arm" (*b'yad chazakah uvizro'a n'tuyah*). But what exactly does that mean? Do we literally believe in a God with hands and arms? What if the scientific study of the Bible convinces us that the Exodus narrative is, at least in part, contrived? At some point, the history may become suspect and the metaphor questionable. And yet, at the moment of performing the seder ritual, the brute fact of our freedom from slavery becomes existentially real. We are able to say the words of the Haggadah and to accept them, as at least a symbolic way of reaching toward a truth that we might not literally believe but that we take to be profoundly true nevertheless.

It is simply not the case that people first believe something and then move on successfully to pray it. The reverse is more likely: people who engage in moving and compelling rituals of prayer find themselves believing matters they might question once the moment of prayer is over. Not that they believe them literally at the time. But they treat liturgical language more like poetry, finding some acceptable message in what they otherwise would probably reject. When we conclude the reading of Torah, for instance, we usually sing, *Zot hatorah asher sam moshe ...* ("This is the Torah which Moses placed before the Israelites, dictated by God and transcribed by Moses"). Almost no one nowadays actually believes that literally; most people I encounter would object if I were to claim in the midst of a conversation that God called Moses to Sinai and told him to "take a letter" and that we now have that very same letter, word for word. For quite some time, in fact, most Reform Jews omitted this passage from their worship because they didn't believe it.

We know now, however, that their excision of this familiar prayer was premature. Most people who say it don't believe it either—not literally. When they encounter it ritually, they know better than to think they have to believe each and every word. It becomes, in that context, like a national anthem where we do not believe each and every claim either, but do not on that account abolish the anthem. Prayer is a dramatic enactment of a story in which we are all actors; a story that we make our own; a story with layers of meaning beyond the purely literal one.

To be sure, some words of prayers are hurtful to others—anti-Semitic claims about Jews that were commonplace in traditional Christian liturgies and that most modern churches have deleted by now; or our own claim, once upon a time (in the *Alenu*) that people of other religions "bow down and pray to vanity and emptiness," a line that we ourselves censored out and still (in most communities) have not put back in. Where prayers are morally offensive, we may properly decide to omit them; where they are merely contrary to our literal beliefs, however, we may sometimes retain them as a means of finding deeper meaning within them because they are recited in the ritual mode, not the belief mode.

Ritual is the regularized affirmation of order that matters; inherited rituals are reminders of patterns that other people saw.

Ritual is a sacred drama of our fondest aspirations: what we were, what we are, and what we hope to be.

Ritual provides the exclamation points for our lives, more than it does the periods.

Ritual is the wrapping that makes outrageous ideas believable.

The ritual mode of presenting ourselves is the mode by which we dare to aspire at all; it is the way we exclaim—not just define—ourselves into being, passionately and affirmatively; it is our deepest sense that we fit into patterns larger than ourselves; it is the way we come to believe in matters that would otherwise be too great to hope for.

In sum, the three great issues of human life—theology, religious anthropology, and cosmology—are beyond what the scientific method can affirm or deny. Yet our believing mode of self-expression is nowadays so unassailably determined by scientific judgment that the minute I say anything about God, human destiny, the goodness of the soul, and the like, I am likely to wonder whether I believe it. When I act it out in ritual, however, I enter a mode of presentation that convinces me of some reality to which those beliefs at least point, even if the beliefs in question cannot fully convey the reality with the kind of literal truth that scientific claims achieve.

The high and holy days are moments of high and holy ritual. They provide compelling occasions for affirmations in the ritual mode. They thereby permit us the luxury of exercising human imagination in all its glory. We picture human character at its worst but also at its best; we imagine the great possibility of a transcendent power we call God, who is present as we seek to make life worthwhile and who reaches out to us in ways we cannot fathom; we develop the case for making the most of being human; we define the privileges and responsibilities that come with the gift of life.

The High Holy Days provide uniquely memorable moments for exclaiming and proclaiming who and what we are at our finest, at our best, and as we truly want to be and to become. In that regard, the question "Why be Jewish?" becomes answerable. We Jews are a people who stand not only for ourselves and our own destiny but also for the greater purpose of humankind as a whole. Were the Jewish People not to exist in the world, the world would be impoverished. Jews are a historic and historical chain of individuals who have been part of civilization since the dawn of human memory. We continue to impact humanity as a whole because—at least in our ritual moments—we come to believe that God put us here to do just that. We have a mission to the world, not to convert it but to better it; to help it remember the God whom we discovered at Sinai but who, we believe, is available in one form or another to all humankind. This is the universal message of the High Holy Day service, our raison d'être, our very reason for being—nothing less.

The High Holy Day Countryside Revisited

Liturgy is indeed like a journey through the countryside. The High Holy Day itinerary provides a set of anticipated high points along the terrain, everything from the shofar service on Rosh Hashanah to the confessions of Yom Kippur. But the journey as a whole has a tale to tell, a message that is easy to miss because we overlook it as simple backdrop for the more familiar prayers.

Jewish tradition itself warns us against making that mistake. If the liturgy is the journey, Rabbinic writings are the guidebook, and the guidebook is very clear about what we are supposed to notice. On Rosh Hashanah, says the Mishnah, "all who come into the world" (*kol ba'ei olam*) are summoned to appear before God—not just Jews, that is, but every human being—which is to say, we Jews appear before God but in our capacity as universal man or woman, not simply as a member of the Jewish People. To be sure, it is Jewish tradition that summons us to the synagogue on that day, but once there, we appear naked before God as the human descendants of Adam and Eve in Eden. We are either worthy of continued existence in God's world or we are not; and if we are not, we engage in repentance (*t'shuvah*). The ritualized prayers for the occasion may be Jewish, but the act of contrition is not. *T'shuvah* is not a Jewish enterprise but a human one.

Six months after Rosh Hashanah and Yom Kippur we mark the month of Passover, another new year, in Jewish computation. Passover is our specifically particularistic day of days, the time to remember how we Jews were slaves to Pharaoh in Egypt and how we then journeyed to Sinai and the Promised Land as the particular people we were. Passover is one bookend in Jewish time, the particularistic one, the High Holy Days are the other bookend, the universalistic one, recalling that as much as we are Jews, we are also members of the world community, with a mission to advance the well-being of the world in which we find our existence.

All of this is the backdrop to the High Holy Day terrain, hardly the high points of the journey, but the ongoing message that becomes notice-able to those who know what to look for. Traditionally, for example, the cantor begins services a few lines earlier than is the norm the rest of the year. The first word out of the cantor's mouth is now "the ruler" (*hamelekh*) to provide the New Year theme: God's rule over the entire universe, and ourselves as subjects of that universal rule. When the sho-far is blown somewhat later in the day, it begins with a section called "Sovereignty" (*Malkhuyot*), a reiteration of that theme. Three times dur-ing the shofar blasts we say, "Today the world was conceived," as if, on this very day, the world as a whole, not just the Jewish People, came into being. Rabbinic tradition insists that Adam and Eve were formed on this day; it is the birth date of the human race. Our most familiar prayer calling on us to repair the world, *Alenu*, is best known to us as the conclusion to every service, but it began as the introduction to the "Sovereignty" section of the shofar service. The poetic highlight of the day is the familiar *Un'taneh Tokef*, a prayer that pictures all creation, not just Jews, facing the reality of its responsibility before God.

That responsibility, broached first on Rosh Hashanah, becomes the overall message for Yom Kippur, a day that is overwhelmingly dedicated to the responsibility we Jews take upon ourselves as universal men and women. The fixed liturgical confessions (*Ashamnu* and *Al Chet*) are notably lacking in references to commandments relevant only to the Jewish People—we find nothing, for example, regarding the failure to keep Shabbat, to observe kashrut, or to fix mezuzot on our homes. Instead, we get a set of alphabetic acrostics, each letter standing for a different sin that we ourselves may not have committed, but that someone, somewhere in the world, surely has. Some of the sins may seem more Jewish than not—demeaning teachers, for example (*zilzul morim*); but most of them are universal to human experience—insolence, slander, cheating, and the like. An afternoon highlight in the Yom Kippur service is a recollection of the Temple sacrificial cult, the distinctively Jewish mode of worship established by the Bible and elaborated by the Rabbis. But we remember this Jewish experience of worship in the context of the longer narrative of world history—the liturgical recollection begins with a lengthy poetic reminder of how the world was first created and how Israel's history and sacrificial worship are only part of a larger universal whole.

Finally, there are the prayers that this volume features, parts of the liturgical journey that are easily overlooked even though they are the purpose of the journey in the first place. As the survey in the few paragraphs above indicates, it would have taken a considerably larger volume to list and comment upon all the universalistic prayers that make up the High Holy Day experience. In the interest of space, we settled for just these.

V'khol Ma'aminim, "Everyone Believes"

We begin with *V'khol Ma'aminim*, "Everyone Believes," a medieval *piyyut* (poem) that has been traced to one of the most prolific Jewish poets of all time, a man named Yannai (circa fifth to seventh centuries CE).[3] Yannai was one of three great poets who constitute the classic age of Jewish poetry in the Land of Israel in those years. Readers of this series will already have encountered him as the author of *Un'taneh Tokef,* a *piyyut* mistakenly attributed to a rabbi of the later Middle Ages said to have written the poem as a response to being persecuted.[4] That legendary attribution, it will be recalled, fit well the era of the Holocaust and before, when persecution was indeed the norm for so many Jews. But its true origin, the Byzantine era when both Jewish and non-Jewish poets addressed the larger issues of human life together, is far more relevant to today, when the question "Why be Jewish?" demands precisely the sort of transcendent vision of the human condition that *Un'taneh Tokef* provides. Yannai addresses the same concern here in his conviction that everyone, not just Jews, can find their way to certain universal beliefs that ought to be evident to everyone.

The original Yannai composition seems to have been introduced with the words "Therefore, may your name be sanctified, Adonai our God, over Israel your people" (*Uv'khen yitkadash shimkha adonai eloheinu al yisra'el amekha*),[5] a formula that marks it as part of a longer composition known as a *k'dushta.* The *k'dushta* was, typically, a poem with nine parts running throughout the *Amidah* for festivals and holy days, the various parts being inserted into different sections of that prayer. The first and second parts were interjected into the first and second blessings; the other seven parts were allocated throughout the third blessing, the *K'dushah*—hence the name of the poem as a whole, a parallel Aramaic word, *k'dushta.*

Yannai's poem provides twenty-six stanzas that indicate the reasons for God to be sanctified or the ways in which such sanctification occurs: God is a faithful judge, who sees within us, for example. The number and order of the things mentioned are dependent on the fact that the poem is an alphabetic acrostic, a common poetic form of Yannai's time—the introductory words of the verses begin with successive letters of the Hebrew alphabet. But Yannai could have crafted the verses to say anything, and the content of the verses is altogether universal. We do not have references to God delivering us from Egypt, for instance, even though saving Israel is surely a good reason for God's being sanctified! The only exception is *zokher habrit,* "God remembers the covenant," an apparent reference to God's covenant with Israel at Sinai. The Rabbis held, however, that God makes covenants with all peoples, not just with Jews; God's "remembering of the covenant" is therefore part of God's relationship with all human beings, not just Jews. By contrast, as obviously universal references, we are told that God is "good to everyone" (*tov lakol*); "ruler of the universe" (*melekh olam*); and "the sole judge of the world's inhabitants" (literally, "to [all who] enter the world—*hadan y'chidi l'va'ei olam*), a recollection of the Mishnah, which (as we saw above) reserves Rosh Hashanah as a time when "all who enter the world" must be judged by God.

Uv'khen, "Therefore"

The second liturgical selection here is *Uv'khen*, "Therefore." To some extent that single word epitomizes the entire demand that Judaism have a transcendent purpose behind it. Our deepest level of human identity, the place where we find our "moral space," is recognizable precisely because it implies a moral consequence, a "therefore." *Uv'khen* is divided into three paragraphs, each one beginning with "therefore."

Tellingly, the first is entirely universal in that it is addressed to "all that has been made," with the expectation that all will acknowledge God's sovereignty. Only in the second paragraph does the author turn to Israel specifically, requesting honor for the Jewish People in particular. Verse 9, the beginning of the third paragraph, and our third "therefore," is actually a continuation of the second. Most manuscripts begin it with the word "then" (*az*) not "therefore" (*uv'khen*). Most of our printed prayer books, however, repeat the word "therefore" instead, and we have reproduced the "therefore" version here, since that is, by and large, what people are used to. In either case, however, whether beginning with "then" or "therefore," this third section of the prayer returns to the universal, all "the righteous ... the upright ... and the pious," who will rejoice because "injustice will shut its mouth, and all wickedness will vanish like smoke" as God "will abolish tyranny from the earth."

We are unable to say exactly when these lines were composed, but they seem to go back to relatively early stages of our liturgy. They are present already in the ninth-century *Seder Rav Amram*, our first known comprehensive prayer book. Older scholarly opinion placed them as early as the second century, believing them to be an outgrowth of a debate between Rabbi Akiva and the lesser-known Rabbi Yochanan ben Nuri.[6] At stake is a debate between these two authorities regarding the blowing of the shofar, which is to be sounded in three sets of blasts: one to herald God's sovereignty of the universe (the *Malkhuyot*, mentioned above); one to celebrate God's remembering us through history (*Zikhronot*); and one devoted to referencing the many times that the Bible recalls shofar blasts (*Shofarot*) with the implicit hope that the shofar will sound once again at the messianic end of time.

By the time of the two rabbis in question, the latter two sets had already been allocated to the middle of the *Amidah*. The positioning of the first set (*Malkhuyot*, "Sovereignty"), however, was still in question, possibly because the issue of God's rule was just then becoming an increasingly crucial matter of debate. Both Rabbi Akiva and Rabbi Yochanan ben Nuri lived during the Bar Kokhba revolt against Rome (132–135 CE), an uprising that was fought on the grounds that only God, not the emperor, was the true ruler of the universe. Whether directly related to revolt or not, Akiva thought the sounding of the shofar to mark God's sovereignty belonged alongside the two other sets of blasts (the *Zikhronot* and *Shofarot*), while Yochanan preferred placing it altogether separately as part of the third benediction of the *Amidah*—exactly where our *Uv'khen* is located. Early scholarship, therefore, believed that *Uv'khen* went back to Yochanan ben Nuri, as a compromise with his position: the shofar blasts regarding God's rule were positioned according to Rabbi Akiva's stipulation, but a discrete reference to God's universal rule remained in the benediction prior.

There is no evidence to support this interesting but speculative conclusion. All we can say is that *Uv'khen* does, in fact, denote God's universal rule. But whether it goes all the way back to the second century is debatable. Whenever composed, however, it was a staple to the liturgy by the time Rav Amram composed his prayer book around 860 CE.

V'ye'etayu, "And Everyone Will Arrive"

Finally, we provide a prayer that is little known in the Hebrew but quite famous in Liberal and Reform Jewish circles, where an English translation attracted music that became standard fare in the period following World War II. The full history of the music is provided by one of our commentators (Dr. Mark L. Kligman) and referred to by several others (e.g., Dr. Annette M. Boeckler). The composition that is generally sung today goes back to Abraham Wolfe Binder (1895–1966), the director of music at Stephen Wise Free Synagogue in New York and professor of Jewish music at Hebrew Union College–Jewish Institute of Religion next door. Binder was attracted to the translation of an anonymously composed medieval *piyyut* called *V'ye'etayu* (its opening Hebrew word, meaning "and everyone will arrive"). The translation in question was by Israel Zangwill (1864–1926), a fascinating personality in his own right.

Zangwill is discussed several times in these pages, but a summary of his colorful views and influence is surely in order here. Raised and educated in England, Zangwill had established himself by the 1890s as an author and a playwright, fascinated with the traditional ghetto life of Eastern Europe, but convinced that the Judaism for which it stood had been rendered irrelevant by science and modernity. From 1895 to 1905, he was not only a confirmed Zionist but also the man who introduced Theodor Herzl (Zionism's charismatic founder) to British Jewry. In 1905, however, when the Zionist Movement rejected a British offer of Uganda as the site for a Jewish state, Zangwill left Zionism for Jewish territorialism, the search for a Jewish homeland anywhere Jews might be safe—not necessarily in the historic Land of Israel. He then returned briefly to Zionism with the Balfour Declaration (which he helped bring into being), the British government's promise to establish a Jewish state in Palestine. At times, however, he pictured the demise of Judaism as an independent religion and its merger with the best of Christianity and Hellenic culture. Since *V'ye'etayu* was in keeping with his overall universalist sentiments, Zangwill found the *piyyut* appealing.

Binder had come across Zangwill's translation, with the opening line "All the world shall come to serve Thee"—hence its popular title "All the World." In 1932, he edited a revised version of the North American Reform Movement's *Union Hymnal* and inserted his setting of Zangwill there. Eight years later that movement's *Union Prayer Book* was itself revised, with "All the World" included as a liturgical poem. Thereafter, the piece became standard in many Reform and Liberal congregations worldwide.

We include *V'ye'etayu* here as a quintessential statement of Jewish universalism going back to the anonymous poet who authored it sometime in medieval days; we borrow Zangwill's title for it as the title of this book, and we reproduce Zangwill's poem as well.

What is striking about these three liturgical inclusions—"Everyone Believes," "Therefore," and "And Everyone Will Arrive"—is not simply their reiteration of the universal theme that the High Holy Day liturgy as a whole provides, but the fact that the three pieces occur together, one after the other, making up a unit in which their juxtaposition to one another underscores their overall message. Traditionally, they are found in the *Musaf* service.

Reform Jews dispensed with that service on the grounds that it was largely redundant to what was found elsewhere in the liturgy and because it was so heavily invested in references to the sacrificial cult that the traditional liturgy hoped to see restored but that Reform Jews were happy to relegate to history. Whatever *Musaf* prayers Reform Jews wished to keep were apportioned elsewhere, usually to the morning service (*Shacharit*) prior. *Uv'khen*, "Therefore," was found anyway within every *Amidah* (not just *Musaf*). *V'ye'tayu*, "And Everyone Will Arrive," was put in various places, depending on the prayer book, often as a concluding song to sum up the message of the day. The remaining *V'khol Ma'aminim*, "Everyone Believes," has, regrettably, disappeared from most Liberal and Reform liturgies, on the grounds that many of the tenets of belief contained there are not, in fact, believed at all anymore. Omitting this ancient prayer on such grounds may, however, have been misguided, given the role of ritual and the way ritual provides grounds for affirmations that are not necessarily compatible with a scientific statement of cold rational belief. At the very least, "Everyone Believes" is one further exclamation of Judaism's universal optimism: the hope for a better era when the rule of God will indeed become a reality that shapes a peaceful era for all humankind.

Cᴜᴜꙅ

Monotheism, Mission, and Multiculturalism

UNIVERSALISM THEN AND NOW

Dr. Annette M. Boeckler

Progressive Judaism from its beginning stressed its universalism. The Pittsburgh Platform of 1885, the very first manifesto of Reform Judaism in America, begins with it: "We recognize in every religion an attempt to grasp the Infinite, and in every mode, source or book of revelation held sacred in any religious system the consciousness of the indwelling of God in man."

But American Reform Judaism did not invent the idea. Already its European forebears some decades earlier had striven for universalism (paired with anti-Zionism, the ultimate statement of particularism at the time). Universalism has since then become a kind of progressive "dogma," unquestioned, with debates at times about whom to *include*, but a general intention to be welcoming to all, seeking dialogue with all religions and tackling issues of the wider society.

But Judaism is, in its essence, a religion of separations. We separate Shabbat from days of work, holy from profane, and Israel from "the

---

Dr. Annette M. Boeckler is lecturer for liturgy at Leo Baeck College in London and manager of its library. She studied theology, Jewish studies, and Ancient Near Eastern Studies in Germany and Switzerland and *chazzanut* both privately (with cantor Marcel Lang, *z"l*, and cantor Jeremy Burko) and at the Levisson Instituut in Amsterdam. She contributed to *All These Vows*—Kol Nidre, *We Have Sinned: Sin and Confession in Judaism*—Ashamnu *and* Al Chet, and *May God Remember: Memory and Memorializing in Judaism*—Yizkor (all Jewish Lights).

nations [of the rest of the world]." We are Jews precisely because we were separated first from the Egyptians and later (by prophets and the Rabbis) from various other peoples over the course of time. The nineteenth century emphasized our commonality with all peoples, but in our time, with Jews firmly accepted as citizens in most Western countries and with the founding of Israel as an independent Jewish state, the uniqueness of Jews and Judaism has regained attractiveness to some extent. Do we today still *want* to be universal? Or has "universalism" perhaps just become an empty word, no longer a principle by which we live? Have we ever been truly universal?

Among the insertions within the High Holy Day *Amidah* are three texts that long for a universal acknowledgment of the God of Israel.

1. The liturgical poem *V'khol Ma'aminim* lists biblical attributes of God, which "all believe."
2. The *Amidah* insertion *Uv'khen* describes the religiosity of all creatures.
3. *V'ye'etayu* is based on the prophetic vision that all people will some day come to worship in Zion.

All three have extraordinarily beautiful musical renditions; the first and last one, however (at least in traditional synagogues), are often abridged or just quickly mumbled through for the sake of time. As much as all three seem at first glance to be universalistic, however, none of them creates *true* universalism by any modern standard of the term. As a concept, universalism has gone through several manifestations over time in Jewish tradition. Only with our current moment has true universalism emerged as a possibility. As we shall see, all past forms of universalism are actually rooted in expressions of Jewish particularism.

The Hope for Peace

Uv'khen is inspired by a phrase in the *Megillah*. *Uv'khen avo el hamelekh*, "And therefore I shall go to the king" (Esther 4:16), says Queen Esther, to plead for the Jews to be spared following the divine decree that they shall perish. Esther expresses her *uv'khen* without knowing whether she will survive the encounter, because those who approach the throne unsummoned are subject to death. *Uv'khen* in our liturgy conveys the same atmosphere of dread, for it is on the High Holy Days that Israel approaches its divine king, not knowing whether it is to be punished or pardoned.

More than one poem begins with the word *uv'khen*, not just the ones we have here. The *Un'taneh Tokef* too begins with the word. The one we have here, however, draws conceptually on the Greek book of Sirach (written in the second century BCE, and still a part of most Christian Bibles) to express *how* Israel will survive. God will appear to enemy nations, casting fear upon them.

> Have mercy on us, O Master, the God of all, and cast the fear of You upon all the nations. Lift up your hand against the foreign nations, and let them see your dominance.... Have pity on the city of your holy precinct, Jerusalem, the place of our rest.... Give a reward to those who wait for You.... (from Sirach 36)

These Sirach verses are a younger version of an old prophetic theme: the future universal pilgrimage to Zion. The peoples of the world will say:

> Come, let us go up to the mount of the Eternal One, to the house of the God of Jacob, that He may instruct us in his ways and that we may walk in his path. For instruction shall come forth from Zion, the word of the Eternal One from Jerusalem. Thus God will judge among the nations ... and they shall beat their swords into ploughshares ... and they shall never know war any more. (Isaiah 2:3–4)

This is just one—probably the most famous—of several prophetic texts describing this pilgrimage of the peoples to worship the God of Israel, a theme that was first developed in the prophecy of the eighth century BCE.[1]

A later prophet, Zechariah (sixth century BCE) reversed the image (Zechariah 14): yes, all the nations will indeed come to Jerusalem, but for war and only to be smitten by God; on that day great panic from God will fall upon the peoples, only some of whom will survive in order to worship Israel's God. Then, "Adonai will be ruler over all the earth; on that day Adonai will be one and his name will be one" (Zechariah14:9). This very verse concludes the *Alenu* and appears as well just before *Uv'khen* in the High Holy Day *Amidah*.

The prophets promise security, safety, and peace, as Israel's former enemies become part of Israel itself. *V'ye'etayu* restates this prophetic vision. That all the world shall come and serve God is thus not a universal wish, but a very particularistic longing that we—we!—can worship where and how we want in an undisturbed manner, because the whole world will be like us, even a part of us.

Monotheism

This first vision from Zechariah and the early prophets was the product of pre-exilic times. Scholars assume today, however, that Israel had yet to be fully monotheistic. God was seen as one of many deities, albeit the highest and strongest, the one protecting Israel. But the Babylonian exile (sixth century BCE) brought a national and theological crisis that forced a rethinking of this equation. How had Babylonia, which worshiped other gods, been victorious? Why hadn't Israel's God prevailed? God had promised an everlasting Davidic kingdom and an enduring divine presence on Zion, and both were now gone. To reconcile this promise with reality, the exilic prophets explained Israel's destiny as the result of Israel's sin, not of God's weakness; indeed, the God of Israel was in fact the *only* universal ruler over the whole world—no other gods existed. "I am Adonai and there is none else; ... I form light and create darkness, I make peace and create woe" (Isaiah 45:5–7).

The same author (known as Second Isaiah), envisions all Israel regathered so that all peoples will recognize that no other god exists: "Come, gather together, Draw nigh, you remnants of the nations!... Who announced this aforetime, foretold it of old? Was it not I Adonai? There is no god besides Me ..." (Isaiah 45:20–21).

Monotheism is the universal claim that all the world needs to acknowledge the *one* God of Judaism because there is no other.

Throughout the Middle Ages, Jewish universalism was assumed to imply these two prophetic approaches: an eventual pilgrimage of the nations to Zion and their acceptance of Israel's God as the true and only deity. Jewish liturgy reiterated these points: there is only one God, our own; that God will eventually prevail, at which time, all peoples—or at least their remnants—will come to worship God in a rebuilt Temple. *Uv'khen* and similarly sounding poetic insertions (like *V'ye'etayu*) are medieval expressions of this thinking. Only with the Enlightenment and Emancipation, in the eighteenth and nineteenth centuries, was this view questioned.

Acculturation

By the nineteenth century new approaches to universalism developed within Judaism. It was prompted by the desire for Jews to be accepted as citizens with full civil rights, and it followed from the Age of Reason, which had revealed all human beings as similarly gifted with the quintessential faculty of reason. In addition, it mirrored a self-critical reflection within Protestantism in Germany at the time, self-questioning of the absoluteness of Christianity.[2] *V'ye'etayu* especially was now seen in a new light.

Its newfound significance was stressed by its outstandingly majestic setting in Berlin by Louis Lewandowksi (1821–1894) for choir, tenor, and organ.[3] The piece begins with a tenor solo ("cantor") singing *W'je-e-sso-ju chol l'owdecho* ... (the Ashkenazi Hebrew pronunciation as given in the musical transliteration), accompanied by an organ, and is sung extremely slowly in a majestic style (*molto lento maesto*); the four-part choir joins in with *Wi-ha-l'-lu-cho kol af-sse orez* ... ("all parts of the world will sing your praise") and then develops into a dialogue between cantor and choir, imitating the universal response to the one voice of Judaism. Finally, the choir sings slowly (*andantino*) and extremely softly (barely heard, in fact—*pinanissimo*), with every voice sharing the same rhythm, *Wi-lam-du sso-im bi-noh* ... ("and those who go astray shall impart insight"), finishing again with a dialogue between cantor and choir in the initial tempo (*tempo primo*), slow and majestic. The chords of the organ highlight the rhythm, starting loud (*forte*) but finishing with the last four notes, singing *ke-sser m'lu-cho* ("the crown of his kingship") extremely loud (*fortissimo*), with all voices singing their highest notes.

In English-speaking progressive congregations the translation of *V'ye'etayu* by the British writer Israel Zangwill (1864–1926)—"All the world shall come to serve Thee"—attracted majestic melodies, the most popular one by Max Janowski (1912–1991) in Chicago, but Abraham Wolfe Binder (New York, 1895–1966) had already composed a tune for the American *Union Hymnal*, which he was editing.[4]

In the progressive liturgies that include it, "All the World" attracts the full attention of the congregation because of its dramatic music, even though the piece had traditionally not been central at all and in traditional congregations still is not so. *V'ye'etayu* is an example of Reform Judaism not just alternating or abridging the liturgy, but actually changing its meaning and impact by the way certain prayers are "performed." This poem seems surely to stress universalism, and it does so in the vernacular, which worshipers understand as they sing along—thus giving the liturgy of progressive Judaism its own distinctive voice within the voices of Judaism.

The reason for highlighting this text was to develop a form of Judaism that was fully responsive to modernity and thereby to enhance the opportunity for Jews to be given civic equality. The old expressions of chosenness were incompatible with this goal. Petitions for God to overcome the nations with dread or to bring Israel home to Zion were inconsistent with gratitude for the opportunity to join those very nations as citizens.

This universalism was altogether novel in that it sought loyalty to the countries in which Jews lived, rather than a return of Jews to their homeland, where other nations would someday join them by converting to the Jewish message of the ages. This is not to say that Judaism was abandoned as being just like all the other religions of the world. On the contrary: these classical Reform Jews remained proud of the ethical mandates of their heritage and expected Israel, now spread throughout the world, to carry God's moral message to the four corners of the earth.

The person who best systematized these principles was Abraham Geiger (1810–1874). In his guidelines for a new prayer book, he explained:

> With particular regard to the world-historical position of Israel, it has to be strongly emphasized that Judaism is the religion of truth and light, that Israel had received a mission and remains committed to it, to be the carrier and herald of this doctrine, and that this is linked with the confidence that this doctrine will more and more become common for all the world and that thus one day Israel will expand to humanity. Expressions that narrow down these sublime thoughts are unsuitable and are not permitted [in the prayer book].[5]

V'ye'etayu underscored this universal striving and was stressed all the more.

The most universal approach may have been voiced by Claude Montefiore (1858–1938), a founder of British Liberal Judaism, who thought:

> The religion of the future will be, as I believe, a developed and purified Judaism; but from that developed and puri-fied Judaism, the record which tells, however imperfectly, of perhaps its greatest, as certainly of its most potent and influential teacher, will not be excluded. The roll call of its heroes will not omit the name of Jesus. Christianity and Judaism must gradually approach each other. The one must shed the teachings which Jesus did not teach, the other must acknowledge, more fully, more frankly than has as yet been done, what he did was for religion and for the world.[6]

As radical as it is, however, even Montefiore's notion is not fully inclusive. As long as the religion of the future is "a developed and purified *Judaism*," it is a particularistic expression of enormous self-confidence. Judaism was a *particular* religion charged with the *universal* task of spreading God's ethical will throughout the world.[7]

The Jewish Mission

The preferred term for this sacred task was "the Jewish mission." Rabbi Israel I. Mattuck could even say, "Judaism was the first missionary reli-gion."[8] But already in the Talmud the following statement can be found: "The Holy One, blessed be He, exiled Israel among the nations only in order to increase their numbers with the addition of proselytes" (Pesachim 87b). But it became an independent chapter in Jewish thought and prac-tice only with modernity and the need to devise a Judaism that was both independently important (else, why remain Jewish?) but also respectful of others; both particularistic in its practices but universally ethical in its goals. Modernity was the time for this mission to reach fruition. As Samuel Holdheim (1806–1860) put it in a sermon:

> It is the destiny of Judaism to pour the light of its thoughts, the fire of its sentiments, the fervor of its feelings upon all souls and hearts on earth. Then all of these peoples and nations, each according to its soil and historic character-istics, will, by accepting our teachings, kindle their own

lights, which will then shine independently and warm their souls. Judaism shall be the seed-bed of the nations....[9]

The nations of the world would not disappear; they would each retain their own religious particularities, but they would all be influenced by Judaism's core teachings, the universalist ethics of the one true God.

Leo Baeck (1873–1956), who already in 1905 had outlined the specific Jewish ethical mission (*sittliche Missionspflicht*)[10] as part of the "essence of Judaism," used the clearest language in an address given in 1949: "It is the missionary work of Judaism that is to be created now."[11] After summarizing the "missionary work" of Islam, Buddhism, and Christianity, he appeals to Judaism to follow suit and not be silent; Judaism, as well, had "to send out missionaries" as a continuation of a practice known from the time of the Mishnah.

Already at the Fifth International Conference of the World Union for Progressive Judaism in 1946, Baeck had explained his reasons:

> Judaism must not stand aside, when the great problems of humanity, which are reborn in every new epoch, struggle in the minds to gain expression, battle in the societies of mankind to find their way. We must not, as Jews, deny ourselves to the problems of the time, nor hide ourselves, as Jews, in face of them.... We are Jews also for the sake of humanity; we should be there, quite especially in this world after the war; we have our questions to raise....[12]

In our times "proactive conversion" has become a popular term to describe the changed attitude of not only *welcoming* people interested in becoming Jews but also actively *advocating* at least the ethical values of Judaism that ought to hold everywhere. "All the world shall come to serve Thee" can thus be understood not only as a description of a future event but also as today's task to make Judaism known and to lead the world to ethical values. This, again, is not a "universal" notion, but a particularistic expression of Jewish self-consciousness.

On the Verge of True Global Universalism?

Do we really want all the world to come to serve our God? Not according to Abraham Joshua Heschel (1907–1972), who wondered:

> Is it really our desire to build a monolithic society: one party, one view, one leader, and no opposition? Is religious uniformity desirable or even possible?... Does not the task of preparing the Kingdom of God require a diversity of talents, a variety of rituals, soul-searching as well as opposition? Perhaps it is the will of God that in this eon there should be diversity in our forms of devotion and commitment to God.[13]

The various stages of Jewish universalism described thus far have been particularistic in the end. Heschel, however, points to the possibility of a new post-denominational universalism. Despite a deep-seated theology of particularism defining their roots, Jews can *act* in a fully universal way by welcoming a variety of personalities and people from all backgrounds into their congregations and by an open-minded dialogue with everyone—not just the other monotheistic traditions, but even atheists.

The opportunities to learn about other positions while adding our own particular voice are much greater than even Heschel could have imagined because of the new technologies of our era. The Internet, its various social networks, and its tools for translations of foreign languages make this the first time in history when we can actually be truly universal in a physical sense. The point of our global exchange would not be just to tolerate the existence of those who are utterly different than we are, but also to be open to learn from and to be questioned by them. It would mean entering into a dialogue without knowing in advance its outcome and would bring the possibility of encounters that might change both dialogue partners.

The goal of this practical universalism would not be merging our liturgies, which would remain particularistic reminders of our roots and past, as well as being celebrations of our own distinctive present; this very distinctiveness would be part and parcel of a global community where we share issues common to all humanity.

The most difficult dialogue might well turn out to be not with other religions, which would retain their own distinctive liturgies and identity, but with those who are closest to us: other Jewish denominations. We would have to reach a position of mutual respect within Jewish denominations themselves, since reaching out to the whole world without fully respecting our own Jewish brothers and sisters would be inconsistent. We Jews, too, would have to listen to each other while being open to change as we hear other Jews speak of their understanding of Judaism's teachings. Jews speaking openly to Jews would be part of our universalism, too.

Such an attitude cannot flourish without complete security in one's own position. Jews of every stamp would have to be knowledgeable in their understanding of Jewish tradition, because precisely on that account might we be able to develop this practical universalism. It would express the reality of our newly connected global society as a worthy successor of the old prophetic dream of universalism—renewed explicitly for our time.

A Sage among the Gentiles?

A HALAKHIC LESSON ON MORAL UNIVERSALISM

Rabbi Daniel Landes

The soaring, joyous majesty of *V'khol Ma'aminim* has an overt, rigorous halakhic parallel in the doctrine of the *b'nei no'ach* ("children of Noah," or "Noahides")—the term of choice that presents the non-Jew as covenanted with God. This covenant with the world at large is said to have begun with Adam and Eve but completed only with Noah after the Flood. The Rabbinic conversation about this covenant revolves around the *mitzvot* demanded by it, the commandments incumbent on humanity at large, as men and women descended from Noah. The two major Rabbinic descriptions are found in the Babylonian Talmud, tractate Sanhedrin, and in the code of Moses Maimonides. We will focus on the Maimonidean version.

Rabbi Daniel Landes is the director and *rosh hayeshivah* of the Pardes Institute of Jewish Studies in Jerusalem. Pardes brings together men and women of all backgrounds to study classical Jewish texts and contemporary Jewish issues in a rigorous, challenging, and open-minded environment. Rabbi Landes is also a contributor to the *My People's Prayer Book: Traditional Prayers, Modern Commentaries* series, winner of the National Jewish Book Award; *My People's Passover Haggadah: Traditional Texts, Modern Commentaries*, a finalist for the National Jewish Book Award; *Who by Fire, Who by Water*—Un'taneh Tokef; *All These Vows*—Kol Nidre; *We Have Sinned: Sin and Confession in Judaism*—Ashamnu *and* Al Chet; and *May God Remember: Memory and Memorializing in Judaism*—Yizkor (all Jewish Lights).

Maimonides's description of the Noahide code is not incidental to his global vision of the purpose and end of Jewish law. It appears in the culmination of his magnum opus, the *Mishneh Torah*, which is a complete and incredibly designed work of 1,005 chapters, within fourteen volumes. The last book is *The Book of Judges*, and the last set of chapters is the "Laws of Kings and Their Wars." The final discussion (chapters 11–12) is devoted to King Messiah and the messianic age he will usher in at the end of history. The penultimate discussion (chapters 9–10) contains the laws of the Noahide covenant. This discussion is highly relevant, even crucial, for Maimonides's notion of civil society in the here and now and his vision of a perfected world of the future. Maimonides writes:

> The original Adam was charged regarding six matters: idolatry, the "blessing" of God, the shedding of blood, sexual immorality, theft, and civil law. Even though all of these are a tradition received by us from Moses our Teacher, and even though reason [alone] inclines us toward them, it is implied by the Torah that he [Adam] received them by divine command. To Noah, God added [the prohibition against eating] a limb of a live animal, as it says, "You must not eat flesh with its life-blood in it" (Genesis 9:4). We thus find seven commandments. (Laws of Kings and Their Wars 9:1)

We see, first of all, that Maimonides considers these seven moral laws to be rational in nature. First and foremost (1 and 2), one may not disregard the one God, the force behind the moral law, either (1) rejecting Him (through idolatry) or (2) denying Him (through "blessing," a euphemism for "cursing," an act considered too horrendous even to be mentioned). In addition, the bans on (3) murder, (4) adultery and incest, (5) theft, and (6) barbaric cruelty to animals are all obvious, part of the natural moral law that is available to reason. They are also of a certain "minimal" status in that they are only prohibitions. One must "simply" not do them. The one positive and active command is (7) civil law, the obligation to establish basic societal (e.g., ethical, commercial, relational) laws and to set up of courts of justice.

This look at Maimonides's work demonstrates the profound respect that Jewish law has for the Noahide. It assumes that non-Jews will willingly adopt and carry out laws that are rational, moral, and, therefore, universal, in that they are also observed by Jews. They are indeed essential to Jewish law: the three issues over which a Jew must choose martyrdom over transgression are idolatry, sexual immorality, and the wanton shedding of blood. Further, theft is considered by the Bible and the Rabbis as the reason for the Flood in the time of Noah (Talmud, Sanhedrin 109a), and establishing courts of justice is among the highest civic achievements that humanity can achieve:

> A judge should always see himself as if a sword were being pressed against his throat with *Gehinnom* [the equivalent of hell] lying open beneath his feet.... Any judge who judges truthfully, even for just an instant, is considered as if he has rectified the entire world. (Laws of Sanhedrin 23:8–9)

The last command to be given—not eating a limb from a live animal—is likewise very influential in Jewish consciousness, as reflected in the prohibition of eating blood, the Jewish avoidance of hunting, and the laws of kashrut in general.

What emerges is a shared social vision of Jew and non-Jew. Our rituals and narrative are often quite different; even if they share a common, overlapping source, as in Christianity and Islam, they diverge. But there is a shared moral monotheistic vision and law that we need to recover—even when we disagree on how they are to be manifested in all their details.

A second passage now needs to be added to the first if we are to understand the significance of this claim of sharing a common morality:

> All who accept the seven *mitzvot* and are careful to perform them are considered among the pious gentiles and have a share in the world to come. This is the case for those who accept and do them because they were commanded by the Holy One blessed be He in the Torah, which informs us through Moses, Our Teacher, that the children of Noah from of old were commanded to do them. But those who do them out of intellectual conviction [alone] are neither resident aliens, nor pious gentiles, nor one of their sages. (Laws of Kings and Their Wars 8:11)

Once again we must read carefully and precisely. Maimonides greatly values the Noahide who performs the seven *mitzvot*. If done properly, as covenantal acts, they have transcendent meaning; indeed, that is why the performer has a "seat at the table," the heavenly table, that is—a "share in the world to come." Jews are promised no more than that: "All of Israel has a share in the world to come" (the prelude to the classic *Ethics of the Fathers—Pirkei Avot*).

But Maimonides explicitly states that the source of the moral command is God-given within the Torah, a fact that the Noahide needs to acknowledge, either explicitly or by implication. This is certainly true in Christianity, regarding the moral law, and in Islam, where Moses is seen as a prophet.

But for those Noahides who accept the moral law out of intellectual conviction alone, Maimonides seems to have no place of honor. First of all a Noahide is not acceptable as a *ger toshav* ("resident alien"). Classically, the *ger toshav* is someone who is allowed to reside in the Land of Israel because he or she (and his or her family) has taken upon themselves the seven *mitzvot* within a ceremony confirmed by the Great Sanhedrin within the Temple precinct. Halakhically we Jews are commanded to take care of *all* gentiles who live in our midst, but only for reasons of practical concern—so as not to inflame hatred and to contribute to a civilized society and the ways of peace (*mipnei darkhei shalom*). But the *ger toshav* has a higher status in that a *ger toshav* is granted extensive entitlement to support, encouragement, and help in the Jewish community. Although not quite a brother or a sister, a *ger toshav* is most definitely a treasured cousin.

The accompanying term "pious gentile" (*chasidei umot ha'olam*) is nowadays associated popularly with those non-Jews who saved Jewish lives during the Shoah, but in Maimonides's time, it had a far broader meaning, going back to Mishnah Avot, which promises such pious people a share in the world to come but stipulates nothing specific about them. The third term, "their sages" (*chokhmeihem*), classically refers to someone who is both intellectually adept and of excellent moral stature. In Maimonides's view, those who perform the moral law without a divine basis are not part of these three overlapping circles. This perspective makes it difficult to envision a shared moral mission with dedicated atheists and even agnostics.

A different understanding of Maimonides is possible, however, through the ancient and venerable Yemenite Manuscript of the *Mishneh Torah*. To repeat the standard version that we have employed, Maimonides states, "But those who do them out of intellectual conviction [alone] are neither resident aliens, nor pious gentiles, nor [Hebrew: *v'lo*] one of their sages." The Yemenite Manuscript is identical except for the end, where it states: "*but rather* [Hebrew: *ela*] they are [!] one of their sages." The difference in the Hebrew versions is ostensibly only a matter of two three-letter words, *v'lo* ("nor") and *ela* ("but rather"). Actually the difference is even less: the second and third Hebrew letters are the same, *lamed* and *alef*. *V'lo* ("nor") begins with a *vav*, however, while *ela* ("but rather") begins with an *alef*. (Indeed, in cursive texts, these two letters are frequently confused.)

The version with *ela* ("but rather") is inclusive. It means that even though the moral atheist is neither a *ger toshav* nor a pious gentile, he or she is nonetheless "one of their sages," which is to say morally wise, a character trait highly prized by Maimonides, who appreciated moral non-Jewish philosophers.

Which version should we choose?

We should choose both. The Yemenite *ela* ("but rather") includes the nonbeliever as a potential moral agent and partner in creating civil society. But philosophically sophisticated as such a nonbeliever is, we exercise some concern about the person's depth. *Mishnat Rebbe Eliezer* says concerning such people, "If they do the seven *mitzvot* and say '[We do it because] we heard it from so and so, or we made our own decision because reason inclined us so ... they receive the reward only in this world."[1] By contrast, the rational monotheist performs the seven *mitzvot* because they are reasonable and crucially commanded by God. Thus he operates within a dual context of both the here and now of this world but also within a transcendent reality that is called "the world to come."

All the above provides the potential for a three-track moral community. We as Jews proceed with our unique system that has served us morally well for millennia. We can reach out to non-monotheists and even atheists to work together, going so far as to appreciate them as sages. We should especially acknowledge the strong bonds that we have with Christians, Muslims, and other monotheists, in creating a kingdom of God. Indeed, that kingdom is celebrated in *V'khol Ma'aminim*.

On the High Holy Days when I sing with my community, "Everyone believes He remembers the covenant; He allocates life to every living being," I will intend not only our Jewish covenant, but also the covenant that honors our larger moral world, the one God made with the sons and daughters of Noah.

‿〜〜⦿

Universalism, Transnationalism, and the Challenge of Triumphalism

Rabbi David A. Teutsch, PhD

When I was a child, I both loved and puzzled over the messianic visions of the Bible: everyone sitting in the shade of their vines and fig trees with plenty to eat; the lion lying down with the lamb; the law going forth from Zion; widows, orphans, and the poor well taken care of. On the one hand, I earnestly wanted to live in that world. On the other, I intuitively understood that this could not be the next stage for the world we live in.

It took decades for my intellect to catch up with my intuition. One reason it took so long is that I was raised on the notion that universal right and wrong exist alongside universal truth and that it is within the grasp of each individual to discover and do what one ought. Gradually,

---

Rabbi David A. Teutsch, PhD, is the Wiener Professor of Contemporary Jewish Civilization and director of the Center for Jewish Ethics at the Reconstructionist Rabbinical College, where he served as president for nearly a decade. He was editor in chief of the seven-volume *Kol Haneshamah* prayer book series. His book *A Guide to Jewish Practice: Everyday Living* (RRC Press) won the National Jewish Book Award for Contemporary Jewish Life and Practice. He is also author of *Spiritual Community: The Power to Restore Hope, Commitment and Joy* (Jewish Lights) and several other books. He contributed to *Who by Fire, Who by Water*—Un'taneh Tokef, *All These Vows*—Kol Nidre, *We Have Sinned: Sin and Confession in Judaism*—Ashamnu *and* Al Chet, *and* May God Remember: Memory and Memorializing in Judaism*—Yizkor (all Jewish Lights).

however, I learned that moral intuitions are shaped by personal experience, by language and concepts, and by the people we are around—family, peers, and communities. That means our moral lives are profoundly formed by the cultures in which we find ourselves. Ethics looks different in different cultural and historical settings. And as the philosopher Alasdair MacIntyre points out, virtues differ, even from occupation to occupation—computer programmers, for instance, need different virtues than do subsistence farmers. And yet, who does not cling to a hope, however faint, for universal justice, plenty, and peace?

We human beings are social animals. Although weaker than many species, we make up for what we lack physically with brains that support speech and complex, cooperative interaction. Our ancestors used those gifts to form small clans and tribes, where they developed shared identities with those around them. It was not so much that we found our way because of individual conscience, therefore, so much as we were guided by the shared life of clan and tribe. Because group pride and loyalty were critical, clans defined themselves not only by who they were but also by who they were not. To support tribal solidarity, judgments often took the form of "We are better because ..."

Over the millennia, little has changed in that regard. Modern nationalism still assumes competition. Nations—and even families—still tend toward triumphalism. As one commercial puts it, "My dog's better than your dog!"

By contrast, I think of Woodrow Wilson's dream for the League of Nations following World War I, where nations would resolve conflicts and competition without violence in order to live in harmony. It was a vision far short of universalism because its highest goal was not the end of individual nations but their peaceful coexistence—call it transnationalism. Given the propensity of people to identify with smaller groups, I believe transnationalism is actually preferable—it is certainly much more likely to work. Our cultural identities are too important for us to willingly abandon them.

These thoughts provide a useful perspective for exploring the messianic visions embodied in the liturgy of the *Yamim Nora'im* ("Days of Awe"). The core of the Rosh Hashanah service, the re-enthronement of God as sovereign of the universe, announces a world that is a spiritual and moral whole with only one ruler to whom we owe loyalty. But the universalism of this vision assumes that Zion will be the center of God's reign and that the Torah, God's central teaching, will become universally accepted. That is precisely the vision of the *Uv'khen* paragraphs, central to this book's focus.

Much as I love the imagery of these paragraphs, I find them enormously challenging. Their image of world harmony does imply the possibility of every individual coming to awareness of God, but only through the Jewish vision of God's will. If we recognize that other cultures also seek to commune with God, each in its own way, is it not a problem to say that the Torah and the Jewish People are the only basis for universal justice and peace?

The second *Uv'khen* paragraph begins by asking God to "install honor in your people," which is to say, Jews. It then requests "happiness in your land and joy in your city," clearly a reference to the Land of Israel and city of Jerusalem, which are to be the center of divine rule. A universalism that places a single people at its center is not just universalism; it is also triumphalism. The small group of Jews who genuinely believe that God gave every word of Torah to Moses on Mount Sinai can cite belief in the absolute truth of Torah as the source for their view. The rest of us, however, are more likely to believe that failure to recognize other sources of revelation constitutes hubris and triumphalism.

What can we do with the particularism of this language? One answer is to interpret it in a way that is acceptable to us. I hope that the Jewish People is a people of God, that we feel beloved, and that we act as a people of God should. But I also grant that there are others who are people of God. My relationship does not dismiss theirs, any more than one beloved daughter makes another beloved daughter less cared about by her mother. I truly want God to shine forth from Zion (and the State of Israel could certainly benefit from a stronger divine presence there!), but I would love it if God shone forth simultaneously across the world. I envision no messianic days where we abandon particularity or all speak the same language. Rather, I hope for the replacement of triumphalism with concern for others and appreciation of our differences. Then, in the last words of the *Uv'khen's* final paragraph, "Injustice will shut its mouth." The capacity to better the world through transnationalism is wonderfully illustrated by the near eradication of such scourges as polio and smallpox. We can vastly improve the world if we cooperate to do it.

The brilliant twentieth-century poet W. H. Auden once wrote, "The error born into the bones of each man and each woman is to want not universal love but to be loved alone." Translated to the level of tribes and nations, the error is to want our own group's triumph over others. That error alone is responsible for a huge portion of the destruction that human beings visit upon each other. A messianism tainted with triumphalism makes for a poisonous brew—it can be fatal to drink the wrong Kool-Aid.

The acrostic *piyyut* *V'ye'etayu* contains none of the challenges embodied in *Uv'khen*. It too speaks of God becoming universally celebrated, the whole world acknowledging God's sovereignty, and those embroiled in more mundane concerns awakening to the divinity that unifies our world and infuses it with meaning. The vision of *V'ye'etayu* imagines all people turning to God from wherever they happen to be. There is no hint of triumphalism or ethnocentrism here. *V'ye'etayu* embodies a palpable yearning for a world redeemed, not by the triumph of Israel but of God and of all humanity. Here is a messianic vision for which I can pray and work with a whole heart and without hesitation.

Nowadays, *Alenu* is a concluding prayer for our daily, Shabbat, and holiday liturgy, but it was composed for the Rosh Hashanah service specifically. Appropriately, it shares many of the themes of *V'ye'etayu*, also a New Year addition, even though it expresses them quite differently. The theme of *Alenu* is our responsibility to keep God central in our thoughts, our speech, and our deeds in order to "repair the world with the divine presence." It anticipates a time when all will submit to God's rule, unifying God's name and redeeming the world.

Ever since the spread of *Alenu* throughout our liturgy, its messianic hope has provided a crescendo to every service. It is the highest form of the Jewish messianic vision. Like *V'ye'etayu*, it too prays not for the triumph of the Jewish People alone but also of God and all humanity. Much as we hope for the safety and success of the Jewish People, the highest Jewish hope is for the triumph of all the world's peoples, with each one turning toward God in its own way and living with the others in the light of God's presence.

⚬⟋⟋⟋⟋⟍⟍⟍⟍⟍⟍⟍⟍⟍⟍⟍⟍

The Prayer for the State of Israel

UNIVERSALISM AND PARTICULARISM

Rabbi Dalia Marx, PhD

It is a well-known fact that traditional Jewish prayer books contain unflattering wording when referring to non-Jews.[1] Perhaps these exclusive, and sometimes even insulting, expressions served as a coping device: a remedy for Jewish feelings of physical insecurity; a reassurance that God was still on their side; and a reminder that their powerless and, sometimes, humiliated state did not mean that God had abandoned them (as was often claimed by their Christian detractors). The language of chosenness was for many centuries a survival mechanism, the weapon of the weak, a form of spiritual resistance.

In this context, the situation in the State of Israel is unique in Jewish history of the last two millennia. In Israel, Jews are the majority,

Rabbi Dalia Marx, PhD, is a professor of liturgy and midrash at the Jerusalem campus of Hebrew Union College–Jewish Institute of Religion and teaches in various academic institutions in Israel and Europe. Rabbi Marx earned her doctorate at the Hebrew University in Jerusalem and her rabbinic ordination at HUC–JIR in Jerusalem and Cincinnati. She is involved in various research groups and is active in promoting progressive Judaism in Israel. Rabbi Marx contributed to *Who by Fire, Who by Water—Un'taneh Tokef*, *All These Vows—Kol Nidre*, *We Have Sinned: Sin and Confession in Judaism—Ashamnu and Al Chet*, and *May God Remember: Memory and Memorializing in Judaism—Yizkor* (all Jewish Lights). She writes for academic journals and the Israeli press, and is engaged in creating new liturgies and midrashim.

holding political and economic power in a state where their religion and language are dominant. I prefer to read Balaam's blessing (or, maybe, curse) describing the Israelites as "a people who live apart and does not consider itself one of the nations" (Numbers 23:9) as a question: can a people truly exist separately that way? Israeli Jews must regularly grapple with their connections to non-Jews who dwell in the same land or in neighboring territories.

To some extent, Jewish liturgy is hardly affected by all this—the traditional communities worship from a book that evolved through the centuries but is relatively immune to change today. Still, it is the nature of liturgy to reflect the life of those who use it, especially in progressive circles that welcome new compositions. The liturgy can be expected to reflect the ambivalent situation of Jews who live in a Jewish state but reside alongside Arab Palestinians with whom they are often in a state of tension and hostility.

How, then, does the liturgy capture a Jewish and Israeli perspective on non-Jews living in Israel and outside of it—the various Arab countries all around, and most specifically, the Palestinians? To answer that question, I turn to the Prayer for the State of Israel (PSI). I begin with its predecessors, Jewish prayers for the well-being of the various states and governments where Jews have lived. I then turn to special prayers composed exclusively for the Jewish state, the State of Israel. All of this will lead to some observations on universalism and particularism, inclusivity and exclusivity, in Jewish liturgy.

Prayers for the State

The charge to pray for the welfare of the government goes back all the way to the destruction of the First Temple (587 BCE), when the prophet Jeremiah encouraged the exiles to lead normal lives, to build houses and plant gardens, to marry and have children. Part of this normality would be to "seek the welfare of the city to which I have exiled you and pray to Adonai on its behalf; for with its prosperity you shall prosper" (Jeremiah 29:7).

An interesting paradox underlines this call: the exiles should pray for the welfare of their enemies, but for their own benefit. Jews have known throughout the ages that when the political environment is calm, they are better off.

The rationale for the prayer for the government is reiterated by Rabbi Chanina (first century CE), the assistant high priest, who says, "Pray for the welfare of the government, for were it not for the fear of it, people would devour each other alive" (*Pirkei Avot* 3:2). Many centuries before Thomas Hobbes, Jewish political philosophy understood, as Jonathan Sarna phrases it, "that a government, even an oppressive government, is superior to anarchy."[2]

And indeed, we find prayers that Jews have recited throughout the generations for the well-being of their gentile leaders of state.[3] The fourteenth-century Sephardi commentator on the siddur Rabbi David Abudarham described it as commonplace, citing as a proof text the prophet Jeremiah:

> [After reading from the Torah] it is the custom to bless the king and to pray so that [God] would help him and strengthen him over his enemies, for it is written: "And seek the welfare of the city to which I have exiled you and pray to Adonai in its behalf, for in its prosperity you shall prosper" (Jeremiah 29:7). And the welfare of the city is that one prays for the victory of the king over his enemies.[4]

The most familiar prayer for the government, *Hanoten T'shuah* ("May the One who grants salvation"), appeared in the fifteenth or early sixteenth century and has become the traditional liturgical staple recited in both Ashkenazi and Sephardi congregations after the Torah service on Shabbat. Special versions were sometimes composed for specific leaders, among them King Ferdinand, who together with his wife Queen Isabella expelled the Jews from Spain in 1492![5]

The standard text wishes health, success, victory, and prosperity to the ruler, usually specifying his name, and sometimes his wife and children as well. The prayer ends, however, with the wish to behold the redeemer coming to Zion. Here is one version of *Hanoten T'shuah*:

Hanoten T'shuah

"May the One who grants salvation to kings" (Psalm 144:10) and dominion to princes— His kingdom is an eternal kingdom—

הַנּוֹתֵן תְּשׁוּעָה

"הַנּוֹתֵן תְּשׁוּעָה לַמְּלָכִים"

(תהלים יְמַ"ד, 10), וּמֶמְשָׁלָה

לַנְּסִיכִים,

מַלְכוּתוֹ מַלְכוּת כָּל עוֹלָמִים,

"the One who delivers David his servant from an evil sword" (ibid.), "who opens a way in the sea, a path in the mighty water" (Isaiah 43:16), bless, keep, protect, help, exalt, magnify, and raise up the president and his vice president, and all the public servants of this land. May [God] cause our enemies to be struck down before them. May He send blessing and success to their every endeavor.

In his mercy may the king over the kings of kings grant them life and guard them and save them from sorrow, and harm, in his mercy may the king, the kings of kings grant them and all their advisors wisdom to do well by us and by all of Israel.

In their days and in our days may Judah be saved, and Israel dwell securely, and may a redeemer come to Zion.

May this be God's will. And let us say: Amen.

"הַפּוֹצֶה אֶת דָּוִד עַבְדּוֹ מֵחֶרֶב רָעָה" (שם, 11).

"הַנּוֹתֵן בַּיָּם דֶּרֶךְ וּבְמַיִם עַזִּים נְתִיבָה" (ישעיהו מ"ג, 16),

הוּא יְבָרֵךְ וְיִשְׁמוֹר וְיִנְצוֹר וְיַעֲזוֹר אֶת הַנָּשִׂיא וְאֶת מִשְׁנֵהוּ וְאֶת כָּל שָׂרֵי הָאָרֶץ הַזֹּאת.

מֶלֶךְ מַלְכֵי הַמְּלָכִים בְּרַחֲמָיו יְחַיֵּם וְיִשְׁמְרֵם וּמִכָּל צָרָה וְיָגוֹן וָנֶזֶק יַצִּילֵם.

וְיַדְבֵּר שׂוֹנְאֵינוּ תַּחְתֵּיהֶם, וְיִשְׁלַח בְּרָכָה וְהַצְלָחָה בְּכָל מַעֲשֵׂי יְדֵיהֶם.

מֶלֶךְ מַלְכֵי הַמְּלָכִים בְּרַחֲמָיו יִתֵּן בְּלִבָּם וּבְלֵב כָּל יוֹעֲצֵיהֶם וְשָׂרֵיהֶם לַעֲשׂוֹת טוֹבָה עִמָּנוּ וְעִם כָּל יִשְׂרָאֵל.

בִּימֵיהֶם וּבְיָמֵינוּ תִּוָּשַׁע יְהוּדָה וְיִשְׂרָאֵל יִשְׁכּוֹן לָבֶטַח וּבָא לְצִיּוֹן גּוֹאֵל.

וְכֵן יְהִי רָצוֹן, וְנֹאמַר: אָמֵן.

This prayer, which has many versions, brings to bear, as it were, the power of God and the special connection of the Jewish community with God to the benefit of the leaders, and thereby served as proof of Jewish loyalty to them. When (in 1768) the Russian authorities accused the first Chabad leader, Rabbi Shneur Zalman of Liadi, of treason for sending charity to Jews in the Ottoman-occupied Land of Israel, a copy of *Hanoten T'shuah* written by him was produced as evidence of his loyalty to the czar and his family.[6]

Even during the Soviet era, those Jews who continued to attend synagogue services included (or, more likely, were instructed to include) a prayer for their Communist rulers.[7] We can be sure that many Jews recited this prayer with full intent, but it is also clear that in many cases they said it merely out of duty or even fear. Some even believe that these texts contained some inside jokes, in that the continuation of the biblical citations (which are not quoted in the text) can be read as mockery or even as a curse, hidden beneath the words of praise. "May the One who grants salvation to kings, the One who delivers David his servant from an evil sword" (Psalm 144:10) continues: "Rescue me, and deliver me out of the hand of strangers, whose mouths speak falsehood, and whose right hand is a right hand of falsehood" (Psalm 144:11). The verse "Thus says Adonai, who opens a way in the sea, a path in the mighty water, who brings forth the chariot and horse, the army and the power" (Isaiah 43:16–17) goes on: "They lie down together, they shall not rise; they are extinct, they are quenched as a wick."[8]

By their nature, these texts deal primarily with the "other"—in this case, the ruler and those in power—and reflect the vulnerable state of Jews who lived as minorities in countries other than their own. They prayed for the rulers, it should be noted; only occasionally did they pray also for the welfare of the country itself or its inhabitants.

Obviously, the Prayer for the State of Israel (PSI), especially as recited by Jews in Israel, presents a completely different case because it is a case of Jews praying for the government of their own Jewish state. But the language of the prayer must inevitably confront that government's attitude toward Israelis who are not Jews and Jews (those living in the diaspora) who are not Israelis.

Given this new situation, rabbinic figures in the young State of Israel sought to distance themselves from the older formula of *Hanoten T'shuah* by composing a completely new prayer, namely, our Prayer for the State of Israel. It would not seek the welfare of the rulers alone but of the entire country and its inhabitants. The PSI is a significant liturgical breakthrough because Orthodoxy in general is loathe to add anything at all to what has been passed down by tradition. Yet precisely because it was deemed to be a new prayer without prior halakhic precedents and regulations, the PSI was open to enormous creativity—unconfined by classical liturgical formulae.

The PSI versions are sensitive to prevailing religious, ideological, and political sentiment; they readily expose the intentions of those who create them and those who recite them. Indeed, changes to the PSI, even in the official version of the Israeli Chief Rabbinate, can often be traced to specific changes in the political climate within Israel.[9] These serve as a litmus test for the ongoing tension between universalism and particularism as manifested in the liturgy.

The PSI: A Prayer for the Jewish State

Even before the establishment of the state, some versions of prayers for Israel were composed, either in the traditional formula of *Hanoten T'shuah* or in the form of a *Mi Sheberakh* supplication. Dozens of such prayers have been created since then.[10]

More specifically, however, an official version of the PSI unrelated to these traditionalist formulas came into being in 1948. Its origins have been the subject of some debate, an early opinion being that it originated from the pen of Nobel Prize winner Shmuel Yosef Agnon. We now know, however, that it was composed by Rabbi Isaac Herzog, the Ashkenazi chief rabbi at the time.[11] Let us now look more closely at the version provided by Rabbi Herzog and used not just in Israel but in the diaspora as well.

Our heavenly father,	אָבִינוּ שֶׁבַּשָּׁמַיִם,
rock of Israel and its redeemer,	צוּר יִשְׂרָאֵל וְגוֹאֲלוֹ,
bless the State of Israel,	בָּרֵךְ אֶת מְדִינַת יִשְׂרָאֵל,
the first sprouting of our redemption.	רֵאשִׁית צְמִיחַת גְּאֻלָּתֵנוּ.
Shield it with the wing of your grace	הָגֵן עָלֶיהָ בְּאֶבְרַת חַסְדֶּךָ
and spread over it	וּפְרֹשׂ עָלֶיהָ סֻכַּת שְׁלוֹמֶךָ
your tabernacle of peace.	
Shine your light and truth	וּשְׁלַח אוֹרְךָ וַאֲמִתְּךָ
upon its leaders, ministers, and advisors,	לְרָאשֶׁיהָ, שָׂרֶיהָ וְיוֹעֲצֶיהָ,
and grant them good counsel.	וְתַקְּנֵם בְּעֵצָה טוֹבָה מִלְּפָנֶיךָ.
Strengthen the hands of those who defend our Holy Land,	חַזֵּק אֶת יְדֵי מְגִנֵּי אֶרֶץ קָדְשֵׁנוּ
and grant them deliverance	וְהַנְחִילֵם אֱלֹהֵינוּ יְשׁוּעָה
and the crown of triumph,	וַעֲטֶרֶת נִצָּחוֹן תְּעַטְּרֵם,
and grant peace in the land,	וְנָתַתָּ שָׁלוֹם בָּאָרֶץ
and eternal joy for its inhabitants.	וְשִׂמְחַת עוֹלָם לְיוֹשְׁבֶיהָ.

Remember favorably our kinfolk
of Israel throughout the lands
of their dispersion,
and lead them quickly and upright
to Zion, your city, and Jerusalem,
the dwelling place of your name,
as it is written in the Torah of Moshe
your servant:
"If any of you that are dispersed be
in the uttermost parts of heaven,
from thence will Adonai your God
gather you,
and from there will He take you.
And Adonai your God will bring you
into the land
that your ancestors possessed,
and you shall possess it;
and He will do you good,
and multiply you above your
ancestors.
And Adonai your God will circumcise
your heart,
and the heart of your seed,
to love Adonai your God with all
your heart,
and with all your soul, that you may
live" (Deuteronomy 30:4–6).
And unite our hearts to love and
revere your name,
and to observe all the words of your
Torah.
And bring forth swiftly the son
of David,
your righteous messiah,
to redeem those who eternally await
your salvation.

וְאֶת אַחֵינוּ כָּל בֵּית יִשְׂרָאֵל,
פְּקָדְנָא בְּכָל אַרְצוֹת פִּזּוּרֵיהֶם
וְתוֹלִיכֵם מְהֵרָה קוֹמְמִיּוּת לְצִיּוֹן
עִירֶךָ, וְלִירוּשָׁלַיִם מִשְׁכַּן שְׁמֶךָ,
כַּכָּתוּב בְּתוֹרַת מֹשֶׁה עַבְדֶּךָ:
"אִם יִהְיֶה נִדַּחֲךָ בִּקְצֵה הַשָּׁמַיִם
מִשָּׁם יְקַבֶּצְךָ יְיָ אֱלֹהֶיךָ וּמִשָּׁם
יִקָּחֶךָ: וֶהֱבִיאֲךָ יְיָ אֱלֹהֶיךָ אֶל
הָאָרֶץ אֲשֶׁר יָרְשׁוּ אֲבֹתֶיךָ
וִירִשְׁתָּהּ וְהֵיטִבְךָ וְהִרְבְּךָ
מֵאֲבֹתֶיךָ וּמָל יְיָ אֱלֹהֶיךָ אֶת
לְבָבְךָ וְאֶת לְבַב זַרְעֶךָ לְאַהֲבָה
אֶת יְיָ אֱלֹהֶיךָ בְּכָל לְבָבְךָ
וּבְכָל־נַפְשְׁךָ לְמַעַן חַיֶּיךָ"
(דברים ל, ד–ו).
וְיַחֵד לְבָבֵנוּ לְאַהֲבָה וּלְיִרְאָה אֶת
שְׁמֶךָ,
וְלִשְׁמוֹר אֶת כָּל דִּבְרֵי תוֹרָתֶךָ,
וּשְׁלַח לָנוּ מְהֵרָה בֶּן דָּוִד מְשִׁיחַ
צִדְקֶךָ,
לִפְדוֹת מְחַכֵּי קֵץ יְשׁוּעָתֶךָ.
וְהוֹפַע בַּהֲדַר גְּאוֹן עֻזֶּךָ
עַל כָּל יוֹשְׁבֵי תֵבֵל אַרְצֶךָ,

Reveal Yourself in your glorious
majesty
to all the inhabitants of your world.
Let everything that breathes
proclaim:
his majesty rules over all.
Amen, selah.

וְיֹאמַר כֹּל אֲשֶׁר נְשָׁמָה בְאַפּוֹ:
יְיָ אֱלֹהֵי יִשְׂרָאֵל מֶלֶךְ
וּמַלְכוּתוֹ בַּכֹּל מָשָׁלָה.
אָמֵן סֶלָה.

The prayer begins in a lofty and poetic style before reverting to less flow-
ery prose dependent on proof-texting from biblical verses. It requests the
following:

a. Peace and protection for the state, as the "first sprouting of our
   redemption"
b. Wisdom for its leaders
c. The victory and safety of Israel's soldiers and defenders
d. Ingathering of diaspora Jews
e. Success in Israel for the religious mandates of tradition
f. Redemption and the coming of the messiah
g. Acceptance of God by all the inhabitants of the world

The perspective of the prayer is Israeli and Jewish: it concentrates on the
State of Israel and its role. It deals at length with diaspora Jews, calling
upon God to bring them home to Israel. Non-Jewish citizens of the state
go unmentioned specifically but may be included in the petition for "eternal joy for its inhabitants." Humanity in general is subsumed only in the
traditional context of their ultimate messianic acceptance of God's kingdom. This is, in sum, fully in keeping with traditional Judaism's hope for
the ingathering of exiles and the ultimate triumph of God throughout the
world.

According to Joel Rappel, an Israeli scholar who examined the evolution and history of the official PSI, Herzog deliberately rejected early
versions that began with the traditional words *Hanoten T'shuah* because
he saw them as symbolizing Jewish powerlessness and submissiveness to
the foreign ruler. He made it a point to compose a completely new prayer,
which would stress Jewish sovereignty and independence.

But the PSI is conversant with another emotionally charged document of the time, the Declaration of the Establishment of the State of Israel, signed by the members of the Provisional Government, on the day of the establishment of Israel, May 14, 1948 (5 Iyar 5708). The two texts share linguistic expressions of major national values that characterized the young state. We may go so far as to see PSI as a religious response to the Declaration and to those civil religious sentiments that the Declaration defined. Indeed, the very fact that it has the Declaration in mind may be the reason that ultra-Orthodox circles in Israel have rejected it so fiercely,[12] even though (as we shall see) it by no means accepts the secular views that the Declaration so clearly proclaims.

The Declaration was fully a modern civil document, a reflection of the world in which the fledgling secular state found itself. It necessarily addressed the different categories of "others," people, that is, who did not fall into the category of Jewish Israelis. Here are the relevant paragraphs from the Declaration of Independence, with the categories italicized:

> The State of Israel ... will foster the development of the country *for the benefit of all its inhabitants*; it will be based on freedom, justice and peace as envisaged by the prophets of Israel; it will ensure complete equality of social and political rights to *all its inhabitants irrespective of religion, race or sex*; it will guarantee freedom of religion, conscience, language, education and culture; it will safeguard the Holy Places *of all religions*; and it will be faithful to the principles of the Charter of the United Nations.
>
> We appeal to the United Nations to assist the Jewish people in the upbuilding of its State and to receive the State of Israel into the community of nations.
>
> We appeal—in the very midst of the onslaught launched against us now for months—to *the Arab inhabitants of the State of Israel* to preserve peace and participate in the upbuilding of the State on the basis of full and equal citizenship and due representation in all its provisional and permanent institutions.
>
> We extend our hand to *all neighboring states and their peoples* in an offer of peace and good neighborliness, and appeal to them to establish bonds of cooperation and mutual help with the sovereign Jewish people settled in its own land.

> The State of Israel is prepared to do its share in a common effort for the advancement of *the entire Middle East.*

Next comes an appeal for the diaspora Jews to unite around the cause of the young state:

> We appeal to the Jewish people throughout the Diaspora to rally round the Jews of Eretz-Israel in the tasks of immigration and upbuilding and to stand by them in the great struggle for the realization of the age-old dream—the redemption of Israel.

The PSI, in contrast to the Declaration, contains almost no reference to any of the following: the community of nations, the Arab inhabitants of Israel, or the neighboring states or their peoples.[13] The difference between the texts can partially be explained by the fact that the Declaration is a political statement meant for both Jews and the "community of nations," whereas the PSI is a text specifically meant for Jewish worship.[14] Still, the utter lack of references to non-Jews demands our attention. Rappel maintains that Herzog deliberately refrained from including them, just as he avoided the old, submissive *Hanoten T'shuah* formula. Instead, he created a liturgical text that deals solely with Israel from a Jewish perspective and a call to diasporan Jews to return to it.

We see, then, that Herzog's purview remained within the traditionalistic mind-set that he had inherited from his Jewish past: he viewed the state from the perspective of its heralding the next great stage in God's plan for the ultimate messianic rule that had been promised through the eons. Although couched in new language, the prayer's sentiment remained fully in keeping with traditional Jewish liturgy's accent on the coming of God's kingdom at the end of time.

Later PSIs, however, composed in Israel as well as in the diaspora, and especially in non-Orthodox contexts, deal also with non-Jews in a variety of ways. Let us explore some of them now.

Universalism and Particularism in the Prayers for the State of Israel

The Herzog prayer was not the only one to find its way into Jewish liturgies. Indeed, in the following decades, a variety of alternatives have appeared in

Israel, North America, and Europe. A convenient starting point for our survey is the PSI found in *Ha'avodah Shebalev*, Israeli Reform version (1982), the prayer book of the Progressive Movement in Israel and, therefore, both Reform and Israeli, with a strong Zionist perspective[15] and a liberal point of view. While directly citing the Herzog PSI in part, it also provides significant variations and an altogether different theology and ideology:

Rock of Israel and its redeemer,
bless the State of Israel,
the first sprouting of our redemption.
Shield it with the wing of your grace
and spread over it your tabernacle of
peace.
Shine your light and truth
upon its leaders, judges, and officials.
Grant them good council so
that they may follow the path of
righteousness, liberty, and justice.
Strengthen the hands of those who
defend our Holy Land,
and grant them salvation and life.
Grant peace to this land
and everlasting joy to its inhabitants.
Remember favorably our kinfolk of
the house of Israel
throughout the lands of their
dispersion.
Plant the love of Zion within their
hearts,
and may there be those among
them—may God be with them—
who shall come to Jerusalem,
your city that bears your name.
Spread your spirit over all the
inhabitants of our land.

צוּר יִשְׂרָאֵל וְגוֹאֲלוֹ,
בָּרֵךְ אֶת מְדִינַת יִשְׂרָאֵל,
רֵאשִׁית צְמִיחַת גְּאֻלָּתֵנוּ.
הָגֵן עָלֶיהָ בְּאֶבְרַת חַסְדֶּךָ
וּפְרֹשׂ עָלֶיהָ סֻכַּת שְׁלוֹמֶךָ.
שְׁלַח אוֹרְךָ וַאֲמִתְּךָ
לְרָאשֶׁיהָ, לְשׁוֹפְטֶיהָ וְלִנְבְחָרֶיהָ,
וְתַקְּנֵם בְּעֵצָה טוֹבָה מִלְּפָנֶיךָ,
לְמַעַן יֵלְכוּ בְּדֶרֶךְ הַצֶּדֶק, הַחֹפֶשׁ
וְהַיֹּשֶׁר.
חַזֵּק אֶת יְדֵי מְגִנֵּי אֶרֶץ קָדְשֵׁנוּ,
וְהַנְחִילֵם יְשׁוּעָה וְחַיִּים.
וְנָתַתָּ שָׁלוֹם בָּאָרֶץ
וְשִׂמְחַת עוֹלָם לְיוֹשְׁבֶיהָ.
פְּקָד נָא לִבְרָכָה
אֶת אַחֵינוּ בֵּית יִשְׂרָאֵל
בְּכָל אַרְצוֹת פְּזוּרֵיהֶם.
טַע בְּלִבָּם אַהֲבַת צִיּוֹן,
וּמִי בָהֶם מִכָּל עַמֵּנוּ
יְהִי אֱלֹהָיו עִמּוֹ
וְיַעַל לִירוּשָׁלַיִם עִרְךָ,
אֲשֶׁר נִקְרָא שִׁמְךָ עָלֶיהָ.

Uproot from us hatred and
animosity, zealotry and evil.
Plant in our hearts love and amity,
peace and friendship.
Speedily fulfill the vision of your
prophet:
"Nation shall not lift up sword
against nation, neither shall they
learn war any more" (Isaiah 2:4).
And let us say: Amen.

הָאֵצֶל מֵרוּחֲךָ עַל כָּל יוֹשְׁבֵי
אַרְצֵנוּ,
הָסֵר מִקִּרְבֵּנוּ שִׂנְאָה וְאֵיבָה, קִנְאָה
וְרִשְׁעוּת,
וְטַע בְּלִבֵּנוּ אַהֲבָה וְאַחֲוָה,
שָׁלוֹם וְרֵעוּת.
וְקַיֵּם בִּמְהֵרָה חֲזוֹן נְבִיאֶךָ:
"לֹא יִשָּׂא גוֹי אֶל גּוֹי חֶרֶב
וְלֹא יִלְמְדוּ עוֹד מִלְחָמָה"
(יְשַׁעְיָהוּ ב, ד). וְנֹאמַר: אָמֵן.

The call for the ingathering of the exiles is significantly toned down, while the diaspora is viewed as a valid Jewish choice: to be sure, some "shall come to Jerusalem, your city that bears your name"; but this hope is balanced by the prayer that God "remember favorably our kinfolk of the house of Israel throughout the lands of their dispersion." Requesting victory by the military is replaced by a concern for its soldiers' well-being. Instead of petitions for the coming of the messiah, we get an emphasis on understanding and fellowship among all the inhabitants of the land.

The current situation is viewed, at least partly, as suffering from "hatred and animosity, zealotry and evil," which require healing. In conclusion, we get a wish for the fulfillment of Isaiah's prophecy of peace—a passage that (in practice) is typically sung.

Relating to the State of Israel as "the first sprouting of our redemption" has proved especially problematic over the years. Many have been troubled by its messianic pretensions, holding that the State of Israel does not merit the title. Seeing the state as already redemptive, moreover, has led some extremists to demand a post-historical morality that permits violence toward Arabs.[16] This liberal version of the prayer therefore strikes a balance. It does see Israel as "the first sprouting of our redemption," but the image of redemption is a far cry from the traditionalistic portrait that includes all Jews being restored to their homeland and the rest of humanity converted to the true vision of the one and unique Jewish God.

The parallel prayer found in *Mishkan T'filah*, the North American Reform siddur (2007), abbreviates the official text but adds an English sentence that does not appear in the Hebrew text at all. It turns the petition "Bless the State of Israel, first sprouting of our redemption" into a call for peace: "Bless the State of Israel which marks the dawning of the hope for all who seek peace."

Finding a PSI in a North American Reform siddur is not a given. It is, of course, absent from the older *Union Prayer Book*, whose three editions (1895, 1918, and 1940) were published before the establishment of the State of Israel. Classical reformers were, in any case, wary of Zionism, if not explicitly against it.[17] More surprising is the absence of a PSI in the newer *Gates of Prayer* (1975), which was published in a time of growing affinity toward the young state and support of Zionism. Rabbi Lawrence A. Hoffman, PhD, maintains that the editors were opposed to the phrase "first sprouting of our redemption" and therefore left the prayer out. Instead, a short paragraph asking God's blessing on the state was appended to the prayer "For Our People and Our Nation" (p. 452). The final paragraph requests God's favor "upon Israel, her land, her people" and reframes "first sprouting of our redemption" as "the promise of her beginning," which "may ripen into fulfillment."[18]

The United Kingdom provides three progressive alternatives: the Masorti Movement, akin to North America's Conservative Jews; the Liberal Movement, very much like North American Reform; and the Reform Movement, which shares the philosophy of the Liberal Movement but is somewhat more traditional ritually. The Liberal *Siddur Lev Chadash* (1995) has the following prayer, which appears in English only:

> Eternal God, our Rock and Redeemer, grant blessing to the State of Israel, created to fulfill an age-old dream and to be a haven for the oppressed. Inspire its leaders and citizens with faithfulness to the aims of its founders: to develop the land for the benefit of all its inhabitants, and to implement the Prophetic ideals of liberty and justice. May they live in harmony with one another and in peace with their neighbours, and cause to come true once more the ancient vision that "out of Zion shall go forth Torah and the word of God from Jerusalem" (Isaiah 2:3).

This Liberal offering emphasizes Israel's commitment to its initial aims. If the Herzog original reacts negatively to the Declaration of Independence of the State of Israel, this prayer responds positively, most notably where it says, "To develop the land for the benefit of all its inhabitants, and to implement the Prophetic ideals of liberty and justice." Whether by accident or design, it falls short of explicitly referring to Israel as a Jewish state or as the homeland of all Jews.

The British Reform Movement siddur, *Forms of Prayer* (*Seder Ha-T'fillot*, 2008), pursues the same line of thought as the Liberal siddur but provides a Hebrew equivalent and makes reconciliation and the desire for peace in Israel its main focus:

Our God and God of the generations, we ask your blessing upon the State of Israel and all who dwell in it. Send your light and your truth to the people, and guide them with wisdom and understanding, so that peace and tranquility may reign on its borders and in its homes. May the spirit of friendship and understanding remove all fears and heal all wounds. There, may mercy and truth come together for the good of all, so that your promise is fulfilled: "for Torah shall come out of Zion and the word of God from Jerusalem" (Isaiah 2:3). Amen.

אֱלֹהֵינוּ וֵאלֹהֵי כָּל־הַדּוֹרוֹת שְׁלַח
נָא בִּרְכָתְךָ עַל מְדִינַת יִשְׂרָאֵל
וְעַל כָּל יוֹשְׁבֶיהָ. שְׁלַח נָא אוֹרְךָ
וַאֲמִתְּךָ לְמַנְהִיגֵי־הָעָם וְהַדְרִיכֵם
בְּחָכְמָה וּבִתְבוּנָה כְּדֵי שֶׁיִּשְׂרוֹר
שָׁלוֹם בִּגְבוּלוֹתֶיהָ וְשַׁלְוָה בְּבָתֶּיהָ.
רוּחַ אַחֲוָה וַהֲבָנָה הֲדָדִית תְּרַפֵּא
כָּל פֶּצַע וְחַבּוּרָה. תִּקְוַת עַמָּהּ
וַעֲבוֹדַת בָּנֶיהָ תַּגְשֶׁמְנָה אֶת חֲזוֹן
הַנְּבִיאִים, "כִּי מִצִּיּוֹן תֵּצֵא תוֹרָה
וּדְבַר יְיָ מִירוּשָׁלָיִם"
(ישעיהו ב, ג). אָמֵן.

The prayer was composed by Rabbi Lionel Blue for the British Reform Movement's 1977 liturgy (*Forms of Prayer*) and was reprinted in its 2008 successor with some minor changes for the sake of inclusive language.[19] It is deliberately and emphatically universalistic, in that it seeks God's "blessing upon the State of Israel *and all who dwell in it*." It evokes "the spirit of friendship and understanding" to "remove all fears and heal all wounds." Isaiah 2:3 was chosen as its closing verse, probably because it had been part of the PSI inherited from Great Britain's venerable Singer prayer book,[20] a prayer book that had become synonymous with traditional

British practice and was consulted by non-Orthodox movements there. This verse from the PSI in Singer was also included by the Liberal prayer book (cited above) but had already been borrowed by Blue, who prefaced his Reform version, however, with the universalizing emphasis: "There, may mercy and truth come together for the good of all mankind" (the word "mankind" was changed in the 2008 edition to "all").

The first contemporary German Reform prayer book emerged in 2009, *T'filot l'khol hashanah: Jüdisches Gebetbuch*, under the editorship of Rabbi Andreas Nachama and Jonah Sievers. Its PSI provides a short adaptation of the official version, with some conspicuous changes:[21]

Our heavenly father,	אָבִינוּ שֶׁבַּשָּׁמַיִם,
Rock of Israel and its redeemer,	צוּר יִשְׂרָאֵל וְגוֹאֲלוֹ,
Bless the State of Israel,	בָּרֵךְ אֶת מְדִינַת יִשְׂרָאֵל,
So that it may be the first sprouting of our redemption.	תִּהְיֶה רֵאשִׁית צְמִיחַת גְּאֻלָתֵנוּ.
Fulfill through it the words of the Scriptures:	וְקַיֵּם בָּהּ מִקְרָא שֶׁכָּתוּב:
"For out of Zion shall go forth Torah and the word of God from Jerusalem" (Isaiah 2:3).	"כִּי מִצִּיּוֹן תֵּצֵא תוֹרָה וּדְבַר יְיָ מִירוּשָׁלָיִם" (ישעיהו ב, ג).
Spread a tabernacle of peace over the whole world;	וּפְרֹשׂ סֻכַּת שָׁלוֹם עַל כָּל הָעוֹלָם.
And may all the inhabitants of the world dwell in safety.	וְכָל יוֹשְׁבֵי תֵּבֵל יִשְׁכְּנוּ לָבֶטַח.
And let us say: Amen.	וְכֵן יְהִי רָצוֹן, וְנֹאמַר: אָמֵן.

As with the traditional versions, this one too discusses the rise of the State of Israel as "the first sprouting of our redemption." Like Singer and the other British prayer books mentioned here, it then cites Isaiah 2:3 and moves on quickly to the well-being of the entire world, without special references to Israel or Jews. The "tabernacle of peace" that the official PSI would have God spread over Israel is here generalized, extending to the entire world. Like the European texts from England (cited above), this one too ignores the concept of "others" altogether.

A subtle but important feature of the German version is the way it deals with the implications of "the first sprouting of our redemption."

Rather than have it refer to the past, as if Israel has already entered messianic times, it projects the phrase into the future: "So that it may be the first sprouting of our redemption." It is hard to read this emendation of the English as anything less than a critique of traditionalists who see Israel as necessarily conferring messianic status on the present. In concept, it is reminiscent of *Gates of Prayer* (above), which, as we saw, preferred praying that "the promise of her [Israel's] beginning may ripen into fulfillment."[22]

So far, we have sampled a variety of denominational prayer books, but the liturgical landscape contains as well a number of liturgies published by nondenominational institutions, communities, and even individuals; many of them have published their own versions of PSI. A good example is the prayer composed by Rabbis for Human Rights (RHR), founded in 1988, the only Israeli rabbinic organization comprising Orthodox, Conservative, and Reform rabbis. RHR revises the text from time to time; these are the 2013 Hebrew and English versions:

Sovereign of the Universe, accept in loving kindness and with favor our prayers for the State of Israel, her government and all who dwell within her boundaries and under her authority.

On the sixty-fifth anniversary of her founding, reopen our eyes and our hearts to the wonder of Israel and strengthen our faith in your power to work redemption in every human soul. Grant us also the fortitude to keep ever before us those ideals to which Israel dedicated herself in her Declaration of Independence, so that we may be true partners with the people of Israel in working toward her as yet not fully fulfilled vision.

רִבּוֹן הָעוֹלָם, קַבֵּל נָא בְּרַחֲמִים וּבְרָצוֹן אֶת תְּפִלָּתֵנוּ לְמַעַן מְדִינַת יִשְׂרָאֵל, מֶמְשַׁלְתָּהּ וְכָל הַדָּרִים בִּגְבוּלֶיהָ וְתַחַת שְׁלִיטָתָהּ.

פְּקַח נָא אֶת עֵינֵינוּ וְלִבֵּנוּ מֵחָדָשׁ לַנִּפְלָא שֶׁבְּקִיּוּמָהּ וְחַזֵּק אֶת אֱמוּנָתֵנוּ בְּכֹחֲךָ לְהָבִיא גְאוּלָה לְכָל נְשָׁמָה. תֵּן לָנוּ אֶת הָאֹמֶץ וְהַהַתְמָדָה לִרְאוֹת תָּמִיד לְנֶגֶד עֵינֵינוּ אֶת הָעֶקְרוֹנוֹת שֶׁהִצִּיבָה לְעַצְמָהּ יִשְׂרָאֵל בִּמְגִלַּת הָעַצְמָאוּת. הָבֵא לְכָךְ שֶׁנִּהְיֶה שֻׁתָּפֵי אֱמֶת עִם אֶזְרְחֵי יִשְׂרָאֵל בְּהַשָּׂגַת הֶחָזוֹן שֶׁטֶּרֶם נִשְׁלַם בִּמְלֹאוֹ.

Grant those entrusted with guiding Israel's destiny the courage, wisdom and strength to do your will. Guide them in the paths of peace and give them the insight to see your Image in every human being. Be with those charged with Israel's safety and defend them from all harm. May they have the strength to protect their country and the spiritual fortitude never to abuse the power placed in their hands. Spread your blessings over the Land. May justice and human rights abound for all her inhabitants. Guide them "To do justice, love mercy and walk humbly with your God" (Micah 6:8), and "May justice well up like water, righteousness like a mighty stream" (Amos 5:24). Implant tolerance and mutual respect in every heart, and may all realize that "we were not brought into this world for conflict and dissension, nor for hatred, jealousy, harassment or bloodshed. Rather, we were brought into this world in order to recognize You, may You be blessed forever" (Rabbi Nachman of Breslov). Spread over Israel and all the world your shelter of peace, and may the vision of

תֵּן לְכָל הָעוֹסְקִים בְּצָרְכֵי צִבּוּר אֶת אֹמֶץ הַלֵּב, הַתְּבוּנָה וְהַכֹּחַ לַעֲשׂוֹת רְצוֹנְךָ בְּלֵבָב שָׁלֵם. הַדְרֵךְ אוֹתָם בִּנְתִיבוֹת שָׁלוֹם וְהַעֲנֵק לָהֶם אֶת הָרְאִיָּה לְהַכִּיר אֶת צֶלֶם אֱלֹהִים בְּכָל אָדָם. חַזֵּק אֶת מְגִנֵּי אֶרֶץ קָדְשֵׁנוּ וְהָגֵן עֲלֵיהֶם מִפְּנֵי אוֹיֵב, חֶרֶב, סַכָּנָה וְיָגוֹן. טַע בָּהֶם עֹז לְהָגֵן עַל מוֹלַדְתָּם וְהַאֲצֵל עֲלֵיהֶם אֶת גְּבוּרַת הַנֶּפֶשׁ לִכְבֹּשׁ אֶת יֵצֶר הַשִּׁלְטוֹן וְהַכֹּחַ. הָרֵק אֶת בִּרְכָתְךָ עַל הָאָרֶץ וְעַל כָּל יוֹשְׁבֶיהָ. יִמָּצְאוּ בָהּ צֶדֶק וּזְכֻיּוֹת אָדָם לְכָל אָדָם. הַשְׁרֵשׁ בְּלֵב כֻּלָּם אֶת מוּסַר נְבִיאֶיךָ "עֲשׂוֹת מִשְׁפָּט וְאַהֲבַת חֶסֶד וְהַצְנֵעַ לֶכֶת עִם אֱלֹהֶיךָ" (מיכה ו, ח) "וְיִגַּל כַּמַּיִם מִשְׁפָּט וּצְדָקָה כְּנַחַל אֵיתָן" (עמוס ה, כד) לְמַעַן יִלְמְדוּ דַּרְכֵי סוֹבְלָנוּת וּכְבוֹד הֲדָדִי. יְהִי רָצוֹן שֶׁכָּל יוֹשְׁבֵי הָאָרֶץ יַכִּירוּ כִּי "לֹא בָאנוּ לְזֶה הָעוֹלָם בִּשְׁבִיל רִיב וּמַחֲלֹקֶת וְלֹא בִּשְׁבִיל שִׂנְאָה וְקִנְאָה וְקִנְטוּר וּשְׁפִיכוּת דָּמִים. רַק בָּאנוּ לָעוֹלָם כְּדֵי לְהַכִּיר אוֹתְךָ תִּתְבָּרֵךְ לָנֶצַח (ר' נחמן מברסלב). פְּרֹשׂ עַל יִשְׂרָאֵל וְעַל כָּל תֵּבֵל

your prophet soon be
fulfilled: "Nation shall not lift up
sword against nation, neither shall
they learn war any more" (Isaiah 2:4).
So may it be your will that speedily
and in our day all inhabitants of the
earth will say of the State of Israel,
"It is very good" (Genesis 1:31), for
she will have become a blessing to
the entire world and a "light unto the
nations" (Isaiah 42:6).

אֶת סֻכַּת שְׁלוֹמֶךָ וְקַיֵּם בִּמְהֵרָה
חֲזוֹן נְבִיאֶךָ: "לֹא יִשָּׂא גוֹי אֶל גּוֹי
חֶרֶב וְלֹא יִלְמְדוּ עוֹד מִלְחָמָה"
(ישעיהו, ב, ד).יְהִי רָצוֹן מִלְּפָנֶיךָ
שֶׁיֹּאמְרוּ [בִּמְהֵרָה בְיָמֵינוּ] כָּל
יוֹשְׁבֵי תֵבֵל "הִנֵּה טוֹב מְאֹד",
כִּי יִתְבָּרְכוּ בִּמְדִינַת יִשְׂרָאֵל כָּל
מִשְׁפְּחוֹת הָאֲדָמָה.

The very length of the prayer indicates how important it was to its authors. Rather than settle for general statements regarding peace, it specifies those to whom it refers: "All who dwell within her boundaries and under her authority," a description that seems intended to encompass not only Israeli citizens but also Palestinians in the West Bank. It then expresses its wishes for the redemption of "every human soul." Appropriately, the RHR prayer explicitly references the Declaration of Independence, which the original Herzog version had pointedly omitted. We are to "keep ever before us those ideals to which Israel dedicated herself in her Declaration of Independence," a reminder of the commitments that those who signed it took upon themselves, commitments that bind us as well.

This version emanates from within Israel itself; its authors choose, therefore—like the official PSI and the Israeli Reform version (but unlike many of the diaspora PSI texts)—to call upon God for help in defending the Land from its enemies. God is to strengthen "those charged with Israel's safety." Like the Israeli Reform siddur (and unlike the Herzog text), it does not ask for victory; instead, it focuses on safety and security. Uniquely, however, it also requests spiritual fortitude "never to abuse the power placed in their hands." Unlike diaspora PSI texts, this prayer places Israel at the center of attention even as it seeks for Israel to be a source of well-being for the entire world.

If Rabbis for Human Rights epitomizes institutions intent on publishing alternative PSI texts, then Rabbi Aryeh Cohen, a professor at the

American Jewish University, personifies individuals who have turned to the task on their own. Convinced of "a large and growing number of people who would like to include Israel in their prayers in all of its complexity and are unable to intone the Chief Rabbinate's liturgy,"[23] the author set about creating something better. "In my mind," he continues,

> I framed the prayer between two powerful religious and literary moments. On the one hand, Rabbi Yehudah Halevi's famous line: "My heart is in the east, and I am at the far reaches of the west." On the other hand, Isaiah's statement "Zion will be redeemed with justice, and those who return to her with righteousness" (Isaiah 1:27). The *piyyut* is a movement between those two poles.[24]

In other words, the prayer captures the Jewish People's eternal longing for Zion and, at the same time, a demand that Zion redeemed shall be governed justly. The first verse addresses Zion; the second and third verses address God:

Prayer	תפילה
My heart, my heart goes out to you, Zion. Tears and jubilation, celebration and grieving Did we not dream a dream that came to be? And here it is—both song and lament.	לִבִּי לְבִּי יוֹצֵא לָךְ צִיּוֹן. דְּמָעוֹת וְצָהֳלָה, שִׂמְחָה וְיָגוֹן הֲלֹא חֲלוֹם חֲלַמְנוּ וַיְהִי וְהִנֵּה-גַם רִנָּה גַם נֶהִי.
We are mere matter, and our prayer is to the Creator Toward the Good and the Just, direct the people in refuge in Zion For yours is all the world, and we have but one land, Which we inherited together with the sons and daughters of Hagar.	נַחְנוּ רַק חֹמֶר וּתְפִלָּה לָנוּ לַיּוֹצֵר, לַטּוֹב וְלַצֶּדֶק הַכֵּן אֶת הָעָם בְּצִיּוֹן מִסְתַּתֵּר. כִּי לְךָ כָּל הָאָרֶץ וְלָנוּ אֶרֶץ יְחִידָה, אֲשֶׁר יְרַשְׁנוּ יַחְדָּיו עִם בְּנֵי הָגָר.

Favor us with knowledge with which to understand
The wisdom of Avraham, "If you will go left, I will go right" (Genesis 13:9).
Overflow with mercy on a great and troubled land.
For "Zion will be redeemed in judgment and its inhabitants in justice" (Isaiah 1:27).[25]

חָנֵּנוּ דַּעַת אֲשֶׁר בּוֹן נָבִין
חָכְמַת אַבְרָהָם: "אִם תַּשְׂמְאִילָה
וְאַיְמִין" (בראשית יג, ט)
רַחֲמִים תַּשְׁפִּיעַ עַל אֶרֶץ רָבָּה
הַגְּזֵירָה.
כִּי "צִיּוֹן בְּמִשְׁפָּט תִּפָּדֶה וְשָׁבֶיהָ
בִּצְדָקָה" (ישעיהו א, כז).

Cohen composed his text in the middle of the Second Intifada, and it is used by the members of the Shtibl Minyan in Los Angeles. It concentrates on the relationship between the children of Abraham, both Jews and Muslims—or, to be more exact, the Palestinians. It neglects other matters, however, even the all-important consideration of Israel as a Jewish homeland. It thus constitutes the mirror image of the official PSI, in that Herzog ignores the non-Jewish dwellers in Israel, while Cohen makes them his main issue.

A second individual composition worth looking at comes from Moshe Greenberg, a Bible professor and Conservative rabbi. Greenberg was born in Philadelphia and emigrated to Israel in 1970. Cohen's text, we saw, condensed the PSI into a single solitary theme. Greenberg's 1989 version attempts the opposite: it seeks to include as many relevant topics as possible:

We are grateful to you, the Eternal, our God, for having woken your people to found a nation in the land that you bequeathed to our ancestors, and for having graced us with a surviving remnant and a revival after the murderous destruction that the wicked of the world brought upon us.

מודים אנחנו לך יְיָ אלהינו,
על שעוררת את בני עמך
להקים מדינה בארץ שהנחלת
לאבותינו, ועל שחננתנו
שארית ותקומה לאחר
ההשמדה שהמיטו עלינו רשעי
העולם.

Now, our God, our eyes turn to you to give us wisdom to govern our nation, and counsel to make peace with our enemies, and love for our fellow children of Israel inside our land and beyond it so that we might become one body to sanctify your name across the world, for it is for that that we were created.

Our hands are stained with insolence and blunders that have fenced in our ways with thorns. We hoped for the good and aimed toward justice, but the leaven in our dough soured our deeds. We know not what we are to do; therefore our prayer is laid out before you that you will give us the wisdom to find our paths to our foes' hearts, and that you will direct their heart to make peace with us, and that you will spare our hands and theirs from killing and terror, and uproot from our midst thoughts of destruction and hatred.

Strengthen our hands to build our country, and to pepetuate what we have undertaken:

To prepare for the ingathering of the exiles; to watch over the development of the land for the good of all its inhabitants; to perpetuate social and legal equal rights for each and every citizen; to ensure

ועתה אלהינו, לך עינינו תלויות לתת לנו חכמה לכלכל את מדינתנו, ועצה להשלים עם אויבינו, ואהבת אחינו בני ישראל בארץ ובחוצה לה למען ניעשה אגודה אחת לקדש שמך בעולם, כי לכך נוצרנו. בידינו זדונות ושגגות אשר שכו את דרכינו בקוצים; קיווינו לטוב וכיוונו לצדק, אבל השאור שבעיסתנו החמיץ את מעשינו.
אנחנו לא נדע מה נעשה, ועל כן תפילתנו שטוחה לפניך כי תחכימנו למצוא מסילות ללבבם של צרינו, וכי תטה את לבבם להשלים עמנו, וכי תחשוך את ידינו ואת ידיהם מהרג וחבלה, ותעקור מקרבנו מחשבות הרס ושנאה.
חזק את ידינו לבנין מדינתנו, לקיים את אשר קיבלנו על עצמנו בקומה:
להיכון לקראת עלייה יהודית ולקיבוץ גלויות;
לשקוד על פיתוח הארץ לטובת כל תושביה;
לקיים שיוויון זכויות חברתי

freedom of religion,
conscience, language, education,
and culture to all of our citizens.
May it be your will to help us meet
our obligations for the sake of your
glorious name, whose name we
bear, so that through us the word
of your prophet will be fulfilled:
"You are my servant, Israel, and
through you I shall be glorfied"
(Isaiah 49:3).

וּמְדִינִי לְכָל אֶזְרָח וְאֶזְרָח;
לְהַבְטִיחַ חוֹפֶשׁ דָּת, מַצְפּוּן,
לָשׁוֹן, חִינּוּךְ וְתַרְבּוּת לְכָל
אֶזְרָחֵינוּ.
יְהִי רָצוֹן מִלְּפָנֶיךָ שֶׁתְּסַיֵּיעַ
בִּידֵינוּ לַעֲמוֹד בְּהִתְחַיְּיבוּיּוֹתֵינוּ
לְמַעַן כְּבוֹד שִׁמְךָ הַנִּקְרָא עָלֵינוּ,
וִיקוּיִּים בָּנוּ דְּבַר נְבִיאָן: "עַבְדִּי
אַתָּה יִשְׂרָאֵל אֲשֶׁר בְּךָ אֶתְפָּאָר"
(יְשַׁעְיָהוּ מ"ט, ג).

This PSI begins by offering gratitude and then specifies its petitions. It asks for wisdom to reconcile with the enemy, acknowledging the failure thus far to manage it on our own. Like the Rabbis for Human Rights' PSI, it cites some key sentences relating to "others" from the Declaration of Independence. It ends with a request for help so that we may meet our commitments to God. This is also virtually the only text that explicitly refers to the Holocaust.[26] As far as I know, this text is not in current use.

Having dealt with denominational and then personal PSIs, we should also look at a version that is used in a specific congregation. I chose Mevakshei Derekh, a Reconstructionist-oriented congregation in Jerusalem, which is very engaged with liturgy and its meaning. This is a rather unique congregation on the Israeli liberal scene, since it uses a traditional prayer book (albeit with a few minor changes). In the case of the PSI, Mevakshei Derekh has two alternative versions of the prayer. The first is in use in other congregations in Israel, some modern Orthodox and some Masorti; the second is recited only at Mevakshei Derekh. Here is the first prayer; it is quite well known, but I could not trace its author:

Sovereign of the Universe, merci-
fully accept our prayer for the
State of Israel and its government.
Pour out your blessing upon the
land and upon those who faithfully

רִבּוֹן הָעוֹלָם, קַבֵּל נָא בְּרַחֲמִים
אֶת תְּפִלָּתֵנוּ בְּעַד מְדִינַת יִשְׂרָאֵל
וּמֶמְשַׁלְתָּהּ. הָרֵק אֶת בִּרְכָתְךָ עַל
הָאָרֶץ וְעַל הָעוֹסְקִים בְּצָרְכֵי צִבּוּר

deal with the needs of the public. Guide them according to the laws of your Torah, and teach them to understand your precepts, in order that the land never be deprived of peace and tranquility, happiness and freedom. Please Eternal, God of the spirit of all flesh, reveal your spirit upon all the inhabitants of our land, and instill within them love and fraternity, peace and friendship, and uproot from their hearts all hatred and animosity, jealously and competition. And remember all of our fellow members of the House of Israel, in all the lands in which they are dispersed, and lead them quickly upright to Zion, your city, and to Jeruselam, your habitation. Strenghten the hands of those who defend our holy land, and grant them salvation, and crown them with the crown of victory. And grant peace in the land, and eternal joy to its inhabitants. And so may it be your will that our land be a blessing to all the inhabitants of the world. And may there abide among them friendship and freedom, and quickly establish the vision of your prophet: "Nation shall not lift up sword against nation, neither shall they learn war anymore" (Isaiah 2:4). Amen.

בֶּאֱמוּנָה. הוֹרֵם מְחֻקֵּי תוֹרָתֶךָ,
הֲבִינֵם מִשְׁפְּטֵי צִדְקֶךָ, לְמַעַן לֹא
יָסוּרוּ מֵאַרְצֵנוּ שָׁלוֹם וְשַׁלְוָה,
אֲשֶׁר וְחֹפֶשׁ כָּל הַיָּמִים.
אָנָּא יְיָ אֱלֹהֵי הָרוּחוֹת לְכָל בָּשָׂר,
הַעֲרֵה רוּחֲךָ עַל כָּל תּוֹשָׁבֵי אַרְצֵנוּ,
וְטַע בָּהֶם אַהֲבָה וְאַחֲוָה, שָׁלוֹם
וְרֵעוּת, וַעֲקֹר מִלִּבָּם כָּל שִׂנְאָה
וְאֵיבָה, קִנְאָה וְתַחֲרוּת.
וְאֶת אַחֵינוּ כָּל בֵּית יִשְׂרָאֵל פְּקֹד
נָא בְּכָל אַרְצוֹת פְּזוּרֵיהֶם וְתוֹלִיכֵם
מְהֵרָה קוֹמְמִיּוּת לְצִיּוֹן עִירֶךָ
וְלִירוּשָׁלַיִם מִשְׁכַּן שְׁמֶךָ.
חַזֵּק אֶת יְדֵי מְגִנֵּי אֶרֶץ קָדְשֵׁנוּ
וְהַנְחִילֵם יְשׁוּעָה, וַעֲטֶרֶת נִצָּחוֹן
תְּעַטְּרֵם. וְנָתַתָּ שָׁלוֹם בָּאָרֶץ
וְשִׂמְחַת עוֹלָם לְיוֹשְׁבֶיהָ.
וְכֵן יְהִי רָצוֹן שֶׁתְּהֵא אַרְצֵנוּ בְּרָכָה
לְכָל יוֹשְׁבֵי תֵבֵל. וְתַשְׁרֶה בֵּינֵיהֶם
רֵעוּת וְחֵרוּת, וְקַיֵּם בִּמְהֵרָה חֲזוֹן
נְבִיאֶךָ: "לֹא יִשָּׂא גוֹי אֶל גּוֹי חֶרֶב
וְלֹא יִלְמְדוּ עוֹד מִלְחָמָה".
אָמֵן.

This is a new formulation of the prayer, independent of the structure of the official PSI composed by Rabbi Herzog but bearing some thematic resemblance to it. Instead of referring to Israel as the "first sprouting of our redemption," it expresses the hope that it may become a blessing for the entire world. The last paragraph stresses the role that Israel should play in the world. And although it requests that the defenders of the Land should be crowned with victory (compare this to *Ha'avodah Shebalev*, which asks for the well-being and safety of the soldiers, and the Rabbis for Human Rights' prayer, which asks for the restraint of their power), it seeks peace among the nations.

Aharon Loewenschuss, a chemistry professor and a member of Mevakshei Derekh, was not satisfied with this prayer and composed an alternative:

A Prayer on Behalf of Our People and Our Land

Ruler of the universe,
Accept with favor our prayer for the State of Israel and its people.
Pour your blessing upon this land and upon all its inhabitants.
Cause us to understand your righteous laws,
and implant in our hearts the wisdom of your prophets—
"To do justice, to love mercy, and to walk humbly with your God"
(Micah 6:8).
Pour out your spirit upon all the inhabitants of our land; plant within us tolerance and mutual respect, uproot hatred, violence, coercion, and exploitation from within us.
Spread your tabernacle of peace over the house of Israel in all their dwelling places.

תְּפִילָה בְּעַד עַמֵּנוּ וּבְעַד אַרְצֵנוּ

רִבּוֹן הָעוֹלָם,
קַבֵּל נָא בְּרָצוֹן אֶת תְּפִלָּתֵנוּ לְמַעַן
מְדִינַת יִשְׂרָאֵל וְעַמָּהּ.
הָרֵק אֶת בִּרְכָתְךָ עַל הָאָרֶץ וְעַל
כָּל יוֹשְׁבֶיהָ.
הֲבִינֵנוּ מִשְׁפְּטֵי צִדְקֶךָ, וְתֵן בְּלִבֵּנוּ
אֶת מוּסַר נְבִיאֶיךָ —
"עֲשׂוֹת מִשְׁפָּט וְאַהֲבַת חֶסֶד
וְהַצְנֵעַ לֶכֶת עִם אֱלֹהֶיךָ" (מיכה ו, ח).
הַעֲרֵה רוּחֲךָ עַל כָּל תּוֹשְׁבֵי
אַרְצֵנוּ;
טַע בָּנוּ סוֹבְלָנוּת וְכָבוֹד הֲדָדִי;
עֲקֹר מִתּוֹכֵנוּ שִׂנְאָה, אַלִּימוּת,
כְּפִיָּה וְנִצּוּל לָרַע.

Pray, place the courage in their souls to come to our land, "and may your children return to their own realm" (Jeremiah 31:16).
Teach us to accept with an open heart those who are gathering to our land.
And strengthen those who are coming to us,
so that they endure the difficulties of their absorption.
And may we dwell in it together in fellowship.
Strengthen the hearts of our soldiers,
the defenders of our land,
may their spirit be bold, and their weapons unblemished.
Shield them under the shadow of your wings,
and grant them salvation,
so that they may prevail over our enemies.
But pray, grant peace to this land and may all who dwell in it be blessed by it,
speedily fulfill the vision of your prophets:
"Nation shall not lift up sword against nation, neither shall they learn war anymore" (Isaiah 2:4).

פְּרֹשׂ אֶת סֻכַּת שְׁלוֹמְךָ עַל בֵּית יִשְׂרָאֵל בְּכָל תְּפוּצוֹתָיו.
אָנָּא, תֵּן עֹז בְּנַפְשָׁם לָבֹא לְאַרְצֵנוּ, וְיֵשְׁבוּ בָּה שֶׁבֶת אַחִים גַּם יַחַד.
לַמְּדֵנוּ לְקַבֵּל בְּלֵב פָּתוּחַ אֶת הַמִּתְקַבְּצִים אֵלֵינוּ,
וְאֶת הַבָּאִים אֵלֵינוּ חַזֵּק,
לַעֲמֹד בְּקָשְׁיֵי קְלִיטָתָם, "וְשָׁבוּ בָנִים לִגְבוּלָם" (ירמיהו לא, טז).
אַמֵּץ אֶת לֵב חַיָּלֵינוּ, מְגִנֵּי אַרְצֵנוּ,
וְהָיְתָה רוּחָם עַזָּה, וְנִשְׁקָם — טָהוֹר.
שׁוֹמְרֵם בְּצֵל כְּנָפֶיךָ,
הַנְחִילֵם יְשׁוּעָה וְגָבְרוּ עַל אוֹיְבֵינוּ.
אַךְ, אָנָּא, תֵּן שָׁלוֹם בָּאָרֶץ וְהִתְבָּרְכוּ בָּה כָּל יוֹשְׁבֶיהָ,
וְקַיֵּם בִּמְהֵרָה חֲזוֹן נְבִיאֶיךָ:
"לֹא יִשָּׂא גוֹי אֶל גּוֹי חֶרֶב, וְלֹא יִלְמְדוּ עוֹד מִלְחָמָה" (ישעיהו ב, ד).

Loewenschuss explained to me that it became important to him to replace the traditional PSI, as well as the one from Mevakshei Derekh cited above, with a prayer that would accurately reflect what he considered the actual ideology and beliefs of his community. Toward that end, he brought his proposal to the worship committee in the early 1980s, but it took some time before the committee even agreed to consider his composition. Loewenschuss says he "had to leave the sanctuary in anger" before the proposed text was admitted to discussion. Gradually, however, it became the community's preferred text.

Rather than praying solely for the rulers and governing powers of the state, the Loewenschuss text requests wisdom, understanding, and courage for all. Written during the massive immigration from the former Soviet Union, it specifies the well-being of "those who are gathering to our land." The writer, who immigrated to Israel as a child and recalls his family's initial difficulties in the new land, calls for the acceptance of the newcomers "with an open heart." When referring to the military, he asks that it be both courageous and moral, and he concludes the prayer with a request for the peace that will make Israel a blessing to all who dwell in it.

Most of the prayers discussed here were created for (and recited in) non-Orthodox circles. Orthodox communities show less interest in formulating PSIs; Orthodoxy avoids liturgical innovation in general, and ultra-Orthodox authorities reject the prayer in principle because they reject the very concept of Israel as an official Jewish state among the nations. In the National Orthodox community (not the ultra-Orthodox), the official PSI is recited in most synagogues, though the energy with which it is recited varies; it sometimes depends on their support of the government and its policies. Throughout recent decades, especially following the Oslo agreement in 1993 and even more so following the disengagement process from Gaza in 2005, some communities have chosen to make changes to the PSI reflecting their opposition to the current policy of the state.[27] In some extremely right-wing groups, the identification with the state has decreased so much that the state is no longer considered the "sprouting of our redemption," and consequently, the prayer is not recited there anymore. In that sense, extreme settlers were in the position of many Jews in the diaspora, relating to a state that they did not consider their own.[28] Ironically, some of those in Orthodox circles who were eager to consider the establishment of Israel as a religious event, a stage in the messianic process, now find themselves estranged from it. In most Orthodox synagogues, however, the prayer is still recited with considerable fervor.

Universalism and Particularism, Inclusivity and Exclusivity in the Prayers for the State of Israel

Prayer is conversation. Primarily we speak with God, but we also converse with other people, both those in our community and those outside of it. We even communicate indirectly with those who are not part of our people and religion—although they are probably not aware of our discourse and, indeed, need not be, because the statements we make to or about them are intended for our own benefit as much as for theirs. Prayers reflect the *Sitz im Leben*, the existential context of those who once composed them, those for whom it was composed, those to whom they now refer, those who actually recite them, and even those who reject them.

If you want to know about Jewish history, the hopes and fears of Jews, if you are interested in opening windows to the souls of Jews, you may want to look into their liturgy and rituals before turning to legal statements or systematic theological essays.[29]

The prayers for the State of Israel can therefore serve as a test case not just for liturgical innovation but also for identity writ large, as expressed through theology, ideology, and politics.

In that regard, we have seen how current PSIs reflect a current existential situation for Jews who write or recite them. Prayers for the government have been recited by Jews for many centuries, but the composers of the PSIs deliberately overlooked the classical medieval formula (*Hanoten T'shuah*) and created new ones, precisely because they understood themselves to be living in a new era and an unprecedented situation. As new texts altogether, reflective of the new era not of the liturgical past, the PSI texts have no halakhic (legal), liturgical, or textual constraints and can show significant flexibility. They freely express and assess national, social, and religious sentiments of today.

Finally, what is omitted from the liturgy can sometimes be at least as revealing as what is included. As we saw, for example, the official Israeli Chief Rabbinate PSI contains no reference to the non-Jewish inhabitants of Israel and its neighboring countries. Its composer, Rabbi Herzog, may have wanted to stress its role as an internal Jewish text; he may have seen it as an alternative and religious "Declaration of Independence," this one for Israeli-Jewish use, as opposed to the official Declaration that has been directed to Israelis—to Jews as well as to the world at large. Other texts added but also omitted ideas to express their own changing views of the state's essence, goals, and responsibilities.

Each text aims differently to strike a balance between the need to be part of the family of nations and the desire to stress Israel's own national aspirations.[30] They differ, among other things, in commitment to those who are not Jewish; most of the prayers that overtly relate to non-Jews who live in or near Israel stem from the liberal movements. The Orthodox camp is generally less enthusiastic about liturgical innovation and is less apt to show universalistic sensitivity. The few PSIs composed by Orthodox Jews do not relate to non-Jews at all.[31]

As one might expect, diaspora and Israeli texts differ with regard to Israel's role for the Jewish People as a whole. Israeli prayers deal largely with the actual situation in the country and with its concrete goals—we can say that most of them are Israel centered more than they are Jewish People oriented. Most of the diaspora prayers, by contrast, are more likely to highlight Israel as the birthplace of the Jewish People ("for Torah shall come out of Zion" [Isaiah 2:3]) and the locus for future Jewish hopes—concerns that provide Israel's somewhat different meaning to diaspora consciousness.

Sacred texts in general (but prayers in particular) set boundaries that distinguish one group from another; in so doing, some differentiate more rigidly than others. Traditional Jewish prayers tend to be on the rigid side, having sometimes either a negative view of others or being unconcerned with them—a reflection of the circumstances of having lived for most of Jewish history, especially in Europe, as a *reactive* minority. In the Jewish state, however, where Jews are no longer a minority, Jewish self-definitions can be *proactive*—allowing for concern about others without negating manifestations of Jewish nationality, religion, and peoplehood.

✦

The Music of V'ye'etayu— "All the World"

Dr. Mark L. Kligman

The Ashkenazi tradition of synagogue music is notable for two important features.

First is *nusach*, the modal (or chanting) sounds of Jewish prayer that
signify the yearly occasion and time of day. Shabbat eve, Shabbat morning, Rosh Hashanah eve, and so on, all have their own unique "modal"
sounds based on different scales.

The second is *misinai niggunim*, literally "melodies that go back to
Sinai." They are not that old, of course, but they do go back several centuries. We do not know exactly how far, but the fact that these melodies are
found in eighteenth-century musical manuscripts spread out over hundreds
of miles leads us to conclude that they must have been set sometime earlier
still and then kept alive by strong oral tradition that maintained them in
use throughout Ashkenaz. These *misinai niggunim* include such standbys
as *Kol Nidre* and the Great *Alenu* (the melody used for Rosh Hashanah
as an introduction to *Malkhuyot*, the section of the shofar service that

Dr. Mark L. Kligman is professor of Jewish musicology at Hebrew Union
College–Jewish Institute of Religion in New York, where he teaches in the
School of Sacred Music. He specializes in the liturgical traditions of Middle
Eastern Jewish communities and various areas of popular Jewish music.
Dr. Kligman is an adjunct professor at Columbia University and Rutgers
University, the academic chair of the Jewish Music Forum, and coeditor
of the journal *Musica Judaica*. He has published on the liturgical music of
Syrian Jews in Brooklyn in journals as well as his book *Maqām and Liturgy:
Ritual, Music and Aesthetics of Syrian Jews in Brooklyn*, which shows the inter-
connection between the music of Syrian Jews and their cultural way of life.

highlights God's rule over all creation). Over time, these melodies have become synonymous with the prayers themselves, to the point where they iconically represent those prayers, there being only one melody for them.

Interestingly, *V'ye'etayu* follows neither general rule: it does not follow the *nusach* and there is no *misinai niggun* for it. Rather, *V'ye'etayu* generally goes unemphasized in traditional synagogues; there is no specific tradition for how it is to be sung, and it may not even be sung at all. When it is sung, however, the melody is usually set in a major key. Here it stands out because the *Amidah* of the Rosh Hashanah service—the prayer in which it is inserted—is predominately sung in a minor key.

Unlike *misinai* melodies, then, *V'ye'etayu* has many possible settings. Here is a survey of the most important ones.

Louis Lewandowski (1821–1894) was, perhaps, the most influential synagogue musician in Berlin, whose compositions were sung by Ashkenazi communities in Europe, America, and around the world. His major work, *Todah W'zimrah* (1876–1882), contains synagogue settings for cantor, choir, and organ, including a setting of *V'ye'etayu* with the overall format of ABA—that is, the same melody (A) occurs at the beginning and the end but is separated by a second melody (B). The Hebrew text of *V'ye'etayu* is an alphabetic acrostic—it allocates a line for each letter of the Hebrew alphabet. The first melody (A) encompasses the sentences from *alef* through *tet*. For the sentences from *yod* through *samech*, the B melody intrudes. The A melody then returns for sentences *ayin* to *tav*. The A melody has one note to each syllable, with limited embellishment. The B melody is higher and a bit more dramatic, especially in the words *v'yilm'du to'im binah* ("and those who stray will come to understand"), but also where the text speaks of God's strength, urges us to extol God, and suggests we pray with trepidation.

The ABA form provides a nicely balanced setting in a singable and recognizable melody that effectively conveys a majestic feeling for the text. In this Germanic-synagogue musical style, the cantor sings one phrase and the choir sings the next one—cantor and choir do not sing at the same time. The organ plays throughout.

The Lewandowski melody was commonly sung in traditional communities throughout the late nineteenth and twentieth centuries and even today. *Zamru Lo: The Next Generation*, a popular current publication of congregational melodies, includes the Lewandowski melody for this text, but the choral harmony and organ are not included.[1]

A. W. Binder (1895–1966) was an especially well-known composer of synagogue music from the 1920s to the 1960s. He served as music director at the Stephen Wise Free Synagogue and taught at the School of Sacred Music of Hebrew Union College–Jewish Institute of Religion in New York City. He was signally influential to Reform music in the twentieth century through his compositions, teaching, and encouragement of others. He edited the third edition of the *Union Hymnal*, published in 1933.

As we saw, *V'ye'etayu* had gone largely unemphasized even in traditional circles, so had easily been omitted from Reform liturgies, especially because its complex Hebrew text—a medieval poem following an alphabetic acrostic—was not easily navigated. Its universalistic message, however, fit the Reform Movement's emphasis on social justice and repairing the world (*tikkun olam*), so Binder was attracted to it, especially because a loose translation in rhyming form had meanwhile been composed by the notable British Jew Israel Zangwill. Binder's setting of this English version, called "All the World," after the opening line of Zangwill's poem, became standard fare in Reform circles. This hymn is also in a major key and is composed in steady march-like three-beat patterns, making it a clear demonstration of a hymn with very predictable musical phrases: a phrase with eight syllables (e.g., the opening line, "All the word shall come to serve Thee") followed by a phrase of six syllable (e.g., the following line, "And bless Thy glorious Name"); this pattern continues throughout the poem, giving us a single long melody that is repeated three times. Whereas Lewandowski's setting had an A melody, a contrasting B melody, and the return of the A melody, Binder's "All the World" repeats the same sixteen-measure melody three times.

The heralding and majestic nature of Binder's setting and its predictable and easy-to-sing melody made it amenable to congregational participation, so that—as we have seen—it became quite popular in Reform congregations throughout North America and elsewhere as well. Even though most Reform congregations have moved away from hymn singing, Binder's setting can still be heard in many places. In a sense, it became iconic in its own right for congregations that were used to hearing it as a staple for their New Year worship.

Another Reform setting for "All the World" is by Herbert Fromm (1905–1995), written for cantor, choir, and organ. Fromm was born in Germany, conducted the civic opera in a couple of cities, and then turned to Jewish music specifically after 1933, when German law prohibited

Jews from engaging in German culture. Like so many other Jewish musicians, he fled Nazi Germany (in 1937) and resettled in America, where he accepted a post as music director at Temple Beth Zion in Buffalo and, the following year, Temple Israel in Boston. He eventually became known as a prolific and accomplished composer, with many works intended specifically for synagogue liturgical use.

Fromm's "All the World" was published in 1979, using a text that is updated in terms of English usage. Instead of "All the world shall come to serve Thee," for example, Fromm's version reads, "All the world shall come to serve You." Unlike Binder's setting, however, Fromm reverts to the traditional ABA form (by Lewandowski) of the Hebrew original, *V'ye'etayu*. In Fromm's setting, the A section, in a minor key, begins with a slow majestic setting entirely sung by the choir. The second half of this introductory A section mounts in tempo. The B section (starting with "They shall worship You at sunrise") is to be sung as a solo, presumably by the cantor. The contrast is heightened in that it follows yet a quicker tempo and demands a more elaborate accompaniment on the organ. The A section returns with the choir singing the words "With the coming of your kingdom all the hills will shout with song"—and is like the opening A section in that it follows a slower majestic tempo. It then builds to a slow but grand conclusion. Quite common to classical music—the work of J. S. Bach, for instance—is the final chord of a minor piece using a major chord. This is the case with Fromm. On the final words "You crowned king," the last chord is D major.

An influential cantorial setting nowadays for *V'ye'etayu* comes from Chazzan Israel Alter (1901–1979), a man whose work has influenced generations of cantors. Like Fromm, Alter too fled Germany, in 1935, after serving as the last chief cantor of Hanover. For almost three decades, he served at the largest synagogue in Johannesburg, South Africa, but in 1961, he came to New York, where he served as a cantor and taught in the School of Sacred Music at Hebrew Union College–Jewish Institute of Religion. Alter's setting for *V'ye'etayu* is found in his publication *The High Holy Day Service: The Complete Musical Liturgy of Rosh Hashanah and Yom Kippur for the Hazzan* (published by the Cantors Assembly in 1971). It follows the traditional text in Hebrew, but like his other work, generally speaking, it is quite complex.

He begins and ends in a major key but has a good deal of contrast in key changes and key signatures. As the text of *V'ye'etayu* becomes more emphatic in the middle section, with the words *v'yatu sh'chem* ("they will stand shoulder to shoulder to serve You"), the setting becomes more embellished and provides a higher line in a contrasting key. Unlike the Lewandowski version, Alter's setting does not neatly appear in a three-part form; rather—as is typical of traditional cantorial composition—it changes to express the tone and meaning of various phrases in the text. The middle section is highlighted most significantly. It is not until the very last line (*V'yishm'u r'chokim v'yavo'u*, "And they will hear from afar and arrive") that the melodic line returns to the beginning phrase and key.

Most recently, Cantor Benjie Ellen Schiller, graduate and faculty member of the Debbie Friedman School of Sacred Music at Hebrew Union College–Jewish Institute of Religion, has written a setting titled "*V'ye'etayu*—All the World" (in the Transcontinental Choral Library, published in 1990). The setting is for cantor, choir or congregation, and organ. Unique in her version is the combination of Hebrew and English, a common feature to new synagogue music since the 1970s. Schiller's setting begins with an organ introduction and the cantor or congregation singing in unison the first section of "All the World" in English. The melody is in a moderate tempo in a minor key. We will refer to this as the A section. The B section is the first few lines of the Hebrew text of *V'ye'etayu* sung by the cantor alone. The melody is more complex, with close attention being paid to modern Sephardi Israeli pronunciation of the text. The A section then returns, only to be followed by another B section thereafter. This A and B alternation occurs once more, before ending with a final A section. In all, the form is AB-AB-AB-A. The B sections work their way through the Hebrew, while the A section repeats the first portion of "All the World" in English, as a sort of English refrain. The last B section has a more dramatic ending, fittingly sung by the cantor alone. The contrast in Schiller's setting is more evident than in the others surveyed here, given its Hebrew-English alternation, each one with its own melody. Predominantly in a minor key, like the Fromm setting, the one by Schiller ends with a major chord.

These settings of *V'ye'etayu* and "All the World" demonstrate the ongoing tendency of Jewish synagogue music, generally, to adapt to new aesthetics. Lewandowski's grand style obeyed the aesthetic of nineteenth-century German Reform; Binder wrote for the tradition of hymn singing that was common in the first part of twentieth-century Reform. Chazzan

Alter's setting follows the traditional cantorial approach of a deeper and more complex form of solo chazzanic expression. Fromm and Schiller developed their own unique forms of artistry in keeping with what, for each of them, was a contemporary stylization of the text. What the settings have in common is each composer's interpretation of the text and, in most cases, an encouragement of the congregation to join in the singing, so as to highlight this part of the liturgy for the High Holy Days.

෧ඁඁ෨

PART II
Views from Philosophy and Literature

For a Judaism of Human Concerns

Rabbi Walter Homolka, PhD, DHL

The main force in Jewish thought today often seems to focus on the tribal and particularistic aspects of our tradition. This has not always been the case, however. Rabbi Bradley Shavit Artson, DHL, critiques the change when he remembers that "the great minds of the Medieval period—Saadiah, Rambam, and others—asked broad, universal, human questions" while mobilizing "Jewish tools to address those challenges." The modern period, by contrast, "asks little Jewish questions, while mobilizing universal tools to answer those questions." Typical of these "little questions" are such queries as "How can we survive as a people? What does it mean to be American?"[1]

Artson's critique of modernity targets much of contemporary Jewish intellectual argument. And, indeed, it may apply to some of those Jews who were newly admitted to Western society in the nineteenth century and who worried most, therefore, about Jewish survival in their times. Others, however, managed to make an immense contribution to general human thought by asking general questions relevant to the overall human condition and providing an answer from a distinctly Jewish toolbox. Hermann Cohen was a pioneer in this latter endeavor.

Rabbi Walter Homolka, PhD, DHL, is the rector of the Abraham Geiger College for the training of rabbis, the executive director of the Zacharias Frankel College, and a professor of modern Jewish thought at the School of Jewish Theology of the University of Potsdam in Germany. He is the author of many books, including *Jesus Reclaimed: Jewish Perspectives on the Nazarene*, and coauthor with Hans Kung of *How to Do Good & Avoid Evil: A Global Ethic from the Sources of Judaism* (SkyLight Paths). He is a contributor to *We Have Sinned: Sin and Confession in Judaism—Ashamnu and Al Chet* and *May God Remember: Memory and Memorializing in Judaism—Yizkor* (both Jewish Lights).

Cohen's contribution would have been outstanding in any event, but it is all the more striking given the era in which he lived. In 2014, we commemorate the beginning of World War I, the "Great War," as it is still called by some. It started in 1914 and ended four years later, the very year Hermann Cohen died. Cohen's voice provided a corrective to the self-interested nationalism that had been stoking the fires of war. Except in scholarly circles, Cohen is largely forgotten today, even though his corrective is as relevant now as ever. Particularly in a book dedicated to the High Holy Day message of universalism, Cohen deserves pride of place.

Hermann Cohen (1842–1918) served as a professor at the University of Marburg (Germany), where he became known as the most outstanding representative of the neo-Kantian school of rational thought. But his particular contribution was the development of theories that connected general ethics to Jewish moral teaching. During the final years of his life, Cohen held lectures on both general and Jewish philosophy at the Berlin Hochschule fuer die Wissenschaft des Judentums, a training ground for liberal rabbis (among others). But his main influence was directed to a general audience.

Hermann Cohen concentrated on the universal message of Judaism whereby God is king over all nations and the Jewish People a holy priesthood to serve humankind. In contrast to the petty particularisms that were becoming a world at war, Cohen proposed the view that the ultimate meaning and value of human life lies in the Jewish concept of *shalom*, "peace." Just as the Hebrew root of *shalom* means "perfection," so too the purpose and the goal of humanity are striving toward perfection.

Shalom as Completion of Moral Community

Cohen saw peace as the quintessence of all divine attributes and the highest goal, therefore, of a moral life. Tolerance and openness would have to replace nationalist restrictions, because moral community was, by definition, universal. His argument proceeded from a Kantian view of ethics as universal, but he spoke as a Jew, not just a philosopher, citing the Talmud: "The entire Torah exists solely for the morals of peace" (Gittin 59b).

This universal state of peace would require a compromise between the individual ego and the common welfare of all. In keeping with Kant's philosophy of morality as an imperative of reason, Cohen saw peace as a moral requirement to which reason obligates us, but he thought such universal ethical behavior followed from religious principles as well. It is not just reason, but God as well who obliges human beings to pursue moral conduct; we must bow to God's wishes.

For Cohen, God is a God of love, not just for a few, but for all humanity, and God demands such love of humanity from all human beings in turn, for (as Judaism teaches) humanity is formed in God's image. Because human beings are naturally creatures of reason and because reason requires universal morality—else it is not morality—it follows that the moral law exists naturally within human community. God is the religious equivalent of the universal grounds for this moral law. Peace becomes a symbol of human perfection, individual harmony, and the perfection of humanity.

Shalom as Catalyst for the Messianic Age: War as the Satan of World History

The prophets had already described world peace as the goal and purpose of human history, thereby proving themselves to be true teachers of compassion and speakers for God, who (as we saw) represents the possibility of universal love and the grounds for morality itself.

But peace is more than the absence of war. It is a symbol of the messianic age, the epitome of morality. Only with the dawn of messianic peace will the process of human spiritual salvation be completed. Through peace as the common power of human consciousness, all forms of love will be freed from ambiguity; the individual will be freed of selfishness, for example, and be able to experience love in all its unadulterated wholeness.

Peace as the purpose of humanity is actually the conceptual equivalent of the messiah whom Jewish tradition pictured as freeing humanity of conflict, mediating strife among individuals, and bringing about the reconciliation of Israel with its God. And if "peace" is the way we understand the messiah, then its opposite, "war," can be compared to the Satan of world history.

In Hermann Cohen's eyes, war is a mockery of the thoughts of God, the father of all humanity, just as it contradicts the concept of humanity as an end in itself and the ultimate aim of universal history. He juxtaposes this essentially Jewish view with the perspective of the ancient Greeks, whereby war is the father of the universe and the real meaning of life and of human fate is found in battle.

Cohen places particular significance in the love of one's enemies and, with that, introduces an important new element into thoughts on peace. This universalizing of peace to include even one's foes followed from Cohen's strict and uncompromising argument that peace is the goal of all morality and the primal power for progress in the world. Particularly on the verge of World War I, Cohen's teaching regarding the peace that is due one's enemy stands out as the epitome of the moral life.

Elimination of Hatred Will Bring Global Peace

The highest goal, namely, the fulfillment of peace, is achieved individually, however, as its first step is the self-perfection and peace of the soul. It is not mere faith without understanding that provides the basis for peace of the soul; rather, this peace is itself based on the full exercise of human reason.

This peace of the soul is expressed in a sense of satisfaction that makes one independent of the striving for exaggerated material needs, therefore paving the way for further appreciation of the moral demands of reason.

The opposite of reason is unbridled passion, which prevents the achievement of peace in the soul by building up hatred. The religious doctrine of "virtue"—an extension of love—expresses the necessary fight against hatred: not just to avoid it personally but also to exclude it from operating among people everywhere and to prevent its very existence in the world. Virtue, in other words, is the name we give to the ethical expression of love in pursuit of peace and in opposition to hatred.

The need to eliminate hatred is tantamount to a command to love one's enemies. Only when one knows no enemies at all is it possible to remove all hate from one's heart. "All hatred is in vain," Cohen wrote. "I deny hatred to the human heart. Therefore I deny that I have an enemy, that I could hate a man."[2]

By eliminating hate from the inventory of human motivation, the long-awaited peace of the soul finally approaches. Only through love unfettered by hate can such tranquility and contentment be achieved. We are not yet describing the end result of human peace worldwide, which will follow only after personal peace is a reality. This personal sense of peace, however, gives rise through reason to the further belief that national hatred too must be eliminated from human consciousness world-wide. Kant's entire ethical system, after all, is based on the assumption of what he called the categorical imperative, the sense that one must act as if the entire world were called upon to act the same way. Seeking personal peace for one's own soul thus necessitates the same condition of peace for everyone. When the need for hatred is finally recognized as an illusion, this universalizing of peace becomes possible. As humanity moves ever forward toward imagining the virtue of peace, it will simultaneously unmask the deadly image of hate.

The concept of *shalom*, according to Cohen, is truly indispensable. And the way to achieve it is through religious study that promotes self-perfection and peace of the soul. When hatred is removed from the world (along with the very word "enemy"), then peace will come in the form of the messiah who will reconcile the human race with God. Thus, the messiah is no longer seen as the bringer of peace, but as a personification of the situation once peace has been achieved.

Peace as the Crown of Life

Peace is most certainly the basic will of the human soul, and the goal, therefore, of all humanity. It permeates all things and is above all else in human desire. All this follows from the fact that we are made in God's image: God is peace; human beings who strive to be like God must strive also for peace. Peace is the unity of all powers of life, their balance, and the resolution of all their differences. Peace is, to the mind of Hermann Cohen, the crown of life.

In my opinion, Cohen's teachings complete the transition that Judaism had already been undergoing for several centuries before Cohen burst upon the scene. This transition can be seen in the way we describe the God whom Israel worships. Until the modern period, Jews worshiped God as *Adonai tz'va'ot*, "the Lord of hosts," in the original tribal and particularistic sense of the God of Israel, a God of war, and a God who fought and subdued other ancient peoples of the biblical era. With the dawn of the Enlightenment, however, God was reconceived as an absolute God of peace, an image that is actually presupposed by the author of the book of Genesis. Cohen thus saw himself returning to an original way of Jewish thinking. At the same time, he sought to build a bridge to modernity on the basis of Jewish philosophical thought.

Hermann Cohen marks the epitome and end of the Jewish Enlightenment. His theories offer a consistent and outstanding example of universalism derived from Kantian philosophy on one hand and the very essence of the Jewish tradition on the other. True, in retrospect, Cohen's idealism was too optimistic. But his message remains with us as the ultimate statement of Jewish philosophy wed to universalistic human betterment. His insistence on universal morality as the basic principle and highest aim of humanity addresses both the Jewish and the non-Jewish individual and, at the same time, the entire world.

Rabbi Bradley Shavit Artson, DHL, with whom I began, supplies a contemporary conclusion with which I will close:

> If Judaism is not a tool to become profoundly human, if it is not our entryway, our porthole into humanity, into all of creation, then it is unworthy of its legacy. We must be willing to stand for a Judaism that addresses broad, universal, human concerns, one which mobilizes the great resources of the Bible, of Rabbinics, of Hassidut and Kabbalah, of Jewish Poetry, Philosophy, and Art, to be able to allow us to be fully human.[3]

Hermann Cohen is the quintessential example of the universalistic Judaism for which Artson argues: the insistence that in its very essence, Judaism has time and again found ways to touch humankind with its universal message—best stated, perhaps, in the spectacular prayer featured in this volume, "All the World":

> With the coming of Thy kingdom,
> The hills shall break into song,
> And the islands laugh exultant,
> That they to God belong.
> And through all their congregations,
> So loud Thy praise shall sing,
> That the uttermost peoples hearing,
> Shall hail Thee crowned King.

ᏀᎳᎳᎧ

All Peoples Will Break into Song, but the Song Will Be Hebrew

Rabbi Bradley Shavit Artson, DHL

The Problem

It is generally assumed that universalism and particularism are mutually exclusive: either one precludes the other. We assume as well that one of the options—universalism, usually—is morally superior. Along with that bias goes the accompanying conceit that our own cultural preferences are *truly* universal and that anyone holding the same opinion about their cultures is mired in pernicious and outmoded particularism.

This dichotomy (universal = good, superior, progressive, rational, enlightened; particular = bad, inferior, reactionary, emotional, tribal) seems natural to those who take the modernist worldview that certain foundational truths are self-evidently true. At the core of these assumptions is a picture of the world composed of inert matter governed by eternal objective laws. Given that assumption, the primary intellectual task is explaining how a minute fraction of this inert stuff could erupt first into

Rabbi Bradley Shavit Artson, DHL, an inspiring speaker and educator, holds the Abner and Roslyn Goldstine Dean's Chair of the Ziegler School of Rabbinic Studies and is vice president of American Jewish University in Los Angeles. He is a member of the philosophy department, supervises the Miller Introduction to Judaism Program, and mentors Camp Ramah in California. He is also dean of Zacharias Frankel College in Potsdam, Germany, ordaining rabbis for the European Union. A regular columnist for the *Huffington Post,* he is author of many articles and books, including *God of Becoming and Relationship: The Dynamic Nature of Process Theology* and *Passing Life's Tests: Spiritual Reflections on the Trial of Abraham, the Binding of Isaac.*

life, then mind, then consciousness. Practically speaking, we then work to exploit the inert stuff for the short-term benefit of the tiny percentage of self-conscious stuff, ourselves.

We have made great headway in the practical challenge (however, at great cost), but we consistently fail in the intellectual one. We have yet to generate a coherent understanding of how life emerges from nonlife and how mind emerges from brain. Meanwhile, our very success at ransacking the inert stuff for humanity's short-term gain appears to be killing us.

Something has to give.

The Promising Alternative

Perhaps these failures persist because modernity's metaphysical assumptions are flawed. By integrating the best that science now offers (evolutionary theory, relativity, quantum physics, cosmology, and cognitive neurology, among others), we can reframe better assumptions.

Building on the insights of such thinkers as Henri Bergson, William James, Alfred North Whitehead, Charles Hartshorne, Marjorie Suchocki, John Cobb, Catherine Keller, and others, we can reconceptualize the world as the dynamic, interrelating, self-determining dynamism it truly is. We call this "process thought."

Process thought imagines every aspect of the world not as a substance (unchanging, inert), but as an event in the process of becoming. Each one is self-determining but also impacted by other, similar, self-determining aspects. Each becoming-aspect, while retaining some consistency across time, is also part of a larger world in the process of generating novelty and greater connection.

With each new moment, each event is offered the range of potentialities made possible by its previous choices, the realities of the rest of the world around it, its history, and its own nature. Each event retains the capacity to select from among the possibilities open to it at that moment, although one of those possibilities is the optimal choice (optimal in terms of love, compassion, relating, experience, justice). Process thinkers label that optimal choice "the lure." Like all great possibilities, it is not known rationally from the outside, but is intuited from within (Whitehead called that intuitive grasp "prehension"). At each instant, we and all creation are presented with the lure appropriate to our actual existence, but we retain the self-determination to strive for it or to reject it for other choices.

God, in the process view, is the unifying ground that makes all relating possible. God is the One who lures both us and all creation in the direction of optimal development, experience, and justice, rather than finding ourselves trapped in an endless loop of meaningless repetition of the same natural laws. God is the One who meets us in our particularity and re-creates us as we choose a particular path, with that choice now ratified as a permanent part of our character and history. And God, knowing everything possible to know, retains our choices forever.

In this understanding, God is not all-powerful in a coercive sense, but vastly, persistently powerful in a persuasive way. God does not, cannot, break the rules. God works in/with/through us to advance the vision of a creation of greater relating and caring. We retain our freedom, like God, to be self-surpassing and to choose, within the constraints of our actuality, our next choice.

Process, Particularity, and Universalism

This new, deeper integration allows the recognition that particularism always contains within itself the seeds of universality. We are all distinctive becoming events, self-determining and manifesting dignity. God meets each of us with the lure that is proper to our own specific reality, but our particular becoming takes place in consonance with each and every other becoming. We are all in this together. Isn't that the most universal universalism possible?

So particularity occurs within the larger whole of universalism. And universalism always blossoms in its many particularities. Christianity sought to become a single universal church, but it has flowered into thousands of denominations, each having to accommodate the others. Life that began from a single organism flowered into millions of species, all of them interrelated. There can be no true universalism without particularity, nor any robust particularity that isn't an expression of, and contribution to, universalism.

Universalism and particularism aren't polar opposites, nor are they antagonists. Rather, each is a separate vantage point from which to view the ubiquity of becoming. Together, they form a raucous whole—each enhancing the other.

If we apply this new understanding to prayer, we find precisely this synergy between universalism and particularism that spirals toward greater hope, joy, and connectivity. Indeed, this enhanced vitality constitutes the very salvation to which Rosh Hashanah points.

The Prayers

Our selection contains five principal sections:

1. *V'khol Ma'aminim*: a *piyyut* by the poet Yannai, describing assertions about God's relationship to us and our embrace of that relationship
2. *Tusgav L'vadekha*: a transition or summary paragraph acknowledging that on that future day, God will be one and God's name one
3. *Uv'khen*: three paragraphs, possibly among the earliest insertions into the *Amidah*, delineating three stages of cosmic and human advance
4. *V'ye'etayu*: an alphabetic *piyyut* celebrating God's reign over a humanity redeemed
5. *V'timlokh*: biblical passages celebrating that eventual time when God's rule will be manifest

Refined through the lens of process theology, each of these sections reveals a fusion of universal and particular, grounded in dynamic relationship, and lured toward a salvation that will be ours no less than God's.

V'khol Ma'aminim

The poet mixes descriptions of God ("holder of the scales of justice ... examiner of hidden secrets ... redeemer from death") with affirmations of how those beliefs enter our lives ("inspector of our hearts ... answers silent prayers"). In sum, God not just "is," but God is reliably available to us. This very structure reinforces the realization that however much God's transcendence remains a logical necessity, we know God only through God's immanence—our connection to God, in our individual lives, our communities, and our world. In effect, the poet dances the dynamism of our relationship with the divine. Divine trait and human perception cycle this dance in a helix of ascension.

The poem exhibits little that is explicitly Jewish, leading many to label it "universalist." It speaks to the broadest swath of humanity, indeed to all creation. Yet for all that, it is written in highly structured Hebrew, its scansion familiar to the tropes of its time and place. God is not recalled in the abstract, but in categories familiar to the Hebrew reader—redeemer from death, seeker of repentance, and so on. And God is explicitly *zokher habrit*, the one who recalls the covenant—not just Israel's covenant at Sinai, perhaps, but the covenant with humanity through Noah, making *V'khol Ma'aminim* a song of the most universal aspirations set in the specific language of Jewish faith.

Tusgav L'vadekha

This anonymous transition notes (or requests?—the Hebrew could mean either) that God should rule over united humanity, as the prophet Zechariah (14:9) predicted, "On that day Adonai will be one and his name will be one." The future tense always implies uncertainty—we *hope* that it will be so. God is vulnerable to our choices and to the choices of creation as a whole, as are we. We articulate our fondest hopes as a renewal of our striving for their attainment, and we note our own active role in creating this optimal outcome. Even the words of the prophet share a frank recognition that God's oneness is not yet complete. There is a splintered, fragmented quality to our apprehension of the divine, and we affirm, aspire, advance the commitment to overcome that fragmentation for a more integrated future.

Even here, universalism and particularity circle together: there is no explicit mention of Jews, Torah, Israel, or Jerusalem; but the name for the divine is the Hebrew *Adonai*, traditionally understood as the name revealed to Moses and the Hebrews escaping Egypt ("I am Adonai. I appeared to Abraham, Isaac, and Jacob as El Shaddai" [Exod. 6:2–3] and "tell the Israelites that Adonai ... has sent me to you" [Exod. 3:15]). Yet the reach of Adonai will one day span all humanity. Is that the advance of one particularism to encompass all, or is it the sweep of a universality so grand that all true recognitions of God converge into oneness?

Uv'khen

These three paragraphs plot the advance of humanity and cosmos in the implementation of the lure, God's hopes and plans for the world.

The first paragraph focuses on creation. All humanity—indeed, the entire cosmos—is integrated into this paean of praise and awe. Yet God is still Adonai, the God made known to Israel, specifically.

The second paragraph addresses more explicitly Jewish (particularistic?) concerns: God will bring joy to the Land of Israel and gladness to the city of Jerusalem and shine the light through the descendant of King David, the messiah. Yet even here, the particular erupts into the universal: an age of world peace and harmony, emanating from Jerusalem but extending the whole world over.

Salvation is the topic of the third paragraph, again with no specifically Jewish imagery; the vision emerges from the prophets of Israel but reaches every corner of the globe. Is that particular or universal? Or perhaps it is the particular vision of a universal climax?

Note also what is not present. In any threefold presentation of Jewish themes, we would expect to find creation, revelation, and redemption. Indeed the first and third are there, precisely where we anticipate them—paragraphs one and three. But instead of finding Sinai and revelation in paragraph two, we find Zion and the messianic promise. The poet seems to have gone out of his way to make sure that all particularity leads to universalism and that all universal aspirations are rooted and expressed in specifically Jewish terms.

V'ye'etayu

After this liturgy of progress, the interaction of particular and universal luring all toward a better future, comes this stirring poem that Solomon Schechter called the "Marseillaise of the people of the Lord." Here too the poet speaks of an age in which *all* humanity will recognize the oneness of God. Not just humanity but all of nature will join in a symphony of praise and gratitude. Furthering this cosmic perspective, there is no mention of specifically Jewish themes; Israel, Jerusalem, Torah, *mitzvot* are all conspicuous in their absence.

For all the raucous expansiveness, however, the poet defines some lands as distant ("ends of the earth") and some people as latecomers to monotheism ("nations who don't know You"). In this most universal of visions, there is still a geographic center and a people who occupied it from the beginning. We know the destination of "they [who] will hear from afar, and present You with a royal crown." Jerusalem is no longer exclusively our capital; it belongs to all humanity, all creation. But it remains the center. Our universalism is permeated with particularity; our particularity marinates in universalism.

V'timlokh

V'timlokh offers a liturgical affirmation that God will indeed rule over all creation and will do so from Mount Zion. Then God is *kadosh* ("holy"), with holiness manifest through justice and righteousness. Thus the section ends, as it has been throughout: the dynamic fusion of a particular universality and a universal particularity.

All holiness is one, yet known uniquely as Adonai. All the world praises, but we hear it still in Hebrew. Every nation rejoices, but with hearts centered in a Jerusalem that now belongs to us all. Particularism blossoms into universalism, which erupts into particularism, again and again, without end.

 ∽✲∽

Is Judaism Too Important to Be Left Just to Jews?

THE *SH'MA* AND THE *ALENU*

Rabbi Reuven Kimelman, PhD

Is Judaism too important to be left just to Jews? In other words, is Judaism only for Jews or for all humanity? If Judaism is only for the Jews, then why does the Jewish calendar mark time from the creation of the world or from the creation of humanity, whereas the calendar of the so-called world religions marks time from the decisive event of their own particular histories (the birth of Jesus; Muhammad's escape from Mecca). Nothing distinctively Jewish even crops up in the first eleven chapters of its scripture in Genesis. To deem Christianity and Islam universal and Judaism particular because they seek to foist their religion on humanity while Judaism does not is a case of mistaking imperialism for universalism.

The siddur addresses the transition from particularism to universalism in two interlocking ways through the *Sh'ma* and the *Alenu*. Israel's

---

Rabbi Reuven Kimelman, PhD, is professor of classical Judaica at Brandeis University in Waltham, Massachusetts. He is the author of *The Mystical Meaning of Lekha Dodi and Kabbalat Shabbat* and of the audio books *The Moral Meaning of the Bible* and *The Hidden Poetry of the Jewish Prayerbook*. He contributed to *Who by Fire, Who by Water*—Un'taneh Tokef, *All These Vows*—Kol Nidre, *We Have Sinned: Sin and Confession in Judaism*—Ashamnu *and* Al Chet, and to the My People's Prayer Book volumes P'sukei D'zimrah *(Morning Psalms)* and Kabbalat Shabbat *(Welcoming Shabbat in the Synagogue)* (all Jewish Lights).

recitation of *Sh'ma* ("Hear O Israel, Adonai is our God, Adonai is one") is associated with its acceptance of God's unity—and called by the Rabbis *kabbalat ol malkhut shamayim,* "accepting the authority of God's kingship." The *Alenu* too specifies the reign of God, but in the future and for all the earth, as its conclusion states: "Adonai will reign over all the earth. On that day Adonai will be one and his name will be one" (Zechariah 14:9).

The movement from Israel's acknowledgment of God's rule to the whole world's recognition of it in the future is already echoed in a Rabbinic question about the *Sh'ma.* If God is one, why say "*our* God"? Nobody says two plus *our* two is four. Their answer is that in the present, Adonai is ours; but in the future, Adonai will be one. But isn't God one now? To which the Rabbis daringly respond with Zechariah, "On that day [!] God will be one." If God will be one on that day, then God is not in our day. "One" here thus means "one for all"—a condition yet to be met.[1] The end goal of Judaism is for all humanity to call upon God as their sovereign.

The theological tension the Rabbis found in the *Sh'ma* between the present and the future is writ large in the *Alenu,* the prayer that now concludes all three daily statutory services, but which began as an introduction to the section of the *Musaf* Rosh Hashanah shofar service whose subject is divine sovereignty, *Malkhuyot.* Its two parts correspond to the two parts of the *Sh'ma.*

The first part of the *Sh'ma,* "Hear O Israel, Adonai *our* God," refers to Israel alone accepting God's kingship. So too, the first part of the *Alenu* affirms that we Jews in particular (*alenu*) have the obligation of adoring (*l'shabe'ach*) the sovereign God, the author of creation (*yotzer b'reishit*). Both are particularistic: it is distinctively *our* God—from the *Sh'ma*— whom *we*—of the *Alenu*—are obliged to worship. In fact, the *Alenu* uses a lyrical expression for God's singularity that smacks of the terms that follow the recitation of the *Sh'ma* in the morning and evening.[2]

The question then is how is it that the God who created all is only acknowledged by us? The conclusion of part one of the *Alenu* provides the answer: "For you have come to know this day and thus should take to heart that Adonai is God in heaven above and on earth below; there is no other" (Deuteronomy 4:39). So it is we who acknowledge God alone because it has been made known to us that there is no other anywhere. Apprised of the truth of creation, we are obliged to worship the one God who created all. We saw, however, that the second part of the *Sh'ma* ("God is one") refers obliquely to the future when everyone will recognize

God's kingship. So too, *Alenu*'s part two looks to a future time when others too will acknowledge the one and only God.

Part two deals with bridging the gap between what is and what should be. It begins "We therefore hope." This generalized hope is then spelled out in four specific ones, formulated as infinitives: "to see, to remove, to establish, and to turn." The first is for us, the we of the *Alenu*, to do; the other three are for God to do.

Our first hope is "to see the *radiance* of your might" (*tiferet uzekha*). The expression *tiferet uzekha* recalls *shekhinat uzo*, "the manifestation of His might" of part one, where it is associated with us recognizing that "He is our God, there is no other." What was once reserved for heaven (*Shekhinah*) is now to be radiated (*tiferet*) on earth, thereby making the God of creation acknowledged by all. The association of *tiferet* with *oz* appears also in Psalms 78:61 and 96:6 with reference to the Temple as Psalm 132:8 associates *oz* with the ark. Isaiah too (60:7, 63:15, 64:10) associates *tiferet* with the Temple. The purpose of associating *oz* and *tiferet* here is to press their allusions into the service of the idea of the whole world as a t/Temple wherein all worship God. "To see" further reinforces the Temple/Sanctuary connection by evoking Psalm 63:3: "So I beheld You in the Sanctuary, *to see* your *oz* and presence [*kavod*]." God's ultimate appearance is thus imagined here as making the whole world a Temple for the universal worship of God. The process is that God's *Shekhinah*, which part one locates in heaven and perceptible only to us, becomes in part two God's *tiferet* gloriously radiated to all on earth.

The construction of the Tabernacle in the desert is presented at the end of Exodus on the model of the construction of the world at the beginning of Genesis. Midrashic literature also lists the homologies between the cosmos and the Temple. After all, if, as the Psalms state, "He built his sanctuary like the heavens, like the earth that He established forever" (78:69), then by reverse engineering the world can become the Temple.

The transformation of the world into the Temple is based on two conceptual moves. Both involve the notion of a cosmic Temple. One is bringing down to the world the heavenly Temple; the other is making the earthly Temple coextensive with the world. The verses from Psalms and Isaiah likely imagine the heavenly Temple descending to earth on a vertical axis. For Isaiah (6:1), God's majesty is perceptible in heaven; for the psalmist (11:4), God's holy Sanctuary is identified with God's heavenly throne. Thus Micah (1:2–3) can call on all the peoples, the earth and all its fullness, to note that God will go forth from God's holy Sanctuary to descend to the heights of the earth. The Rabbis, however, foresee the earthly Temple expanding across the world on a horizontal axis. This horizontal understanding corresponds to the standard Rabbinic formula for blessings recited over the enjoyment of food, "Blessed are You, Adonai our God, sovereign of the world...." The purpose of this formulation is to expand the precincts of the Temple to allow one to partake of food wherever one is rather than limiting its consumption to the Temple. According to the Talmud (Berakhot 35a), the verse "the earth and all its fullness is Adonai's" (Psalm 24:1) could theoretically render the enjoyment of the earth's bounty off-limits except in the Temple. By acknowledging God's authority everywhere through affirming God as "sovereign of the world," the blessing makes God's bounty available to all, as it says, "The earth is given over to humanity" (Psalm 115:16). Since the world as God's Temple ("the earth and all its fullness is Adonai's") is made accessible to humanity ("the earth is given over to humanity") through the blessing, the world becomes an extended Sanctuary.

Similarly, the Torah states, "The presence [*kavod*] of Adonai filled the Tabernacle" (Exodus 40:34), whereas according to Psalms, "His presence fills the whole world" (Psalm 72:19). Which is it: Tabernacle or world? The Midrash resolves this by noting the difference between present and future reality, saying, "Just as the *Shekhinah* is found in the Temple in Jerusalem, so the *Shekhinah* will fill the world from one end to the other."[3] The blessing resolves this by extending God's presence over space. Through blessings, the presence of God once concentrated in the Tabernacle is made palpable throughout the world. "Adonai *our* God," becomes *melekh ha'olam,* "sovereign of the world."[4] Both images inform the second section of the *Alenu.*

The *Alenu*'s first hope, "to see" God manifest throughout the world, also matches the section of the Rosh Hashanah *Amidah* that spells out God's universal reign through three parallel Hebrew rhyming strophes:

> Reign over the whole wide world with your presence [*kavod*],
> and be exalted over the whole earth with your glory [*yakar*],
> and appear in the majestic splendor of your might [*oz*]
> to the inhabitants of your world

If we divide the sentences into parallel linguistic units, we get an order of abc, abc, acb. The last, as is common in liturgical formulations, reverses the order of the last two sentences to indicate closure:

> (a1) Reign (b1) over the whole wide world (c1) with your presence [*kavod*],
> (a2) be exalted (b2) over the whole earth (c2) with your glory [*yakar*],
> (a3) appear (c3) in the majestic splendor of your might [*oz*] (b3) to all the inhabitants of your world.

The parallel structure gives us the matching triads of

(a) "reign ... be exalted ... and appear"
(b) "over the whole wide world ... over the whole earth ... and to all the inhabitants of your world"
(c) "with your presence ... your glory ... [and] the majestic splendor of your might."

The overlapping imagery enhances our expectation of what we will someday behold.

The major difference between the two sections is the individual versus the collective orientation. The Rosh Hashanah *Amidah* makes its point through three individual-oriented expressions:

> Then all made will know that You made it,
> and all created will understand that You created it,
> and all that breathes will declare:
> "Adonai, the God of Israel, is king and his sovereignty rules all."

The Alenu makes its point through three collective-oriented expressions:

> all members of humanity,
> all the wicked of the earth,
> all inhabitants of the world.

Both hold that God rules the world by virtue of all accepting God's reign. Indeed, the other section begins and ends with a form of the word "reign" (*melekh*) followed by a phrase for God's universal rule. Both are predicated on the world coming to grasp with the reality of the one God. The Rosh Hashanah *Amidah* says, "all will know and understand"; the second section of the *Alenu* says, "all the inhabitants of the world will recognize and know."

The two corresponding master images are that of the world as God's realm and that of the world as God's Temple. The former is reflected in the just-cited Rosh Hashanah *Amidah*: "appear in the majestic splendor [*hadar g'on*] of your *oz*"; the latter in the *Alenu*: "to see the radiance [*tiferet*] of your *oz*." Just as the second plays on the biblical allusion to the Temple through the association of *tiferet* with *oz*, so the first plays on the biblical allusion to the Temple (see Ezekiel 7:24 and 24:21) through the association of *gaon* with *oz*. Alluding to the Temple while dealing with the world reinforces the convergence between Temple and world.

The order of the *Alenu* corresponds to the Aramaic translation of Isaiah 6:3, cited in *Uva L'tziyon*, which renders "Holy, holy, holy, Adonai of hosts, his presence fills all the earth" as follows:

> "Holy" in the highest of heavens, the home of his
> *Shekhinah*;
> "Holy" on earth exercising his power;
> "Holy" for ever and ever throughout all time;
> "Adonai of hosts," the whole earth is full of the radiance
> of his glory.

The first "holy," like section one of the *Alenu*, locates God's *Shekhinah* in heaven. The second "holy," like section two, places God's power (*g'vurah*) or might (*oz*) on earth. The third "holy" underscores God's eternity, as section two underscores God's eternal rule. The final phrase, "Adonai of hosts," is understood as "the whole earth is full of the radiance of his glory," which not only epitomizes section two, but also the words "radiance of his glory" (*ziv y'karei*) are the Aramaic equivalents of *tiferet* of the first line and *kavod*, which is the final word before the citing of the concluding legitimating verses.

Once God's might is visibly manifest, the second infinitive of hope can take effect, namely, that the might of God will be used "to remove the idols from the earth so that the false gods will be utterly eliminated." This hope reworks the language of the prophetic ideal (in Isaiah 2:17–20,

Ezekiel 30:13, and Zechariah 13:2) of eliminating idolatry and establishing the universal acceptance of God.

The third infinitive is "to establish," *l'takein*; but it should be spelled with a *kaf*, not a *kuf*, as in Saadiah Gaon's siddur (p. 221, l. 15) and in Genizah texts, implying "establishing," rather than "repairing or healing." It is associated with the Temple, as it says, "Your hands *established* the Temple" (Exodus 15:17). The result is not the world's "reparation or healing" but its "templization." In Psalm 96:10, the term for "world" associated with "establish" is *teivel*. The context deals with God's kingship. Here the word is *olam* either because *teivel* is used in the next strophe in a section where synonymy is common and repetition rare or because it is associated with the "kingship of the Almighty" and thus points back to the aforecited Rosh Hashanah *Amidah*'s expression "Reign [*m'lokh*] over the whole wide world [*olam*] with your presence [*kavod*]" and to the blessing formulation of God as "king [*melekh*] of the world [*olam*]."[5] The link with God's kingship accounts for the alternative version of *l'takein* with a *kuf*, following its use in Daniel 4:33, to indicate the reestablishment of kingship. The meaning of *l'takein* as "to repair" or "to heal" here is likely a later development based on the text of the early Ashkenazic liturgy.[6] The result of establishing the world under divine sovereignty is "all flesh calling upon your name." This incorporates Zephaniah's prophecy that the speech of the nations will be so transformed that "all of them will call upon the name of Adonai and serve Him with one accord" (3:9).

The fourth infinitive is "to turn"—"to turn all the wicked of the earth to You." It is unclear whether this is an independent request or the consequence of the third (that "all flesh will call upon your name"). In any case, unlike, for example, the ninth column of the *Eschatological Hymn* (4Q88) of the Dead Sea Scrolls that proposes the elimination of the wicked from the earth, the *Alenu* seeks only their transformation. It thereby conforms to another part of the Rosh Hashanah liturgy that prays that "evil [not evildoers] will be silenced and all wickedness [not the wicked] will dissipate like smoke."

Were all four hopes to reach fruition, then, the *Alenu* continues (following Isaiah 45:23), "all inhabitants of the world would fully realize that to You every knee must bend and every tongue vow loyalty," as we did in the first section. This biblical theme is then translated into classical Rabbinic theological idiom: "And all shall accept the authority of your kingship so that You shall reign over them now and for all time." Unlike biblical covenantal theology, which envisions the stranger joining up with Israel, as in Exodus 12:48, Deuteronomy 29:10, and Isaiah 56:6–8, Rabbinic coronation theology envisions the universal acceptance of God's authority. The goal is not the incorporating of humanity into Israel, but the extending of divine sovereignty to all humanity.

The use of the Rabbinic terminology for divine kingship smooths the transition into the royal theme of the next line, "For kingship is yours and You shall reign in glory [*kavod*] forever," followed by the two verses on God's rule. The first affirms God's rule throughout time: "God reigns for ever and ever" (Exodus 15:18); the second affirms God's rule throughout space: "Adonai will be ruler over all the earth. On that day Adonai will be one and his name will be one" (Zechariah 14:9).

We have come full circle. The *Sh'ma*'s implicit hope is that in the future all humanity will accept divine kingship, as Israel does already. As (with regard to the *Sh'ma*) the Rabbis cite Zechariah 14:9 to interpret "God is one" as "one for all," so the *Alenu* cites it to confirm its vision of universal divine sovereignty.

The universal thrust of part two is unique. True, its vision of the future is matched by the medieval liturgical poem *V'ye'etayu*, but that poem simply reworks the themes and expressions of the *Alenu*. Like the creation narrative of Genesis 1, there is in neither account anything distinctively Jewish about this vision. There is no epithet for the Jews save "we/us," no final judgment or conversion to Judaism, only the universal acceptance of God's sovereignty.

Its universalism matches the first *Uv'khen* section of the Rosh Hashanah *Amidah*, except that it does not go on to posit God's universal rule from Zion, a rule that itself is based on Isaiah (2:2–4), who envisions all the nations looking up to Zion in the end of days to receive instruction from God, and Jeremiah, who envisions a time when people shall call Jerusalem itself "'Throne of Adonai,' and all the nations shall assemble there in the name of Adonai" (Jeremiah 3:17). Even Second Isaiah (45:5, 66:18), who envisions all the nations beholding God's glory, links it to coming to Jerusalem. Unlike most Jewish visions of the future, the *Alenu* is not restorative, looking to revive an ideal past; rather, it is utopian, looking to establish an ideal future. Its universalism is epitomized in the multiple uses of *kol* ("every/all"). Included is *every* human being, *every* wicked person, *every* inhabitant, *every* knee, and *every* tongue, for *all* will accept the sovereignty of God over *all* the earth. It thus seeks the *monotheization* and ethicization ("to turn to You all the wicked of the earth") of all mankind—not its *Judaization*.[7] That the *Alenu* should have become the finale, if not the Jewish national anthem, for the conclusion of daily prayer at the height of medieval religious intolerance is enigmatically marvelous.

The differences between part two and part one underscore the universal vision of the *Alenu*. Part one addresses God in the third person; part two switches to the second person: "He" becomes "You." This reverses the direction of the blessing formula that begins with "You," "Blessed are You," and ends with "He," "king of the world." Part one contrasts us with the nations of the world; part two focuses on how humanity becomes like us. It is not us versus them, but us and them. In part one, we bend the knee and bow down, acknowledging the king of kings; in part two, humanity at large bends the knee, bows, and falls before "Adonai our God," just as we call upon "Adonai our God," in the *Sh'ma*, "Hear O Israel, *Adonai our God*, Adonai is one." In part one, *yakar* ("glory") modifies God's heavenly presence; in part two, it is what humanity will render to God. Part one ends with a verse on the special connection between God and us; part two ends with a verse on the universal rule of God and God's name becoming one.

Both sections begin with the letter *ayin* (*alenu, al ken*) and conclude with a *dalet* (*ein od, echad*), to form the Hebrew word for "witness," *eid*, possibly alluding to the verse "By the testimony of two witnesses the matter will be substantiated" (Deuteronomy 19:15). The last letter of the first word of the *Sh'ma*, is also an *ayin* (*sh'ma*), as the last letter of the last word is *dalet* (*echad*). They appear magnified in the Torah scroll. Together, the *Sh'ma* and the *Alenu* bear "witness" to the liturgical move from particularism to universalism.[8]

๑๛๑

"We" and "They" in Jewish Liturgy

Rabbi Jonathan Magonet, PhD

Every group needs to establish its boundaries: who is in and who is not. If the group is ethnic, territorial, or political, the definition may only require negotiating appropriate borders. But when the group is religious—especially in the case of a monotheistic faith like Judaism, Christianity, or Islam—a further issue arises, because if God is the creator of all humanity, then each of these three faiths, each of which in its own way considers itself chosen, needs to explain the roles both it and the "other" play in the divine plan.

Judaism's starting point for such considerations is the creation story, with the formation of a single human being. As the biblical narrative unfolds, we meet Noah, who becomes the father of all the various strands of humanity. With the choosing of Abraham, however, the narrative moves from the universal history of humanity to the particular odyssey of the Jewish People. But even here, a universal task is specified: Abraham and his descendants are to bring blessing to the families of the world (Genesis 12:3) and to establish righteousness and justice in the world (Genesis 18:18–19). This twofold task remains the vocation of the Jewish People, so that both our uniqueness and our relatedness to the rest of humanity require constant consideration.

Rabbi Jonathan Magonet, PhD, is emeritus professor of Bible at Leo Baeck College in London, where he was principal (president) from 1985 to 2005. He is coeditor of three volumes of *Forms of Prayer* (the prayer books of the British Movement for Reform Judaism) and editor of the eighth edition of *Daily, Sabbath and Occasional Prayers*. He contributed to *Who by Fire, Who by Water*—Un'taneh Tokef, *All These Vows*—Kol Nidre, *We Have Sinned: Sin and Confession in Judaism*—Ashamnu *and* Al Chet, and *May God Remember: Memory and Memorializing in Judaism*—Yizkor (all Jewish Lights).

One way in which we remain aware of this challenge is through the narrative structure underpinning the regular daily prayers. The formal part of the liturgy, that which traditionally requires a *minyan* and begins with the official call to prayer (*Bar'khu*, the invitation to "praise [God]"), is bracketed by expressions of a universal nature. The very first blessing that comes after *Bar'khu* establishes God immediately as creator of day and night, and the second paragraph of the concluding prayer, *Alenu* (*Al ken n'kaveh*, "We therefore hope ..."), provides the ultimate wish that all humanity will one day turn to God. Both the beginning and the end of the service are thus reminders of universalism.

But those two prayers on universalism are coupled with expressions of Jewish specificity. The *second* blessing after the *Bar'khu* expresses the special love God has for Israel, and the *first* paragraph of the *Alenu* expresses our particular task, as Israel, to bear witness to the presence of God in the world. What comes between these bookends—the rest of the service, that is—explores the nature of Israel's intimate relationship with God: we express our love and accept God's commandments (*Sh'ma* paragraphs); we present our petitions to God (*Amidah*). Thus the pattern and tension are established: universal to particular to universal, as follows:

Bar'khu (official call to prayer)
    First blessing (universal): God who creates light and darkness
    Second blessing (particular): God who chooses Israel in love
       [the bulk of the service, Israel's internal conversation with God]
    Alenu: paragraph 1 (particular): Israel's task to recognize God
  Alenu paragraph 2 (universal): Hope for all humanity

However, the nature of the "internal" conversation changes radically in the liturgy featured in this volume, the High Holy Day *Uv'khen* insertions for the third blessing of the *Amidah*, the "Sanctification of God's Name" (*K'dushat Hashem*), as it is called, because of its climactic proclamation of God as "holy holy holy" (*kadosh kadosh kadosh*). Instead of an inward-looking "private" conversation with God, we are forced to look outward beyond Israel alone. There too, we find the structure of universalism bracketing particularism.[1]

The first of the *Uv'khen* paragraphs is universal: it echoes the creation story with its repetition of the verbs *bara*, "to create," and *asah*, "to make/form/do." Indeed, readers familiar with the Bible will recognize in its wording themes that go back centuries. The opening word, *uv'khen*,[2] may itself be a conscious echo of the six-times repeated refrain of Genesis 1, *vay'hi khen*, "and it was so" or "established." In any event, the Isaiah of the Babylonian exile lists the same three verbs (and a fourth, *yatzar*) together in 45:18: "For thus says Adonai, the *creator* [*borei*] of heaven who alone is God, who *formed* [*yotzer*] the earth and *made* it [*v'oseh*], who alone *established* it [*khon'nah*]...."[3]

The second paragraph then moves from the universal to the particular. It characterizes Israel specifically as those who revere, fear, seek, and yearn for God. As a particularistic treatment of Israel, the prayer references petitions common to the daily *Amidah* as well, and interestingly enough, it is the national elements (joy for the land and Jerusalem, the restoration of the Davidic monarchy) that are emphasized rather than the cultic ones (the Temple and its sacrifices).

The third paragraph returns to the universal, emphasizing a future state of human harmony, in which the righteous, upright, and faithful will share, and the parallel end of evil and tyranny.

Like the overall daily pattern, this part of the liturgy too, then, holds in tension the universal and the particular, by sandwiching the particular task of Israel within a universal framework. That framework begins with recollection of creation (the past) and concludes with hope for justice (the future). Thus these insertions dramatize two key understandings of Rosh Hashanah itself: the "birthday of the world" (creation) and *yom hadin*, "the day of judgment." Creation is incomplete without restoring the unity of humanity that marked the hope of Genesis at the very beginning of time. The basis of such restoration is the establishment of justice on an individual and collective basis. In this task, as the descendants of Abraham, charged by God to establish righteousness and justice, Israel has a key role to play.

The same universal/particular relationship is reinforced in the very next blessing of the *Amidah*, the fourth one, which we label "Sanctification of the Day" (*K'dushat Hayom*). Here, however, the pattern is inverted. This time, we begin with the special choice of Israel from among all the nations ("You chose us," *atah v'chartanu*). There then follows the hope that all people and creatures will acknowledge God's kingship ("Rule over all the universe," *m'lokh al kol ha'olam*). Finally, we return to the hope that Israel, specifically, will be sanctified by the commandments and our

hearts purified to serve God in truth ("Sanctify us by your commandments," *kadshenu v'mitzvotekha*). The universal is here located in the *center*—between the two particularistic passages.

In these crucial texts of the High Holy Day *Amidah*, both the particular and universal are given equal weight.[4] That balance, however,
came to be questioned with the Enlightenment and Jewish Emancipation
from medieval conditions. Given the need to stake out our rightful place
as equals among the nations—and influenced, in that regard, by the
universalistic sentiments of the majority Christian culture—we came to
regard Jewish particularism as a narrow product of a ghettoized mentality. As Abraham Geiger expressed it:

> The separation between Israel and the other peoples which
> existed at one time has no right to be expressed in prayer.
> Rather ought there to be an expression of the joy that such
> barriers are increasingly falling.[5]

Instead of balancing the particular and universal, liberal (or progressive)
liturgies began omitting elements of the former and adding newly composed prayers or phrases like "and all mankind" where "Israel" alone was
mentioned, to emphasize the latter. The most obvious target was the first
paragraph of the *Alenu*. Even medieval tradition had begun the task of
moderating the specificity here; in response to fear of anti-Jewish feeling
by their neighbors, Jews had removed the critique "for they [non-Jews]
bow down to vanity and emptiness"—a line that even Orthodox liturgies
had largely long abandoned (although some Orthodox prayer books have
since restored it). Nineteenth-century reformers now reconsidered also
the assertion "who has not made us like the nations of the lands." They
omitted these sentiments entirely or replaced the phrases with more neu-
tral language.

Of late, however, beginning with the liturgies of the post–World
War II era, the particularism of the *Alenu* has made a comeback. The
reasons for this reconsideration include the impact of the Shoah and the
creation of the State of Israel, but also global trends toward more self-
centered expressions of pride among peoples reacting against the increasing uniformity and loss of individual identity in the "global village."

The second paragraph of the *Alenu*—already fully universal—can
actually be seen as raising questions about the nature of our universalistic

hopes. The key aspiration is that "all the inhabitants of the world may perceive and know that to You every knee must bow, every tongue must swear.... Let them all accept the yoke of your kingdom, and reign over them speedily and forever." This sounds universal enough, but is it?

The emphasis on all the inhabitants of the world bowing before Israel's God could be termed "universalistic monotheism."[6] It parallels the assumptions that we find within other monotheistic religions that are tolerant of other spiritual traditions, if at all, provided that they ultimately subsume themselves to the role cast for them and enforced by the dominant faith. Since Jews have never had the power to enforce such a hope on others, this remains a relatively harmless doctrine; nevertheless, for all its universal intention, the passage expresses a kind of spiritual colonialism.

An attempt to reflect a truer form of universalism is found in a change introduced in Kol HaNeshama congregation in Jerusalem and adopted by the UK Reform Movement's *Forms of Prayer*: "Then all who inhabit this world shall meet in understanding, and shall know that we are all partners in the repairing of our world. For yours alone is the true kingdom."

Just as in our liturgy, so in our daily existence as Jews, we are held in this tension between the particularity of our identity and the universalism of our common humanity. How we negotiate a path between the two, individually and collectively, is the challenge dramatized within our traditional liturgy, given special emphasis during the High Holy Days, but played out in every aspect of our daily lives.

෴

All Shall Come to Serve (My Version of) Thee

Dr. Wendy Zierler

Israel Zangwill (1864–1926), celebrated British novelist and playwright, was hardly an Orthodox Jew. Though raised in a traditional home and educated at the Jews' Free School, where he later taught, he abandoned religious observance in adulthood and married a gentile. He was a staunch Zionist and territorialist—a Zionist because he met Herzl and was awed by Herzl's vision for a Jewish state;[1] a territorialist because he believed in seeking a homeland for beleaguered Eastern European Jews in whatever land might be available for Jewish settlement, including Uganda.[2] But he also advocated for the interaction of Jews with the larger community and attempted to reveal the commonalities between Christianity and Judaism.[3]

Neither was he a Reform Jew. In a speech delivered during his first visit to America in 1898, Zangwill vocally criticized American Reform Judaism for what he perceived as its excessive decorum, its minimal congregational participation, and its abandonment of Hebrew liturgy: "With a sacred language far easier to acquire than Greek," he asked, "why write

Dr. Wendy Zierler is professor of modern Jewish literature and feminist studies at Hebrew Union College–Jewish Institute of Religion, New York. She is editor with Rabbi Carole Balin and translator of *To Tread on New Ground: The Selected Writings of Hava Shapiro* (forthcoming) and *Behikansi atah* (Shapiro's collected writings, in the original/Hebrew). She is also author of *And Rachel Stole the Idols* and the feminist Haggadah commentary featured in *My People's Passover Haggadah: Traditional Texts, Modern Commentaries* (Jewish Lights), a finalist for the National Jewish Book Award. She contributed to *Who by Fire, Who by Water*—Un'taneh Tokef, *All These Vows*—Kol Nidre, *We Have Sinned: Sin and Confession in Judaism*—Ashamnu *and* Al Chet, and *May God Remember: Memory and Memorializing in Judaism*—Yizkor (all Jewish Lights).

new prayers in nineteenth century journalese?"[4] It was perhaps this disapproval of Reform English-language liturgy together with his love of medieval Hebrew poetry and his close friendship with one of the editors, Arthur Davis, that led Zangwill, hardly devout himself, to contribute several translations of High Holy Day *piyyutim* (liturgical poems) to a new edition of the traditional British *machzor* (1908). Central to four of these *piyyutim, V'ye'etayu kol l'ovdekha* ("All the World Shall Come to Serve Thee"),[5] is the affirmation of God as king, a major motif in the Rosh Hashanah liturgy. But whereas the other three poems focus primarily on a heavenly divine monarch, crowned "Lord of Infinity," "All the World Shall Come to Serve Thee" deals less with heaven than with earth, less with God than with human transformation, presenting a dynamic vision in which all people, the world over, come to accept God's reign (see p. 151–152).

Zangwill's translation omits the acrostic form of the Hebrew and installs a more regular rhyme scheme than the original text. That aside, the translation remains remarkably faithful to the original Hebrew. Especially because it appears in the Rosh Hashanah *Musaf* service right before *Atah v'chartanu* ("You have chosen us from among all peoples"), it stands out as remarkably ecumenical, transcending Jewish particularity in language and subject matter—so much so that it was adopted also in Reform prayer books across the Atlantic, as well as several Christian hymn websites.[6] It imagines a coming together of all nations, from every end and island of the earth, to recognize and worship God as king—a kind of "theological melting pot."

I am using the term "theological melting point" intentionally in order to point to another work by Zangwill, his best known one, in fact: *The Melting Pot* (1908), a play that he wrote while translating the *piyyutim* for the British *machzor*.[7] Indeed, several connections can be drawn between Zangwill's translation of *V'ye'etayu* and his famous drama about Russian Jewish immigrant composer David Quixano, who, having escaped the carnage of the Kishinev pogrom, ecstatically embraces the promise of America, "the great Melting-Pot where all the races of Europe are melting and re-forming."[8]

The original Hebrew poem is an alphabetic acrostic, a structure that emphasizes inclusivity, as if all the nations, from A to Z, will come to serve the one God. Reinforcing this unity of vision is the repetition of the *vav hachibur* (the conjunctive *vav* meaning "and") at the beginning of every line of the Hebrew poem. The word "and" appears very frequently in the English version as well (although not on every line), underscoring there too the notion of diverse people joining together under a common belief system.

In Zangwill's play, this all-encompassing union of peoples is similarly represented on a plot level, through the romantic union of the Jew David Quixano with the Christian Vera Revendal. All of David's immediate family members were murdered in Kishinev, and the Russian officer who presided over the Kishinev slaughter was none other than Baron Revendal, Vera's own father. Nevertheless, David and Vera's love and shared commitment to the American melting-pot ideal allow them to transcend their backgrounds and personal histories. The play also marshals imagery that is strikingly similar to the poem. As Zangwill scholar Meri Jane Rochelson notes, "The hills, peaks, and islands of the poem evoke lines such as this one, from the protagonist's last speech in the play":[9]

> Yes, East and West, and North and South, *the palm and the pine, the pole and the equator*, the crescent and the cross—how the great Alchemist melts and fuses them with his purging flame! Here shall they all unite to build the Republic of Man and the *Kingdom of God*.
>
> Ah, Vera, what is the glory of Rome and Jerusalem where all nations and races come to worship and look back, compared with the glory of America, where all races and nations come to labour and look forward![10]

If the *piyyut* uses the expression *afsei aretz* ("the ends of the earth"), then Zangwill's play speaks of "the palm and the pine, the pole and the equator" as representing geographical or topographical extremes. If the poem imagines the universal proclamation of God's majesty as a miraculous eruption of the mountains into song, then the play speaks of the cultural fusion of America as a kind of wondrous divine alchemy. Both the poem and the play unequivocally celebrate the coming of the "kingdom of God." *V'ye'etayu* begins with an image of all the nations and races coming *l'ovdekha*, which Zangwill translates as "to serve Thee." In fact, the Hebrew verb *oved* means both "to worship" and "to labor or serve," a double meaning that is reflected in the final sentence of *The Melting Pot*, which contrasts Rome/Jerusalem as places of worship with America as a site of labor.

To be sure, Zangwill's play has had its detractors, both in his own day and in ours. As Edna Nahshon notes, in the aftermath of the performance of the play, a group of Jewish New Yorkers that included philanthropist Daniel Guggenheim, *Jewish Daily News* editor Leon Kamalky, and such rabbis as Judah L. Magnes, Stephen S. Wise, and Dr. Pereira Mendes characterized the intermarriage portrayed in the play "as a recipe for the extinction of Judaism."[11] The multiculturalism of our own day has prompted a similar expression of disdain for the assimilationist ideology promoted in *The Melting Pot*.

Might one level a similar critique of the universalist melting-pot aspirations presented in "All the World"? If all were to come and serve God, what would happen to the distinctiveness of the Jewish People and Jewish religion? Would it all melt down and become extinct? What about the seemingly coercive uniformity of this vision? Is there no value to human beings having different beliefs and traditions?

One way to dispel this concern is to recall that Zangwill was a contradictory figure, a paradoxically particularistic universalist, who did indeed aspire to human unity but who also remained so doggedly preoccupied with Jews that he insisted elsewhere that "the mission of Judaism is either on specifically Jewish lines or on none at all."[12] As David Biale notes, "The most basic tension in *The Melting Pot* lies in the contrast between the play's assimilationist message and its specifically Jewish content."[13] The intermarriage plot notwithstanding, "the end product" of the play

> is to turn all true Americans into Jews. The feisty Irish house-servant, Kathleen, who initially denounces the Quixanos' religious practices in virtually anti-Semitic terms, ends up speaking Yiddish and celebrating Purim. Jews, it transpires, are not just any immigrant group but the quintessential Americans. As David announces to the anti-Semite Davenport: "Yes—Jew-immigrant! But a Jew who knows that your Pilgrim Fathers came straight out of his Old Testament and that our Jew-immigrants are a greater factor in the glory of this great commonwealth than some of you sons of the soil."[14]

Might the same blend of particularism and universalism be teased out of "All the World Shall Come to Serve Thee"? On the one hand, the poem seems to express an unabashedly universalist, even Christian, message.

On the other hand, it loses little in translation—it is authentically part of traditional Jewish liturgy, portraying the specifically Jewish vision of a kingdom of God as alluded to by Isaiah and the psalms. It presupposes the shaming of idolaters "by their graven gods" and is followed in the *Musaf* liturgy by specific references to Mount Zion and Jerusalem. The poem insists that there is a truth out there that "those astray in night" need to learn—a truth, presumably, that Jews already have.

Zangwill was not the only prominent modern Jewish writer to employ the language and thematics of *V'ye'etayu* as a means of expressing universalistic particularity. The same *piyyut* figures centrally in a beautiful and enigmatic 1963 story by Hebrew writer and Nobel Laureate S. Y. Agnon titled *Han'shikah Harishonah* ("The First Kiss"). Like Zangwill's *Melting Pot*, it too invokes romantic love as an occasion for the bridging of human divisions.[15] The story takes place on a Friday afternoon, *erev Shabbat bein hash'mashot*, that magical twilight moment separating Friday afternoon (and not yet Shabbat) from the second that Shabbat actually arrives. According to Rabbinic tradition (*Pirkei Avot* 5:5), on the very first such Friday moment, certain miraculous phenomena were created as God's last-minute addenda to creation. With that legend in mind, Agnon pictures a teenage boy left to watch over the family store in his father's absence—symbolic of a disappearance of religious faith in God "the father" as a result of modernity. Vulnerable, therefore, to new, alien, even universalist ideas, the boy is visited by three Christian monks, who engage him in theological conversation and divert his attention from the approaching Jewish Sabbath. This encounter is dreamlike, even nightmarish, yet true to the spirit of *bein hash'mashot*, the moment is rife with miraculous elements that stand out.

First is the fact that throughout the story, time for the boy seems to stand still. Repeatedly, he thinks the Sabbath has begun, and yet when he looks up to the sky, he finds that "the sun was in the same place it had been when the monks first accosted me."[16] The three Christian fathers finally leave the boy alone, and in their wake come two younger novices, one of whom disappears before the boy's very eyes. The narrator's encounter with the remaining novice constitutes the central miraculous or transformative element of the story. Despite the Deuteronomic prohibition against making a treaty or showing any grace toward the other nations,[17] the narrator finds that he is attracted by the young novice's graceful and sweet appearance: "He had the kind of beauty you used to be able to see in every Jewish town, the beauty of young Jewish boys who never tasted the taste of sin."[18] On one level, the narrator seems to be attracted to the otherness or forbidden quality of the novice, not just as Christian but also as a male object of desire. At the same time, the narrator senses in the novice a deeper, authentically Jewish bond. According to David Biale, the end product of *The Melting Pot* is to turn everyone into Jews. A similar result occurs in Agnon's story, where the narrator discovers that the supposed Christian is a Jew all along. "Listen, my brother," asks the narrator, "aren't you a Jew?" He is indeed: a Jew from Likovitz. The novice's admission of where he comes from prompts the narrator to recall for the novice the time he spent Rosh Hashanah in Likovitz:

> "If you're from Likovitz," I said, "then you must certainly know the Zaddik of Likovitz. I was in his House of Prayer once on New Year's Day, and the Zaddik himself led the prayers. Let me tell you, when he came to the verse 'And all shall come to serve thee,' I imagined that I heard the approaching footsteps of all the nations of the world who fail to recognize the people of Israel or their Father in Heaven. And when he sang 'the wayward shall learn understanding' I imagined they were all bowing down as one to worship the Lord of Hosts, the God of Israel ... My brother, are you in pain?[19]

The story begins with the narrator alone in his father's store, vulnerable to outside influences, and it culminates with the narrator's meeting of this young novice who helps him recall an experience of Jewish spiritual oneness and of almost messianic fulfillment, which in turn, compels the novice to burst into tears and admit her true identity, not as a Christian but as a Jew, and not as a young man but as a woman. And she is not just any Jewish girl but the daughter of the same holy tzaddik referred to in the narrator's story—an uncanny coincidence reminiscent of the unmasking of Vera Revendal's identity as the daughter of David Quixano's Russian persecutor in *The Melting Pot*. Zangwill's David and Vera manage to love and unite *despite* their divergent backgrounds. Agnon's narrator and novice come together specifically *because of* his fond memories of her father's beautiful recitation of "All Shall Come to Serve Thee."

Lurking behind all of this are a number of questions. What, after all, is the daughter of this remarkable holy tzaddik doing here dressed as a Christian (male) novice, following and looking for new (Christian) fathers? As a child, the narrator had perceived the rebbe's prayer leading as so efficacious that the messianic vision of "All the World" seemed almost to come true for him right there before his eyes in the old synagogue. The later appearance of the rebbe's daughter as a male novice suggests something other than the inevitability of everyone coming to serve the Jewish God. Indeed, she has done the very opposite, having fled the fold, perhaps because of the gender-based restrictions, or an undesired match, or because she has adopted completely other beliefs than those of her father. Or perhaps she is specifically seeking access to the broader world or to a more universalistic theology like that represented in "All the World"?

The narrator first identifies the novice as having a beauty that he associates with those who have never tasted sin, and yet this same boy is actually a girl who committed the "double transgression" of hiding her gender as well as her Judaism. It is this double sin that seems entirely to captivate the narrator: when the novice reveals, amid flooding tears, that she is not only a Jew, but the rebbe's "daughter of old age" (evocative of the beloved status of the biblical Joseph), the narrator is drawn to kiss the novice, his first innocent kiss, "the kiss of the mouth," which the narrator associates with a litany of liturgical boons: "goodness and blessing, life, grace and kindness, whereby a man and a woman live together until calm old age."[20]

The story ends there without telling us what becomes of these characters. Do they marry? Does the rebbe's daughter return home? Or to the monastery? The ending of the story intimates that they share a lifelong love, perhaps predicated on their shared willingness to step outside the strict bounds of their religious backgrounds. But perhaps this uncanny tale is really nothing but a dream, a story drawn from that liminal state of consciousness between day and night, an otherworld fantasy?

One thing we do know is that throughout his life and literary corpus, Agnon expressed a yearning to return to that state of religious oneness he experienced as a child in his father and mother's home and in the synagogues of his youth. In the remarkable Hebrew preface to the third edition of *Yamim Nora'im* (*Days of Awe*), Agnon's monumental treasury of High Holy Day legends and commentaries, Agnon recalls the experience of being brought to synagogue as a four-year-old child to sit next to his father and grandfather:

An old man stood bent before the lectern, his tallit sweeping down over his heart and beautiful sweet sounds were emanating from his tallit. And I stood in the synagogue quaking and dumbstruck over the beautiful sounds and the crowns of silver and the wondrous light and the scent of honey that was wafting from the wax candles. And it seemed to me that the earth that I was walking upon and the streets that I had passed through and the entire world were nothing but a corridor to this house.... Even though I had never seen anything like it until that moment, it didn't dawn on me that something like this could ever end.[21]

Is this old man before the lectern a version of the archetypally efficacious leader of prayer whom an older Agnon reimagines as the Tzaddik of Likovitz in "First Kiss"? Are the beautiful sounds that he hears, amid wondrous light and gleaming silver crowns, the sounds of *V'ye'etayu*, representing a vision of universalistic coming together of all peoples to worship God? Like Zangwill, Agnon was a fully modern writer, but far more than Zangwill, Agnon was a Hebraic particularist, who experienced the grace of God through Jewish sources and the Hebrew language. The ecstatic ending of his story "First Kiss" entails not the conversion of non-Jews, but the possible return of Jews who have strayed in the night back to the Jewish fold of love and awe, a reunion of each individual Jew with his or her particular Jewish past.

⌒Ↄↄↄↄ⌒

PART III
"All the World" Remembered
Its Impact on Generations

Two Kinds of Universalism

Rabbi Marc Saperstein, PhD

Growing up in the home of a Reform rabbi, I learned that our liturgy provided a delicate and precarious counterpoint of universalism and particularism, with universalism clearly prevailing. My High Holy Day liturgy then, the newly revised version of the *Union Prayer Book* (*UPB*), was filled with that universalism. "Let this truth shine forth triumphantly," it said, "that all men may acknowledge Thee as their King and render homage to Thy holy name, for Thine is the kingdom and Thy dominion endureth forever."[1] Similarly: "Sustain us with hope that we may confidently await the day when knowledge of Thee shall reach the uttermost parts of the world. O hasten the blessed time when all dwellers on earth shall hearken unto the sound of the Shofar, and shall worship as one brotherhood at Thy holy mountain."[2] I felt proud of the open-minded universalism of these sentiments.

In college, I first encountered the more traditional liturgy of American Conservative Judaism at Hillel services. I realized that my childhood (*UPB*) text of *Alenu* had omitted the first paragraph's particularistic claim that God had "not made us like the other nations of the earth ... for we worship the king of kings of kings, the Holy One praised be He." Encountering that phrase in the traditional siddur, I came to

---

Rabbi Marc Saperstein, PhD, formerly principal of Leo Baeck College, currently serves as professor of Jewish history and homiletics at Leo Baeck College and as professor of Jewish studies at King's College London. Previously he taught for twenty-nine years at three leading American universities. He has published four books on the sermon as source for Jewish history and culture, and contributed to *Who by Fire, Who by Water—Un'taneh Tokef, All These Vows—Kol Nidre,* and *We Have Sinned: Sin and Confession in Judaism—Ashamnu and Al Chet* (all Jewish Lights).

reappraise the particularism/universalism balance in Judaism. The particularistic side was stronger than I thought.

Some time later I learned that the first paragraph originally contained a line so offensive that under pressure from Christian authorities, Ashkenazi Jews had removed it from their liturgical texts already in medieval times: "For they [i.e., everyone other than Jews] bow down to vanity and emptiness, and worship a god that cannot save, while we worship the king of kings of kings."[3] The *UPB*'s further erasure of the first part's particularism now seemed to me to be just the next step in a longer process of universalizing the whole. Its first paragraph now had no particularism at all; instead, it expressed the universalistic idea of God as the creator of the universe ("Who spread out the heavens and established earth").

I have recently begun to question the *kind* of universalism that the second part of *Alenu* provided: the sentiment that all human beings must ultimately recognize the truth that we Jews alone accept at present. My recognition of the problem was stimulated when reading, in March of 2001, that the Taliban dynamited two seventeen-hundred-year-old statues of the Buddha in the Bamiyan region of Afghanistan, in the belief that these statues were an idolatrous violation of core Islamic values. Not long afterward, while worshiping in an Orthodox service, a troubling thought occurred to me: Were the actions of the Taliban fulfilling the ideal expressed in the *Alenu*, "to remove the abominations from the earth, so that the idols will be utterly cut down"? How would Hindus respond to this formulation—or to the phrase from the liturgy represented in this book, "All the world shall come to serve Thee ... their idols overthrown, and their graven gods shall shame them as they turn to Thee alone"? Was the expression of our universalistic hope that all human beings will recognize the one true God whom we now serve fundamentally different from the universalistic Christian prayer that all human beings—and especially the Jews—will recover from their blindness and recognize the one true savior in God the Son? That is, of course, a prayer that many Jews find highly offensive and deeply resent.

I now sense that this "All the world shall come to serve Thee" motif, uplifting as the words and the music once were to me, represents a universalism that is fraught with problems. I call it "They'll all see that we were right" universalism, because it affirms that the whole world will finally recognize the truth—but that the only real truth for them to see is our own.

There is, however, a different kind of liturgical universalism, which we might call "We're all in it together" universalism, in the sense that it addresses a human condition that all human beings already share simply by virtue of being human. It leaves room, therefore, for others to voice their own versions of truths that may be couched in language that we Jews do not share. An example is the rather surprisingly universalistic dimension of *Un'taneh Tokef* that I discussed in a previous volume of this series.[4] Despite its association with the liturgy of the Jewish Days of Awe, it is not at all limited to Jews. Speaking of the metaphorical Book of Memories, the text states:

> Everyone's signature is in it.... And all who enter the world will pass before You.... You record and recount and review all living beings.... You will decide the end of all creatures.... Their origin is from dust and their end is to dust.... They are like shattered pottery, like withered grass and like a faded blossom, like a passing shadow and like a vanishing cloud.

This universalism is not about everyone else finally realizing that we Jews have been right all along; rather, it affirms the existential condition that all human beings already share.

I grew up with the Newly Revised Versions of the *Union Prayer Book* and the *Union Hymnal*. English passages from the *UPB* made such an impression on me that I can still recite full paragraphs from memory. I refer to three examples.

The first begins with paradoxes probably inspired by one of Judah Halevi's most famous liturgical poems, *Yah anah emtza'akha*, "O Lord, where can I find Thee," but moves on to articulate a message that integrates theology with social justice:

> O Lord, how can we know Thee? Where can we find Thee? Thou art as close to us as breathing, yet art farther than the farthermost stars.... When justice burns like a flaming fire within us, when love evokes willing sacrifice from us ... do we not bow down before the vision of Thy goodness? Thou livest within our hearts as Thou dost pervade the world, and we, through righteousness, behold Thy presence.[5]

The second is one that I remember being cited in the 1970s as evidence of the outdated nature of the *UPB* and the need for a new Reform siddur. "Where are there miners anymore?" was the common rhetorical question. Yet the relevance of this passage, not just for Jews but for all human beings, seems to me just as cogent today as when it first entered the Reform liturgy:

> How much we owe to the labors of our brothers. Day by day they dig far away from the sun that we may be warm, enlist in outposts of peril that we might be secure, and brave the terrors of the unknown for truths that shed light upon our way. Numberless gifts have been placed in our cradle as our birthright.... Help us to be among those who are willing to sacrifice that others may not hunger, who dare to be bearers of light in the dark loneliness of stricken lives.[6]

The third is a magnificent formulation of liberal Jewish theology, striking a balance between respect for the great teachings of the past and regard for the insights of later generations, including our own:

> Open our eyes that we may see and welcome all truth, whether shining from the annals of ancient revelations, or reaching us through the seers of our own times, for Thou hidest not Thy light from any generation of Thy children that yearn for Thee and seek Thy guidance.... Bless, O God, all endeavors, wherever made, to lift up the fallen, to redeem the sinful, to bring back those who wander from the right path and restore them to a worthy life.[7]

These favorite passages of mine are all examples of the expansive "We're all in it together" universalism of *Un'taneh Tokef,* not the "They'll all see that we were right" universalism of "All the world shall come to serve Thee." They speak not just to Jews but also to anyone who takes the religious dimension of life seriously, addressing feelings and aspirations pertaining to the essence of being human.

And there is another advantage in these passages. So many of the formulations of the traditional liturgy raise problems for progressive Jews who think about the meaning of the words they are reading. Sometimes these liturgical statements praise God for playing a role in history that does not comport with the actual experience of Jews and gentiles alike ("God ever humbles the proud, raises the lowly, frees the imprisoned, redeems the afflicted, helps the oppressed, answering our people when we cry out").[8] Or they make requests of God that seem impossible or meaningless ("From your place, our Sovereign, shine forth and rule over us, for we wait for You").[9] Or—as in *V'khol Ma'aminim* ("Everyone Believes")—they proclaim beliefs attributed to everyone that certainly are not true for all human beings or even all Jews. The passages I have cited from the *UPB*, by contrast, articulate a common ground of faith without specifying claims that are bound to raise as many objections as affirmations.

The *UPB* was far from being what later generations would call "traditional," and ever since the 1970s, when the *UPB* was replaced by *Gates of Prayer*, Reform Judaism in North America has been anxiously reclaiming tradition. The same is true of progressive liturgies elsewhere. While the return to a more traditional liturgy in progressive circles has significant advantages, I feel it unfortunate that the special universalistic dimension of the classical Reform heritage, emphasizing that "we're all in it together," has largely been lost.

The Missing Hymn

"ALL THE WORLD SHALL COME TO SERVE THEE"

Rabbi Andrew Goldstein, PhD

How I miss it ... Israel Zangwill's Victorian rhyme, sung with gusto in the Liberal synagogue of my youth and early rabbinate. It was the highlight of Rosh Hashanah as well as a frequent concluding hymn on Sabbath mornings—sung in a key that all could manage, unlike the soprano-dominated versions of some of the traditional Hebrew numbers (marked for "Choir" only). And it was in English, so all knew exactly what they were singing.

But then opposing voices began to be heard: "It sounds like I am in a church"; "It reminds me of hymns we sang in school assemblies"; "It's not Jewish." The fact that it was a loose translation by a Jewish poet of an ancient Hebrew *piyyut* first found in *Machzor Vitry* (eleventh century) was somehow insufficient to make it "Jewish." That the English first appeared in the Orthodox *machzor Service of the Synagogue*, "published under the sanction of the late Dr. Herman Adler, Chief Rabbi of the British Empire" (no less), also made no difference.

Its death knell was further set in motion when it was adapted to say "You" instead of the archaic "Thee" and when its sexist language was removed—at the loss of anything approaching Zangwill's poetry. Add to

Rabbi Andrew Goldstein, PhD, is the president of Liberal Judaism, UK, the rabbinic advisor to the European Union for Progressive Judaism, and coeditor of *Machzor Ruach Chadashah*. He contributed to *Who by Fire, Who by Water*—Un'taneh Tokef, *All These Vows*—Kol Nidre, *We Have Sinned: Sin and Confession in Judaism*—Ashamnu *and* Al Chet, and *May God Remember: Memory and Memorializing in Judaism*—Yizkor (all Jewish Lights).

this the growing antipathy to singing anything in English and the rejection of liturgy that sounded triumphalist. Its end had arrived.

In my own congregation, at least, this all predated some parallel questions about *Alenu*. I'm not talking about the phrase forced out by Christian censors in the Middle Ages: *shehem mishtachavim l'hevel varik* ("for they worship emptiness and vanity"); nor even the phrase that stayed in then but was attacked in modern times by most progressive editors (although *Mishkan T'filah* includes it as an option), *shelo asanu k'goyei ha'avatzot* ("He did not make us like the nations of the lands"). I mean the entire second paragraph that juxtaposes idolatry by others with a time to come when all will acknowledge the one God as universal sovereign—the paragraph that ends with the familiar *Bayom hahu yihyeh Adonai echad ush'mo echad*, "On that day, Adonai will be one and his name will be one."

Britain is a multiethnic, multicultural country of several religions—but mostly none. If we pray, "On that day ... God's name will be one," do we offend Trinitarians and Zoroastrians? If we hope for "idolatry to vanish," will Hindus think we are devaluing them? When we yearn for "all to submit to your sovereign rule," will atheists think we are targeting them? In truth, *Mishkan T'filah* and other recent Reform and Liberal prayer books do include alternative versions of the *Alenu*—not for a world united under one God, but for a future world of equality, harmony, and universal tolerance expressed in secular thoughts such as "And then everywhere will be called Eden once again."

With one of these *Alenu* discussions ringing in my ears, I recently set about leading yet another series of High Holy Day services. By *N'ilah* I was thinking: if the anti-*Alenu* brigade got their way, would there be much left of the High Holy Day liturgy altogether? The prayers for those holidays are suffused with hope that "at the end of days" or "soon and in our time" God will be proclaimed sovereign of all the world. Most readily memorable is "All the world shall come to serve Thee."

"All the world" might be Victorian jingoism, beyond its sell date. Yet the traditional *Uv'khen* passages remain, and for me, they are the true heart and soul of the High Holy Day liturgy. I return each year to them with joy and pride—joy because they express in just a few well-chosen words my greatest hopes for the world, and pride when I recall the historical situation with which Jewish memory has associated them.

We do not know for sure when the three *Uv'khen* passages came into being, but a long-held scholarly opinion associated them with ideas that arose during the turbulent times of the early second century CE. It was just decades after the destruction of the Temple, and the Bar Kokhba revolt was just around the corner. Yet precisely at that time, we Jews prayed for the universal realm of God. At some point in time, that fervent wish was condensed into *Uv'khen*, calling on God to instill in *all* people an awe of God and obedience to God's moral law; not just Jews, but all humanity might become an *agudah achat*, "one group," in worshiping the one true sovereign God of the universe.

We might have expected prayers for the redemption of us Jews, but instead we get a prayer that all—not just Jews, but non-Jews, too—unite in redeeming the world. True, the second paragraph singles out Jews, by stipulating our land and city, but the third paragraph returns to the universalistic with a prayer that the "righteous" (Jew and gentile) be justified and that evil vanish like smoke.

As I read the *Uv'khen* passages from year to year, I find that they sum up for me the greatness of Judaism. To be sure (as the second paragraph insists), we can still have our own identity and heritage, our own ways of worship, our own land and holy city. But we exist not just for ourselves. We believe in one God who is the God of all humanity, the God of all creation, and the God who calls us to unite with all humanity to fight evil, persecution, and discrimination.

Still, I cannot forget that other masterpiece of universalistic liturgy, "All the World Shall Come to Serve Thee." It too focuses my attention on what matters truly. It comes from the era when Liberal Judaism was just being founded in Great Britain. Its pioneering spirits (Claude G. Montefiore, Lily Montagu, and Rabbi Israel Mattuck) enthusiastically adopted the prevailing American Reform Movement's acceptance of universalism: the doctrine that calls on Jews to work with all humanity in bringing about a better era. They too sought to proclaim this mission aloud and to herald Judaism as pure ethical monotheism and the way to the Messianic Age. "All the World" captured their hope as no other prayer could do.

Of course the savagery of the World Wars and the Shoah dulled such naive enthusiasm, but as we recite *Uv'khen* and similar thoughts evoked by the High Holy Day liturgy, might we not feel all the more certain that this universalism ought not perish? Does it not follow that we might even want to go out and persuade others of our beliefs? Not, of course, like militant missionaries of the past, nor the Taliban of the present, and not by belittling others, but by expressing more openly a genuine pride in our own religion and the belief we proclaim in the *Sh'ma*, that there is one God who is the God of all creation; as the prophet Malachi put it, "Have we not all one Divine Parent? Has not God created us? Why then do we deal treacherously with one another?" (Malachi 2:10).

And two final thoughts: Lest it be forgotten altogether, Zangwill penned a third verse that was omitted from the North American and British liturgies that included the rest of his poem. Maybe *dayyenu*— enough Victoriana already!

> They shall testify Thy greatness,
> And of Thy power speak,
> And extol Thee, shrined, uplifted
> Beyond man's highest peak.
> And with reverential homage,
> Of love and wonder born,
> With ruler's crown of beauty
> Thy head they shall adorn.

And finally, after extensive research, I discovered who wrote the music I loved so much. It was based on an English folk song and was used for at least three Christian hymns (e.g., "It came upon the midnight clear / that glorious song of old ..."). It was then adapted by Arthur Sullivan of the Gilbert and Sullivan pair who wrote such well-loved operettas as *Pirates of Penzance* and *The Mikado*. No wonder it is so rousing and easy on the ear, yet so uplifting also, when we hear it on a Jewish holy day. But its detractors were right: it does sound nowadays like a Christian hymn even if the words and their origin are Jewish. I will see it as a perfect combination of the universal and particular; Jewish and non-Jewish in perfect harmony.

And, although I regret the passing of the English singing of "All the World," I rejoice at its replacement with the original Hebrew *piyyut V'ye'etayu*, which we now sing to its own lyrical tune.

So all is not lost.

PART IV
The
Liturgy

Translation of the Liturgy and Commentary

Dr. Joel M. Hoffman

A. Introductory Poem:
V'khol Ma'aminim ("Everyone Believes")

[1]The holder of the scales of justice—everyone believes He is a faithful God.

הָאוֹחֵז בְּיַד מִדַּת מִשְׁפָּט.[1]
וְכֹל מַאֲמִינִים שֶׁהוּא אֵל אֱמוּנָה,

[1]Differences between Hebrew and English grammar make this poem difficult to translate. The biggest challenge is the Hebrew word *kol*, which encompasses both "everyone" and "everything," and, more generally, "all." This is why some translations prefer "all believe ..." for our "everyone believes ..." in the second half of each line. But we think that "all believe" is stilted in English in a way that doesn't do service to the original Hebrew poetry.

Furthermore, the Hebrew lines generally take the form of "The one [who] ... everyone believes He is...." The "He" in the second part is a common way of pairing two phrases in Hebrew. For example, the Hebrew rendition of the English "this is the man who is important" might literally be "this is the man who he is important." So the "he" in the second part in Hebrew would most naturally disappear in English. But we don't have that option in our poem here, because, for example,

135

"The holder of the scales of justice everyone believes is a faithful God" is not grammatical for most English speakers.

We could use "The holder of the scales of justice is believed to be a faithful God," which would better capture the way "He is" functions in Hebrew. But then we'd have trouble introducing "everyone," and we'd have to resort to "The holder of the scales of justice is believed by everyone to be a faithful God." That version is hardly poetic and, worse, serves to diminish the impact of "everyone," while the Hebrew stresses that word. So we are stuck with "He is ..." in the second half of the English lines, which deviates a little from the impact of the original Hebrew and suffers from the additional drawback of forcing us to use a masculine word in English for God, even though the Hebrew is less specific.

Finally, the poem is built around a double alphabetic acrostic that serves two purposes. It gives the poem structure, in the form of lines that begin (after the initial letter *heh*, which means "the one who") with successive letters of the alphabet: *alef, bet, gimel*, etc. And it connects the first part of each line with the second, because the letter that starts the first part of the line also starts the second. For example, in verse 1, "the holder" and "God" both begin with *alef*.

Our translation cannot capture this structural pattern, but where the Hebrew uses identical words in both halves of a line, we try to do so in English, too.

[1]*Holder of the scales of justice*: Based on Deuteronomy 32:41, part of the Song of Moses, where God says: "... when I whet my shining sword and my hand takes hold of justice...." Another interpretation of Deuteronomy here understands the word "shining" more literally as "lightning" and suggests that God can send forth lightning from his sword and then take it back, unlike humans, who once they shoot an arrow cannot recall it. In this second case, the Hebrew *mishpat* is rendered not as "justice" but rather as "punishment." In this sense, the opening line of the poem sets the stage for thinking deeply about the differences between human and divine justice and between justice and punishment.

²The inspector and examiner of hidden secrets—everyone believes He is an inspector of our hearts.
³The redeemer from death and savior from destruction—everyone believes He is a mighty redeemer.
⁴The sole judge of the world's inhabitants—everyone believes He is a true judge.

²הַבּוֹחֵן וּבוֹדֵק גִּנְזֵי נִסְתָּרוֹת.
וְכֹל מַאֲמִינִים שֶׁהוּא בּוֹחֵן כְּלָיוֹת,
³הַגּוֹאֵל מִמָּוֶת וּפוֹדֶה מִשַּׁחַת.
וְכֹל מַאֲמִינִים שֶׁהוּא גּוֹאֵל חָזָק,
⁴הַדָּן יְחִידִי לְבָאֵי עוֹלָם.
וְכֹל מַאֲמִינִים שֶׁהוּא דַּיַּן אֱמֶת,

²*Hidden secrets*: Or, "secrets of the secrets," with two words for "secret." The first Hebrew word for "hidden" or "secret" here comes from the same root that gives us *genizah*, the storehouse of holy texts that are buried, being too valuable to destroy.

²*Our hearts*: Literally, "innards." We add "our" because English frequently requires possessives for body parts where Hebrew does not. We use "heart" instead of "innards" because the Hebrew word here, *k'layot*, is a poetic one that metaphorically expresses something essential about a person. The line is based on Jeremiah 11:20, where God inspects our "innards" and "hearts," as well as "judges righteously."

³*Redeemer from death and savior from destruction*: Based on Hosea 13:14, "Shall I save them from Sheol and redeem them from death?"

³*Mighty redeemer*: Based on the phrase "their redeemer is mighty," which appears twice in the Bible, once in Proverbs 23:11, where "their" refers to orphans, and once in Jeremiah 50:34, referring to the People of Israel.

⁴*World's inhabitants*: Literally, "all who enter the world," from Mishnah Rosh Hashanah 1:2. The line also appears in the *Un'taneh Tokef* and is discussed more fully in the prayer (see Prayers of Awe, *Who by Fire, Who by Water—Un'taneh Tokef*, p. 38, "All who enter ... will pass").

⁵The one who is called "I am what
I am"—everyone believes He was,
is, and will be.
⁶The one whose name is certain,
and whose glory is too—everyone
believes He is unmatched.

הֶהָגוּי בְּאֶהְיֶה אֲשֶׁר אֶהְיֶה. ⁵
וְכֹל מַאֲמִינִים שֶׁהוּא הָיָה וְהֹוֶה
וְיִהְיֶה,
הַוַּדַּאי שְׁמוֹ כֵּן תְּהִלָּתוֹ. ⁶
וְכֹל מַאֲמִינִים שֶׁהוּא וְאֵין בִּלְתּוֹ,

⁵*I am what I am*: God's name in Exodus 3:14, where the phrase occurs
as one of two ways Moses is to explain who sent him. The other appears
immediately after, in Exodus 3:15: "The God of your ancestors,
the God of Abraham, the God of Isaac, and the God of Jacob." It is
common though misleading to cite Exodus 3:14 in isolation, as if that
alone presented God's name. The name in Exodus 3:14 is part of a more
complex answer to Moses's question "Who shall I say sent me?"

Additionally, the Hebrew verb for "am," both here and in Exodus
3:14, is actually in what is commonly used for the future tense (for
complex grammatical reasons), so it matches "will be" in the second half
of the line. To keep the match in our text here, we have included the
verb "is" in the second half, though some versions of the poem omit it.
⁶*One whose name is certain*: Or, "whose name is 'Certain.'" In the
Talmud (Berakhot 33b), "Certain" is part of a long list of God's names/
attributes. The list starts with "great, mighty, and awesome," a trio that
made its way into the daily liturgy at the start of the *Amidah*. The list in
the Talmud continues, "... and potent, and powerful, and held in awe;
strong, and brave, and certain...."
⁶*He is unmatched*: Literally, "there is none but Him," after 1 Samuel 2:2,
"There is none holy like Adonai, for there is none but You, and there is
no rock like our God."

⁷The one who remembers to reward those who call upon him—everyone believes He remembers the covenant.

⁸The one who allocates life to every living being—everyone believes He lives and endures.

⁹The one who is and does good to the wicked and to the good—everyone believes He is good to everyone.

¹⁰The one who knows the cravings of every creature—everyone believes He creates them in the womb.

⁷ הַזּוֹכֵר לְמַזְכִּירָיו טוֹבוֹת זִכְרוֹנוֹת.
וְכֹל מַאֲמִינִים שֶׁהוּא זוֹכֵר הַבְּרִית,
⁸ הַחוֹתֵךְ חַיִּים לְכָל חָי.
וְכֹל מַאֲמִינִים שֶׁהוּא חַי וְקַיָּם,
⁹ הַטּוֹב וּמֵטִיב לָרָעִים וְלַטּוֹבִים.
וְכֹל מַאֲמִינִים שֶׁהוּא טוֹב לַכֹּל,
¹⁰ הַיּוֹדֵעַ יֵצֶר כָּל יְצוּרִים.
וְכֹל מַאֲמִינִים שֶׁהוּא יוֹצְרָם בַּבֶּטֶן,

⁷ *To reward those who call upon Him*: Our English here, a rewording of the Hebrew, misses both the assonance ("call upon" sounds like "remember" in Hebrew—*zokher*) and the poetic impact of the original. This repetition of words that mean or sound like "remember" is common in the High Holy Day liturgy.

⁹ *Is and does good*: The Hebrew has two separate, related words for "good." We mimic the effect by using "is" alongside "does."

¹⁰ *Cravings ... creature[s]*: The Hebrew here has two related and similar-sounding words, the first meaning "nature" (*yetzer*), and the second meaning, as we have it, "creature[s]" (*y'tzurim*). We opt for "cravings" instead of "nature" to reinforce the poetic connection in the Hebrew. Another option would have been "knows the nature of everything in nature ...," but that would give us no way to capture the connection to the second half of the line ("He creates them ...").

¹¹The one who is all-powerful
and who completed everything
together—everyone believes He is
all-powerful.

¹²The one who dwells in secret
in the shadow of the almighty—
everyone believes He is the only
One.

¹³The one who rules over rul-
ers and who is regal—everyone
believes He reigns forever.

¹⁴The one who behaves lovingly
with every generation—everyone
believes He watches over love.

¹⁵The one who is patient and over-
looks offense—everyone believes
He forgives eternally.

¹¹ הַכֹּל יָכוֹל וְכוֹלְלָם יַחַד.
וְכֹל מַאֲמִינִים שֶׁהוּא כֹּל יָכוֹל,
¹² הַלָּן בְּסֵתֶר בְּצֵל, שַׁדָּי.
וְכֹל מַאֲמִינִים שֶׁהוּא לְבַדּוֹ הוּא,
¹³ הַמַּמְלִיךְ מְלָכִים וְלוֹ הַמְּלוּכָה.
וְכֹל מַאֲמִינִים שֶׁהוּא מֶלֶךְ עוֹלָם,
¹⁴ הַנּוֹהֵג בְּחַסְדּוֹ כָּל דּוֹר.
וְכֹל מַאֲמִינִים שֶׁהוּא נוֹצֵר חָסֶד,
¹⁵ הַסּוֹבֵל וּמַעֲלִים עַיִן מִסּוֹרְרִים.
וְכֹל מַאֲמִינִים שֶׁהוּא סוֹלֵחַ סֶלָה,

¹¹*All-powerful ... completed everything together*: We have no way to
capture the poetry of the Hebrew here in English. Three Hebrew
words—"all," "able," and "complete"—form the structure of the line:
"The one who is all-able, and who completed them ... is all-able." In
Hebrew, those three words are all built from the letters *k* and *l*: *kol*,
yakol, and *kolel*, respectively (though grammatical changes turn the
pronunciation of the words into *kol*, *yakhol*, and *kol'l* in the actual text).

¹²*Dwells in secret in the shadow of the almighty*: Based on Psalm 91:1,
where the word we translate as "secret" means "shelter": "You who live
in the shelter of the most high, dwell in the shadow of the almighty."

¹³*Rules ... rulers ... regal ... reigns*: In this case we are lucky that we have
four English words to match four related Hebrew ones.

¹⁶The one who sits on high and who sees those who fear Him—everyone believes He answers silent prayers.

¹⁷The one who opens his door to those who knock in repentance—everyone believes his hand is open.

¹⁸The one who sees the wicked and wants to turn them to righteousness—everyone believes He is righteous and just.

¹⁹The one who is enraged but patient—everyone believes He is slow to anger.

²⁰The one who is merciful and who prefers mercy to rage—everyone believes He is eager to be appeased.

16 הָעֶלְיוֹן וְעֵינוֹ אֶל יְרֵאָיו.
וְכֹל מַאֲמִינִים שֶׁהוּא עוֹנֶה לָחַשׁ,
17 הַפּוֹתֵחַ לְדוֹפְקֵי פִּתְחוֹ
בִּתְשׁוּבָה:
וְכֹל מַאֲמִינִים שֶׁהוּא פְּתוּחָה יָדוֹ,
18 הַצּוֹפֶה לָרָשָׁע וְחָפֵץ בְּהִצָּדְקוֹ.
וְכֹל מַאֲמִינִים שֶׁהוּא צַדִּיק וְיָשָׁר,
19 הַקּוֹצֵף בְּזַעַף וּמַאֲרִיךְ אַף.
וְכֹל מַאֲמִינִים שֶׁהוּא קָשֶׁה
לִכְעוֹס,
20 הָרַחוּם וּמַקְדִּים רַחֲמִים לְרֹגֶז.
וְכֹל מַאֲמִינִים שֶׁהוּא רַךְ לִרְצוֹת,

¹⁶*Sits*: Hebrew, just "is." We add a verb to preserve the rhetorical strength of the text.

¹⁶*Sees*: Hebrew, "eye is upon," based on Psalm 33:18, "The eye of Adonai is upon those who hold Him in awe."

¹⁶*Fear*: Or more accurately, "those who hold Him in awe." We avoid the longer phrase because its awkwardness interferes with the poetry of the line.

¹⁸The Hebrew is in the singular ("a wicked person ..."). We use the plural to avoid the awkward translation "turn him/her to righteousness."

¹⁹*Enraged*: Literally, "enraged with anger." An alternative version of the prayer reads "slow to anger" here—though not with the same words that we translate as "slow to anger" in the second half of this line.

²⁰*Eager to be appeased*: Or, "easy to appease," but we avoid that phrasing because of its potentially negative connotations in English.

²¹The one who is uniform and who treats the meager and great uniformly—everyone believes He is a righteous judge.
²²The one who is perfect and who behaves blamelessly with the blameless—everyone believes He is blameless in all his works.

²¹ הַשָׁוֶה וּמַשְׁוֶה קָטָן וְגָדוֹל.
וְכֹל מַאֲמִינִים שֶׁהוּא שׁוֹפֵט צֶדֶק,
²² הַתָּם וּמִתַּמֵּם עִם תְּמִימִים.
וְכֹל מַאֲמִינִים שֶׁהוּא תָּמִים פָּעֳלוֹ.

²¹*Uniform ... uniformly*: In Hebrew we have two closely related verbs here.
²²*Behaves blamelessly*: From 2 Samuel 22:26. The Hebrew words for "perfect" and "blameless" are closely related.

B. Transition:
Tisagev L'vadekha ("You Alone Will Be Exalted")

¹You alone will be exalted and You will rule over all in unity, in accordance with what your prophet wrote: "Adonai will be ruler over all the earth. On that day Adonai will be one and his name will be one."

¹ תִּשְׂגַּב לְבַדֶּךָ, וְתִמְלֹךְ עַל כֹּל
בְּיִחוּד, כַּכָּתוּב עַל יַד נְבִיאֶךָ: וְהָיָה
יְיָ לְמֶלֶךְ עַל כָּל הָאָרֶץ, בַּיּוֹם הַהוּא
יִהְיֶה יְיָ אֶחָד וּשְׁמוֹ אֶחָד.

¹*Over all*: Or, "over everyone" or even "over all things." We opt for "over all" here to match the quotation that follows, "... over all the earth."
¹*Ruler*: Or, "king," but the Hebrew words here and in "You will rule," earlier in the line, match. So we prefer "ruler" here to match "You will rule" in English.

C. Uv'khen ("Therefore")

[1]Therefore, Adonai our God, instill fear of You in all of your creatures,
    and dread in all that You have made,
[2]So that all creatures will revere You,
    and all that has been made will bow down before You,
[3]And all of them will form one group
    to do your will with complete dedication.

וּבְכֵן תֵּן פַּחְדְּךָ יְיָ אֱלֹהֵינוּ עַל כָּל מַעֲשֶׂיךָ ¹

וְאֵימָתְךָ עַל כָּל מַה שֶּׁבָּרָאתָ

וְיִירָאוּךָ כָּל־הַמַּעֲשִׂים ²

וְיִשְׁתַּחֲווּ לְפָנֶיךָ כָּל־הַבְּרוּאִים

וְיֵעָשׂוּ כֻלָּם אֲגֻדָּה אֶחָת ³

לַעֲשׂוֹת רְצוֹנְךָ בְּלֵבָב שָׁלֵם.

[1]*Instill*: Commonly, "put." But in English "fear" (and "awe"—see the next note) is instilled, not put into people.

[1]*Fear*: Some people prefer "awe" here (even though that English word is usually reserved for another Hebrew one, which we see in verbal form in line 2), because the concepts of "awe" and "fear" were more closely related than they are now. The general idea is that God, as, for example, a tornado, is awe-inspiring and also terrifying.

[1]*Of You*: Commonly, "your," as in "your fear." But the point is that people fear God, not that God has fear.

[1]*Dread*: Hebrew, "your dread," as in "dread for You." But "dread for You" doesn't make sense in English.

[2]*Revere*: Better here would be "hold in awe," but the verbal form we translate as "revere" recurs throughout the poem, and "hold in awe" becomes too awkward in English to capture the poetry of the Hebrew.

[2]*All creatures ... all that has been made*: Both in Hebrew and in our translation, "creatures" and "made" mirror "your creatures" and "You have made" in verse 1, creating a progression from what God specifically did to what has been done.

[3]*Complete dedication*: Others, "perfect heart." But the Hebrew word here, *l'vav*, refers to both emotion and intellect, a combination that we can express in English with "dedication."

4As we know, Adonai our God,
that authority is yours,
    your hand strong and your grasp
mighty.
5And your name is revered beyond
anything that You have made.

6Therefore install honor in your
people, Adonai,
    glory in those who revere You
and hope in those who seek You
out,
    and the opportunity to speak in
those who yearn for You,
7Happiness in your land,
    and joy in your city,
    and blossoming strength in
David your servant,

⁴ כְּמוֹ שֶׁיָּדַעְנוּ יְיָ אֱלֹהֵינוּ
שֶׁהַשִּׁלְטוֹן לְפָנֶיךָ
עֹז בְּיָדְךָ וּגְבוּרָה בִּימִינֶךָ
⁵ וְשִׁמְךָ נוֹרָא עַל כָּל מַה
שֶּׁבָּרָאתָ:

⁶ וּבְכֵן תֵּן כָּבוֹד יְיָ לְעַמֶּךָ
תְּהִלָּה לִירֵאֶיךָ וְתִקְוָה לְדוֹרְשֶׁיךָ
וּפִתְחוֹן פֶּה לַמְיַחֲלִים לָךְ.
⁷ שִׂמְחָה לְאַרְצֶךָ וְשָׂשׂוֹן לְעִירֶךָ
וּצְמִיחַת קֶרֶן לְדָוִד עַבְדֶּךָ

⁴*Authority ... mighty*: Literally, "authority is before You, might is in your
hand, and power is in your right hand." We reword the translation to
make it grammatical, using "hand" and "grasp" for the Hebrew "hand"
and "right hand" because, unlike Hebrew, English doesn't have a single
word for "right hand."
⁵*Anything that You have made*: This is the same Hebrew phrase that
we translated in line 1 as "all that You have made." Quirks of English
grammar prevent us from using the exact same wording here.
⁷*Blossoming strength*: Literally, a blossoming or sprouting "horn," used
symbolically for strength. The line is based on Psalm 132:17, which
juxtaposes the images of blossoming strength and of a light. We find the
light metaphor next, in line 8.

[8]And the ordained light in Jesse's descendant—your messiah—quickly in our day.

⁸וַעֲרִיכַת נֵר לְבֶן יִשַׁי מְשִׁיחֶךָ בִּמְהֵרָה בְיָמֵינוּ:

[9]Therefore the righteous will revere You and rejoice,
     the upright will celebrate, and the pious will jubilantly delight.
[10]And injustice will shut its mouth,
     and all wickedness will vanish like smoke,
[11]For You will abolish tyranny from the earth.

⁹וּבְכֵן צַדִּיקִים יִרְאוּ וְיִשְׂמָחוּ וִישָׁרִים יַעֲלֹזוּ וַחֲסִידִים בְּרִנָּה יָגִילוּ

¹⁰וְעוֹלָתָה תִּקְפָּץ פִּיהָ וְכָל־הָרִשְׁעָה כֻּלָּהּ כְּעָשָׁן תִּכְלֶה. ¹¹כִּי תַעֲבִיר מֶמְשֶׁלֶת זָדוֹן מִן הָאָרֶץ:

[10]*Injustice will shut its mouth*: From Job 5:16.
[10]*Vanish*: Literally, "come to an end."
[11]*Abolish*: From the Hebrew root *ayin vet resh*, which forms the backbone of the mainstream High Holy Day prayer *Un'taneh Tokef*. (See Prayers of Awe, *Who by Fire, Who by Water*—Un'taneh Tokef, p. 43, "Help the hardship of the decree pass.")

D. Concluding Poem:
V'ye'etayu ("And Everyone Will Arrive")

[1]And everyone will arrive to serve You
and praise your glorious name,
[2]And proclaim your righteousness by
the water. And nations who don't
know You will seek You out.
[3]And the ends of the earth will praise
You, and forever recite, "Adonai is
great."

וְיֶאֱתָיוּ כֹל לְעָבְדֶךָ [1]
וִיבָרְכוּ שֵׁם כְּבוֹדֶךָ
וְיַגִּידוּ בָאִיִּים צִדְקֶךָ [2]
וְיִדְרְשׁוּךָ עַמִּים לֹא יְדָעוּךָ
וִיהַלְלוּךָ כָּל אַפְסֵי אָרֶץ [3]
וְיֹאמְרוּ תָמִיד יִגְדַּל יְיָ

---

[1]*Arrive*: Commonly, "come" (as in the familiar "All the world shall come to serve Thee"), but that translation misses two aspects of the Hebrew. First, the Hebrew verb here is rare, unlike the exceedingly common "come" in English. More importantly, the English "come to serve You" is ambiguous. "Come" can indicate movement or, more generally, a change in state, as in "How did that come to be?" The Hebrew clearly refers to movement. Another option here would be "present themselves," but then we would be stuck with the awkward "everyone ... themselves," a dubiously grammatical mixture of singular and plural, or with the gender-restrictive "everyone ... himself."

[2]*By the water*: The Hebrew word here, *iyim*, means "islands" in modern Hebrew and probably referred to coastal towns in antiquity. The phrase is based on Isaiah 42:12, however, which forms part of a poem in which *iyim* is in parallel with "sea" and in opposition to "desert."

[3]*Ends of the earth*: These "ends of the earth" are personified in Hebrew (as they commonly are in Psalms and in Isaiah), so we personify them also in English. Other translations include variations on "they will praise You to the ends of the earth" and "they will praise You in all parts of the earth."

[4]And they will offer their sacrifices to You, and they will denounce their idols.

[5]And they will stand shoulder to shoulder to serve You, and those who seek You out will revere You.

[6]And they will recognize the might of your reign, and those who stray will come to understand.

[7]And they will proclaim your power, and exalt You, the one who is exalted above everyone.

‏⁴וְיִזְבְּחוּ לְךָ אֶת זִבְחֵיהֶם
וְיַחְפְּרוּ עִם פְּסִילֵיהֶם
‏⁵וְיִטּוּ שְׁכֶם אֶחָד לְעָבְדֶּךָ
וְיִירָאוּךָ מְבַקְשֵׁי פָנֶיךָ
‏⁶וְיַכִּירוּ כֹּחַ מַלְכוּתֶךָ
וְיִלְמְדוּ תּוֹעִים בִּינָה
‏⁷וִימַלְּלוּ אֶת גְּבוּרָתֶךָ
וִינַשְּׂאוּךָ מִתְנַשֵּׂא לְכֹל לְרֹאשׁ

[4]*Offer their sacrifices to You*: Hebrew, "sacrifice their sacrifices to You," using the typical Hebrew style of doubling up a root in a verb and its object. We don't usually do this in English, preferring instead generic verbs with nouns. Other examples include the Hebrew "dream a dream" ("have a dream") and even—in modern Hebrew—"shoe a shoe" ("put on a shoe").

[4]*Denounce*: Or "be ashamed of."

[5]*Stand shoulder to shoulder*: The Hebrew expression is similar, "stretch out a single shoulder." The phrase a "single shoulder" comes from Zephaniah 3:9, also in the context of serving God.

[6]*Come to understand*: Hebrew, "learn understanding."

[7]*Proclaim*: Hebrew, "utter," the same verb we find in the common Hanukkah song *Mi Y'malel* ("Who Can Retell?"; literally, "Who Can Utter?"). But in English, "power" isn't "uttered."

[7]*The one who is exalted above everyone*: The Hebrew here, from 1 Chronicles 29:11, has also made its way into the daily liturgy. (See *My People's Prayer Book*, Volume 3, P'sukei D'zimrah *[Morning Psalms]*, pp. 156–158.) The Hebrew word for "everyone" here (*kol*) is the same one that started this poem.

[8]And they will praise You ecstatically,
and crown You with a glorious diadem.
[9]And the mountains will break out in
song, the shores shout aloud when
You are king.

⁸וִיסַלְּדוּ בחילה פָנֶיךָ

וִיעַטְּרוּךָ נֵזֶר תִּפְאָרָה

⁹וִיִפְצְחוּ הָרִים רְנָּה

וִיצְהֲלוּ אִיִּים בְּמָלְכֶךָ

[8]*Praise You ecstatically*: Based on Job 6:10, where the rare verb *salad*
("praise," here) appears. Though we don't know what that word means
in the book of Job, later interpretation assigned it the meaning of
"praise." The word for "ecstatically," from the same original context,
often means "writhing in pain." Here that originally negative word takes
on a positive connotation.

[8]*Crown ... diadem*: The Hebrew, too, has two different roots, one for the
verb, the other for the noun. This is an uncommon pattern in Hebrew.
We capture it in English with the uncommon word "diadem."

[9]*Song*: Or, "celebration," more generally. The imagery of mountains
breaking out in song is from Isaiah (49:13, for example), where the sky
too sings and the earth rejoices. In Isaiah 55:12, the fruit trees clap their
hands.

[9]*Shores*: Again from the Hebrew word *iyim*, which we translated above
(line 2) as "by the water."

[9]*Shout aloud*: From a Hebrew verb commonly used for "neigh."

¹⁰And they will accept the yoke of your kingdom, and extol You in public assemblies.

¹¹And they will hear from afar and arrive, and present You with a royal crown.

¹⁰ וִיקַבְּלוּ עַל מַלְכוּתֶךָ
וִירוֹמְמוּךָ בִּקְהַל עָם
¹¹ וְיִשְׁמְעוּ רְחוֹקִים וְיָבֹאוּ
וְיִתְּנוּ לְךָ כֶּתֶר מְלוּכָה:

¹⁰*Yoke*: A harness used to control beasts of burden. While rare in the West now, yokes were common in agrarian societies, and they feature in this common metaphor. The idea is part of a more general theology that has people shaking off the yokes (and, therefore, the external control) of other humans, replacing it with control by God.

¹⁰*Extol*: Or, "exalt," but we already used that English verb for a different Hebrew one.

¹⁰*Extol You in public assemblies*: Based on Psalm 107:32, "They will extol Him in public assemblies and praise Him in the council of the elders." The "public assembly" thus contrasts with the privacy of the council of elders. The Hebrew for "public assemblies" is singular, suggesting that the phrase functions adverbially, so "publicly" might also be a good translation here.

¹¹*Arrive*: Or, "come." This metaphor of arriving from afar, combined with the opening line of "arriving," brackets the poem nicely.

E. Transition Back to Standard Liturgy: *V'timlokh* ("You Will Reign")

¹You alone, Adonai, will reign over all your creatures,

²On Mount Zion, your glorious habitation, and in Jerusalem, your holy city,

³As is written in your holy scriptures, "Adonai will reign forever, your God, Zion, from generation to generation. Hallelujah."

⁴You are holy and your name is awe-inspiring, and there is no God but You.

⁵As is written, "The Lord of Hosts is exalted through justice, and the holy God becomes holy through righteousness."

⁶Blessed are You, Adonai, the holy God.

¹וְתִמְלוֹךְ אַתָּה יְיָ לְבַדֶּךָ עַל כָּל מַעֲשֶׂיךָ

²בְּהַר צִיּוֹן מִשְׁכַּן כְּבוֹדֶךָ וּבִירוּשָׁלַיִם עִיר קָדְשֶׁךָ

³כַּכָּתוּב בְּדִבְרֵי קָדְשֶׁךָ. יִמְלֹךְ יְיָ לְעוֹלָם אֱלֹהַיִךְ צִיּוֹן לְדֹר וָדֹר הַלְלוּיָהּ:

⁴קָדוֹשׁ אַתָּה וְנוֹרָא שְׁמֶךָ וְאֵין אֱלוֹהַּ מִבַּלְעָדֶיךָ.

⁵כַּכָּתוּב. וַיִּגְבַּהּ יְיָ צְבָאוֹת בַּמִּשְׁפָּט וְהָאֵל הַקָּדוֹשׁ נִקְדַּשׁ בִּצְדָקָה.

⁶בָּרוּךְ אַתָּה יְיָ הַמֶּלֶךְ הַקָּדוֹשׁ:

---

³*As is written*: In Psalm 146:10.

⁴*Awe-inspiring*: Commonly, "awesome." But because the word "awesome" has mutated in meaning, shifting away from its core sense of "awe," that English no longer reflects the meaning of the Hebrew.

⁴*God*: We capitalize the word in keeping with common usage, though a more pedantic grammatical approach would have a lowercase "g" here.

⁵*As is written*: In Isaiah 5:16.

☙

"All the World," by Israel Zangwill

FROM *UNION PRAYER BOOK*, NEWLY REVISED VERSION

All the World Shall Come to Serve Thee

All the world shall come to serve Thee
    And bless Thy glorious Name,
And Thy righteousness triumphant
    The islands shall acclaim.
And the peoples shall go seeking
    Who knew Thee not before,
And the ends of earth shall praise Thee,
    And tell Thy greatness o'er.

They shall build for Thee their altars,
    Their idols overthrown,
And their graven gods shall shame them,
    As they turn to Thee alone.
They shall worship Thee at sunrise,
    And feel Thy Kingdom's might,
And impart their understanding
    To those astray in night.

They shall testify Thy greatness,
    And of Thy power speak,
And extol Thee, shrined, uplifted
    Beyond man's highest peak.
And with reverential homage,
    Of love and wonder born;

With the ruler's crown of beauty
    Thy head they shall adorn.

With the coming of Thy Kingdom
    The hills shall break into song,
And the islands laugh exultant
    That they to God belong.
And all their congregations
    So loud Thy praise shall sing,
That the uttermost peoples hearing,
    Shall hail Thee crowned King.

☙

PART V
Interpretations from the Field

Worshiping in Technicolor; Seeing Others in Black and White

Rabbi Tony Bayfield, CBE, DD

The old canard of Judaism as a petty, legalistic religion concerned only for its own well-being and dismissive of other faiths still raises its ugly head. An example is *In The Shadow of the Sword*, a 2012 book by British classicist and writer Tom Holland.[1] He focuses on the formation of the Babylonian Talmud (c. 200–450 CE), portraying the project as an all-consuming quest for rules. Holland then mischaracterizes even this distortion by referring to such dismissive and titillating marginalia as "geese should not be permitted to copulate" and a discussion of "the size of the Sages' penises."[2] Holland is clearly not interested in the context, which, in the latter case, is a jibe about the paternity of the children of obese men and almost certainly intentionally humorous.[3] To hear Holland tell it, the entire Rabbinic enterprise was obsessive and introverted to the point of being not just ridiculous but—more to the point—caring nothing about the non-Jewish population round about. What should we make of that?

To be sure, the Rabbis' central motif is the covenant between God and the Jewish People. Even the penis discussion has a serious basis in an

---

Rabbi Tony Bayfield, CBE, DD (Cantuar), is professor of Jewish theology and thought at Leo Baeck College in London. He is also president of the Movement for Reform Judaism in the United Kingdom. He contributed to *Who by Fire, Who by Water*—Un'taneh Tokef, *All These Vows*—Kol Nidre, and *We Have Sinned: Sin and Confession in Judaism*—Ashamnu *and* Al Chet (all Jewish Lights).

insistence that the men in question did indeed fulfill their sexual responsibility to their wives and that sexuality is both licit and desirable. That lesson is a characteristic reflection on Jewish marital obligations and human nature. The Rabbis were both particularistically Jewish and universalistically well aware of the world at large—at one and the same time.

To me, the most compelling metaphor is of lovers. The Rabbis and God were often so wrapped up in each other that their world was in glorious Technicolor, while the world around them was in black and white. Such a metaphor continued to hold true for many rabbis down the ages, with the black and white continuing to owe much to the intensity of the lovers' passion. Later, it also reflected a "backs to the world" defensive embrace compelled by the ongoing hostility that was regularly directed at Jews by their neighbors. Neither response is evidence of indifference to others.

But Holland is right, albeit inadvertently, in pointing to a major difference between Judaism on the one hand and Christianity and Islam on the other. As for Christianity, the Roman emperors Constantine (272–337) and, more importantly, Justinian (527–565) wedded Christianity to imperial ambitions that made Christianity a world-conquering power. So, too, Islamic rulers, following Muhammad's death (632), spread Islam throughout the known world. Both Christianity and Islam developed imperialistic theologies, proclaiming it their duty to bring the one true faith to all nonbelievers.

In that, Judaism differed radically. It had long established that God is the God of the whole world, but did not, on that account, feel the need to impose the Jewish covenant on others—who had their own.[4] There can be no more explicit statement of this than the book of Jonah.[5] Jonah is chosen to leave his comfortable life and make the long and perilous journey to Nineveh, the capital of the Neo-Assyrian Empire (the most violent and brutal empire of the day). He doesn't understand what the Ninevites have to do with him. Why did he have to undertake such a personally disruptive and dangerous mission just to "proclaim judgment" upon them "for their wickedness" (Jonah 1:2)? Jonah is perplexed both by God's compassion for the non-Jews of Nineveh and also by God's insistence that it *is* Jonah's business. But those are the very teachings that the book of Jonah provides.

Jonah's perplexity has continued to feature, albeit understandably, in attitudes among some Jews. But the teaching is definitive. God is the

God of the whole world. God's teachings of justice and compassion are universal. Judaism demands that Jews bear witness to God and God's values not by conquest and imposition, but by visible, personal, and collective example. The Technicolor nature of the Jewish relationship with God—the product of both the passion of lovers and the persecution inflicted by non-Jews—must not obscure those truths. God is also to be found in the black and white beyond the Jewish world. Indeed, our understanding now goes further. The distinction between Technicolor and black and white is a subjective one, and the Technicolor exists—at least for Christians and Muslims—just as much as it does for Jews.

Liturgy is not the place where you would expect the black and white to be dominant. Prayer has its roots in the lovers' conversation, in the Technicolor. Yom Kippur is deeply introspective, focusing on each member of the praying community and his or her *own personal* judgment by God. So the High Holy Day *machzor* is not the place where you would expect to find the uncomfortable, universalistic message of Jonah. It is therefore quite remarkable that we read him on Yom Kippur, and I'm not convinced that we do so only because the theme of the book is repentance. On the afternoon of Yom Kippur we are likely to be at our most Jonah-ish, most engaged with our lover-turned-judge, most indifferent to the black and white of the world beyond the Jewish one. The book of Jonah was, I am convinced, included to remind us that Jonah "didn't get it."

Rabbi Jonathan Magonet, PhD, describes the opening of services as preparation to enter the divine presence. The *Bar'khu* is the point at which the individual and the community actually enter. At the end of the *Amidah* we bow out of the presence, and the *Alenu*—with its more world-aware second paragraph—represents our return to the world. Attempts to include others at every point do not fit well with this traditional liturgical paradigm. Britain's greatest Liberal liturgist Rabbi John Rayner brought an added measure of universalism to his Liberal prayer book, *Service of the Heart*.[6] When it was first published, he famously received a letter from a giant among American liturgists, Jakob Petuchowski *z"l*. The letter ended, "With best wishes to you, your family and all mankind."

British Reform's High Holy Day liturgy follows the same pattern and is still stamped with the hallmarks of the love affair. Its focus is on the praying community and its relationship with God. It talks a lot about our sins toward our fellow human beings, but we infer that these sins are first and foremost within family and community. It largely fails to emphasize the black-and-white affirmation of our commitment to Jewish values within wider society and the globe. On Yom Kippur, we are "in here," not "out there."

How much should the book of Jonah impact the Yom Kippur service? How much universalism shall we have in a liturgy that still emphasizes the Technicolor? How much room is there for the black-and-white substance of the external world: our relationship with others, not just with our God; and God's presence among others, not just among Jews?

The liturgical texts featured in this volume are fascinating in that regard. The first, *V'khol Ma'aminim*, does not appear in our current British Reform liturgy. It would have followed the *Un'taneh Tokef* (which we retain despite its problematic theology) and preceded the *Avodah* (which we retain also, as a dramatic reenactment of the Temple rite). Within the latter, the most significant and powerful innovation is a radical extension and exploration of the martyrology and Jewish sacrifice, all of which lengthens *Musaf* considerably. Presumably something had to give, and it was *V'khol Ma'aminim*.

"All the world shall come to serve Thee" *is* included, however—but at the end of *Minchah*,[7] where it appropriately echoes the Jonah reading with which *Minchah* begins. But I have never heard it read or sung. This is, firstly, because it comes just before *Yizkor*, for which a fixed time is set. God forbid that those returning to the synagogue should have to wait while the afternoon prayers are being completed! Secondly, British Reform Jews loathe singing in English—it reminds us of the Orthodox slur that Reform services are like being in church. Then, too, there is the curious choice of a poem by Israel Zangwill as one of the lone voices of Jewish universalism. Zangwill, you will recall, renounced his Zionism in favor of a Jewish homeland anywhere but in Palestine. Later, his play *The Melting Pot* expressed a vision of a world from which all ethnicity and particularity have vanished. Rabbi Jonathan Sacks recently wrote of Zangwill that he was "a Jew who no longer wanted to be a Jew. His real hope was for a world in which the entire lexicon of racial [*sic*] and religious difference is thrown away."[8] Zangwill's philosophy is not at all what Judaism means by universalism.

Our universalism has therefore been more aptly represented by the varied, innovative repetitions of the *Vidui* ("confession") that recognizes our failures toward the modern-day Ninevites—the many nations and peoples who inhabit our shared globe—and to the globe itself. If the detailed specification of our sins quickly becomes dated, no matter: revise it.[9] On Yom Kippur each generation has to wrestle with the language of falling short and its brutal consequences.

We continue to worship in Technicolor but recognize that others worship in Technicolor as well. We acknowledge, with the perplexed and argumentative Jonah himself, that God is the God of others, even our enemies, and that they, too, are capable of genuine repentance. The black and white of our universalism may not be as vivid as our multicolored particularism, but it is there and it is theologically and ethically essential.

⟨⟩

"I Didn't Do It!"

A Rosh Hashanah Nightmare

Rabbi Will Berkovitz

The old man sleeping on the moldering carpet a few feet away called out in the darkness, "I didn't do it. I didn't do it." Some of the other men blanketing the floor grunted in their sleep. "I didn't do it," he called again. I rearranged the plastic bag I was using as a pillow and wondered about the nightmares plaguing the old man. Who was accusing him, and of what?

Such are the dreams of many who are homeless and who find their way into the shelters, underpasses, and doorways across the country.

I had been volunteering in the shelter for a time, coming and going, and realized that despite my close proximity to its residents, I was subtly creating barriers that kept them at a safe distance from me. So one day I asked if I could stay the night. The woman running the shelter said, "Come back at check-in and we will treat you like everyone else." I did, and for a very brief period, some barriers did come down. But like weeds in the garden, they quickly returned. Understanding is transient—shifting and moving in and out of focus. It's not a onetime affair.

Rabbi Will Berkovitz is the CEO of Jewish Family Service of Seattle, where he oversees nine program areas, from refugee resettlement to emergency services. He leads JFS in mobilizing philanthropic, volunteer, and advocacy support to meet the needs of those who are most vulnerable in the Seattle community. Before JFS, he was senior vice president and rabbi in residence at Repair the World, where he developed innovative partnership initiatives with organizations across the United States. He is a contributor to *We Have Sinned: Sin and Confession in Judaism*—Ashamnu *and* Al Chet (Jewish Lights).

The next morning, while eating a stale glazed donut, I introduced myself to the old man whose nightmare I had intruded upon. "The hardest thing," he said, "isn't that people don't give me a quarter. The hardest part is the way people walk past me. I get it if you don't want to give me anything. But I am still human. You could look at me."

The desire to avert our gaze is not new. And our ancient Rabbis understood this. One of my professors, Dr. Aryeh Cohen, cited a two-thousand-year-old debate as to whether one can coerce a neighbor to build a gatehouse around property held in common. Rabban Shimon ben Gamaliel says, "Not all courtyards need a gatehouse" (Mishnah Bava Batra 1:5). Seeking to understand the disagreement, the Talmud describes a tzaddik with whom Elijah the prophet regularly spoke. He collaborated with his neighbors on building a gatehouse, however, "and Elijah no longer spoke with him." Why would Elijah stop speaking to the tzaddik just because he allowed his neighbors to build a gatehouse at the entrance to their property?

A couple of important details to note here: It wasn't just anyone with whom Elijah spoke. It was a tzaddik, "a righteous person," a term reserved for a select few: not us common folk, but those who, either by cultivation of spirit or gift from God, have a heightened sense of goodness. And why a "gatehouse"? What did the gatehouse in particular create or destroy in the world that ended the conversation?

One of the striking things to know about Elijah is that he often appears in the guise of a homeless person. It is that very sympathy with the poor, perhaps, that qualifies him for his quintessential role in Judaism: the messenger who will announce the arrival of the messiah. We sing *Eliyahu Hanavi* at Havdalah to end Shabbat, reserve the chair of Elijah at a bris or baby naming, and keep Elijah's cup on our seder table because we hope that with this week, this newborn, this seder, the messiah will arrive and the walls of separation and blindness will permanently come down. I picture the tzaddik and Elijah speaking like neighbors across a fence or friends on the sidewalk of the front yard. What happened that caused Elijah to keep walking?

Rashi, the famous medieval French rabbi, leaves no ambiguity about why it was a gatehouse specifically that ended the relationship. A gatehouse, he says, muffles the voices of the poor who are calling from the street so that their cries cannot be heard within. I would push Rashi a bit further. It isn't that they go completely unheard; but they are heard only occasionally, transiently, partially. Rather than an immediacy that haunts and confronts us, poverty is held at a safe distance where it can be escaped and—temporally, at least—ignored. The poor are on one side and we are on the other comfortably watching TV, reading in quiet, or entertaining friends at dinner with only our laughter and conversation breaking the silence. The voices of the poor calling out from the shantytown, the refugee camp, or just outside our doors are so far away that we forget they exist at all.

This debate appears in a section of the Talmud called Bava Batra, the tractate that deals with contractual relations between people. At issue is a contract about our mutual humanity and the risk of breaking that contract. "If I look at the mass, I will never act," said Mother Teresa. "If I look at the one, I will." Those who are poor have a face, a name, and a voice. Poverty becomes abstract when the specificity of its faces and voices is obscured.

A couple of months back, I passed a woman curled up in a doorway in the French Quarter of New Orleans. She looked burnt out and cast aside. I would have placed her in that giant heap of society's discarded had I not passed her again a half hour later. No longer hunched over, she was furiously attacking her violin, playing notes that sounded likes accusations. I had utterly misjudged this woman, thinking she was someone she wasn't. That is true for so many in the world of the down and out. The only difference is they can't pick up a violin and call attention to our ignorance or prejudice.

One of the most striking verses in the Torah—the Jewish People's founding document, said to have been written by God and handed to Moses, no less—states emphatically, "There will always be poor in the land." And we will never be let off the hook of collective responsibility, as the verse continues, "Therefore I command you, 'Open your hand to your brother, to your needy one in your land.... Remember you were slaves in the land of Egypt'" (Deuteronomy 15:11, 15:15). Remember we were slaves.

The messiah will come when we stop building gatehouses and start opening our doors. Redemption will come when the questions about homelessness are not left to a dedicated few, but are felt as commands for our entire community. Whether we are learning, praying, or celebrating together, the cries from the street and the dreams of the poor should haunt us, lest the nightmare calling out, "I didn't do it. I didn't do it," become our own, the description of choices we *didn't* make, time we *didn't* commit.

Elijah will arrive only if we hold each other accountable to hearing the voices of the needy and become able to say, "I *did* do it; I *did* do it!"; the values we teach our children must be lived out with our hands, not just our words.

I think of the gatehouse story when I visit the liturgy for Rosh Hashanah. *Uv'khen*, it says—"and then ..." Yes, and then—then what? When services end, where do I go? To my home behind a "gatehouse"? The fresh start that comes from doing *t'shuvah* can delude me into thinking that the whole world is returning home to celebrate the possibilities of a life well led, a life well rewarded, a life well worth living. But the wonderful feeling of a new year, newly begun, can hide the reality of people who never have the chance to begin all over again. God help me not erect a gatehouse around my newfound new year comforts. God save me from the Rosh Hashanah nightmare that when it comes to what I really need to do, "I didn't do it."

Stopping by the grocery store not long ago I told my sons I had to pick up a few things. Nativ, my seven-year-old, said, "We also need to get something for Margret." Try as I might I couldn't figure out who he was talking about. "Nativ," I finally said, "who is Margret?" "She is the woman who sells those newspapers on the sidewalk," he replied. Surprised, I wondered out loud. "Nativ, how do you know her name and what she needs?" He looked me straight in the eye and said, "Abba. I ask."

ॐ

An Open Door

Dr. Erica Brown

V'khol ma'aminim, "Everyone believes ..."

In my synagogue, this *piyyut* is belted out loudly—as the song of prayer that it was probably meant to be when it was composed in late antiquity. The congregation sings it with the kind of musical, majestic confirmation that makes it sound genuinely persuasive. "Everyone believes ... Everyone believes ... Everyone believes." Of course, if it were sung in English, it might not garner the same enthusiasm. "Some believe ... Some question ... Some doubt ... Some object." We sing what we might not say. We sing in another language because our confidence may be weakened by understanding. Ignorance here feels oddly comforting.

But when you are a Hebrew speaker, and the words suffer your mental simultaneous translation, you have to keep pushing the demon of literalism away—much like we send away Yom Kippur's scapegoat to the remote parts of the wilderness where it cannot touch us. On these holiest days of the year, we want to keep our faith in tow. We want to be part of the community of the sacred and sincere.

Absolute faith is never easy; but some years are harder than others, and I confess: my *V'khol Ma'aminim* suffered especially this year. A

Dr. Erica Brown is a writer and an educator. She is a faculty member of the Wexner Foundation, an Avi Chai Fellow, and the recipient of the Covenant Award. She is author of *Inspired Jewish Leadership: Practical Approaches to Building Strong Communities*, a National Jewish Book Award finalist; *Spiritual Boredom: Rediscovering the Wonder of Judaism*; and *Confronting Scandal: How Jews Can Respond When Jews Do Bad Things* (all Jewish Lights); and coauthor of *The Case for Jewish Peoplehood: Can We Be One?* (Jewish Lights), *Return, In the Narrow Places, Leadership in the Wilderness*, and *Happier Endings*. She contributed to *Who by Fire, Who by Water—Un'taneh Tokef, All These Vows—Kol Nidre*, and *We Have Sinned: Sin and Confession in Judaism—Ashamnu and Al Chet* (all Jewish Lights). Her articles have appeared on the *Newsweek/Washington Post* website "On Faith."

close, young friend had died just months before Rosh Hashanah arrived. For the Days of Awe, her seat was never far from mine, and I sat with her daughters this year, feeling her absence. There were moments when the words of the prayer book felt like a condemnation, an accusation, a tease. The girls and I went in and out of services when the language became overbearing and the loss felt insurmountable. The empty chair. The empty prayer.

> Everyone believes He is an inspector of our hearts;
> The redeemer from death and savior from destruction.

That wasn't happening.

> Everyone believes He remembers the covenant;
> The one who allocates life to every living being.

That wasn't happening either.

> Everyone believes He is a righteous judge;
> The one who is perfect, who behaves blamelessly with
> the blameless.

I want to believe this—and in the perfect world, I might, but this year it was so hard. It took extra doses of modesty to remind myself that I am not privileged to know the larger master plan, that our world could still be perfect even if my world was not. I took comfort from an odd source: Big Elk, an eighteenth-century Native American chief and orator, who advised his tribe to put personal pain within collective perspective:

> Do not grieve. Misfortunes will happen to the wisest and best of men. Death will come, always out of season. It is the command of the Great Spirit, and all the nations and people must obey. What is past and what cannot be prevented should not be grieved for.... Misfortunes do not flourish particularly in our lives—they grow everywhere.[1]

I would think it again and again: "Misfortunes do not flourish particularly in our lives—they grow everywhere." Both joy and suffering are so much larger than ourselves. I looked around. The High Holy Day seating chart held mourners everywhere. And I took comfort in the fact that someone from a very different place and time could placate me with universal wisdom in the face of universal anguish in the very particularistic life that I lead.

Since I rarely leave services on the High Holy Days, my walks to accompany my friend's daughters made me aware that there were a number of people I'd never expect to be outside during *Kol Nidre* or the dramatic parts of *Musaf*—not just people who might get bored with the service because of infamiliarity with it, but learned people, whose Judaism was intense, authentic, and deep. And it made me realize that they were outside not because services were tiresome or long, but because they, too, took the words of prayer seriously—so seriously that, at times, the language was strangulating. They needed to breathe. Their existential angst was in a headlong collision with their faith, and they chose to avoid the accident.

I made peace with myself and God through accommodation. I focused on the parts of prayer—specific words and lines—that took on positive meaning. And one such stanza of *V'khol Ma'aminim* packed a particular punch.

> Everyone believes He answers silent prayers;
> The one who opens his door to those who knock in
> repentance.

Here was no "king and master and father"—words for God that felt authoritative and distant. Here was no bold declaration of praise that felt almost overconfident. This was the language of humility and tenderness and embrace that I needed. It was the language of the quiet, the meek, the confused, the unsure, the weak-hearted confronting their deficiencies and anxieties and offering them on the altar of a threshold, a door. Nervous about rejection, they wait before knocking.

But they do not have to wait long. Before they even knock, the door opens a crack. The whispering hush of a humble penitent in front of this shut door is accepted, and suddenly, a gate hinged with contrition opens. Maybe it only opens a little bit. But it's enough to create possibilities. The door is not closed shut. The relationship still exists. The door can be pushed open wider when the penitent is ready to enter.

If prayer is to mature and grow within us as we age, then it will be through the cycle of distance and closeness that we experience in our truest relationships. We achieve intimacy and then back off. We are disappointed, and we pull away. We have moments of profound trust and then moments of suspicion. Our relationships travel these cycles because we do. Human beings are not static.

And if we are not static, then neither are our prayers. Rather than turn away from them when they do not speak to us, we might turn toward them in hope of finding that one expression, that one tune, that one song, that still touches our deepest places and opens the door to intimacy once more.

> Everyone believes He answers silent prayers;
> The one who opens his door to those who knock in repentance.

෧෩෨

Our Jewish Golden Rule

Rabbi Lawrence A. Englander, CM, DHL, DD

Several years ago at an interfaith gathering, I saw a beautiful multicolored poster that displayed the "Golden Rule" as expressed by different religions. The Jewish version was Hillel's summary of Torah "while standing on one foot": "What is hateful to you, do not do to another."[1] I felt proud that Hillel's message embraced every single person in that room. It also reminded me of a passage in the High Holy Day liturgy that I had read a few short weeks before: the *Uv'khen* trilogy anticipates the messianic time when all humanity will "form one group to do your will with complete dedication."

But then I thought ahead to the next paragraph, which beseeches God to "install honor in *your* people" and "joy in *your* city." I have no doubt that the authors of this prayer regarded only Jews as God's people and Jerusalem as God's city; and so this prayer, at heart, is really particularistic. This thought prompted me to go back to the High Holy Day *machzor* in an attempt to find a prayer that would include the entire human race. Sure enough, the Rosh Hashanah morning service records *V'khol Ma'aminim*—"Everyone believes ... God is the sole judge of the world's inhabitants." And let's not forget the melodic strains of the prayer "All the world shall come to serve Thee / And bless Thy glorious name."

But even these prayers are not as universalistic as I had hoped. True, they praise God as maker and ruler of all humankind—but not all of God's children are created equal. These prayers imply that the people of Israel is charged with a special mission to teach the truths of the universal God to the nations of the world, who otherwise would continue

---

Rabbi Lawrence A. Englander, CM, DHL, DD, has been rabbi of Solel Congregation of Mississauga, Ontario, since its inception in 1973. He is author of *The Mystical Study of Ruth*, former editor of the *CCAR Journal*, and a contributor to *We Have Sinned: Sin and Confession in Judaism—Ashamnu and Al Chet* and *May God Remember: Memory and Memorializing in Judaism*—Yizkor (both Jewish Lights).

to wallow in ignorance and immorality. This may have made sense in a world where idolatry demanded child sacrifice and where the powerful deemed it their privilege to enslave the weak. But surely those days have passed. By now, the Jewish values of freedom, justice, and peace have been incorporated into our wider society.

Yet if such is the case, then we are presented with a question from the other side of the particularist-universalist spectrum: why bother remaining Jewish? Wouldn't it be easier to assimilate into the secular mainstream without all the extra baggage? If our moral work is now done, what reason is there to remain as a unique people?

I know there are Jews who answer these questions by saying, "Judaism is a part of my cultural identity. I enjoy the holiday dinners with family, the special Jewish foods, and the beauty of the Jewish life-cycle ceremonies. Otherwise, I'm a citizen of the world." Such people emphasize universalism to the point of making their Jewish identity a personal choice with no necessary impact on anyone or anything else. But Jewish teachings should be more than a matter of convenience; they should be necessary, not only for the benefit of Jews who hold them, but also for the world, which is better off because of them.

Then I remembered *Worlds in Collision*, a 1950 book by Immanuel Velikovsky, a Jewish psychiatrist who also did research into comparative mythology. At that time, it was generally agreed among biblical scholars that the stories about the ten plagues, the Exodus from Egypt, and the splitting of the Sea of Reeds were fictional constructs that make up our "foundation story"—that is, they were designed to explain how the people of Israel came into being. Velikovsky argued instead that some global upheaval may indeed have happened, because other cultures, from South America to China, had recorded catastrophic events that seemed to coincide with the period of the biblical Exodus. So he tried to determine whether these narratives all had a common cause. He developed a theory that the planet Venus began its journey through our solar system as a comet; as it solidified into a planet, its gravitational force collided with that of Mars and sent shock waves that caused the phenomena on Earth recorded by these stories.

In the intervening years, much of Velikovsky's science has been called into question,[2] and his dating of biblical events has been rejected. However, I believe his true discovery lies in his comparison of the tales, because they reveal how their respective cultures perceived themselves and their role in the world.

We can take the ancient Greeks as an example. The Trojan War took place within a century or so of the Exodus. Homer's *Iliad* interprets the war to extol the Greek way of life and, along the way, provides two lessons. First: the gods favored the Greeks. In the thick of the battle, Zeus says to his wife, Hera:

> So you have acted, then, lady Hera of the ox eyes.
> You have roused up Achilles of the swift feet [against the Trojans],

to which Hera replies:

> As for me, who am highest of all the goddesses ...
> how could I not weave sorrows for the men of Troy,
> when I hate them?[3]

Like spectators at a football game, the rest of the Olympians take sides; but in the end, Zeus allows Hera to win the day. The Greek hero Achilles slays the Trojan defender Hektor, and the city is sacked.

From this outcome Homer derived a second lesson: the Greeks were endowed with a manifest destiny. Their superior lifestyle of democracy and freedom allowed the disparate city-states of Greece to unite and rule over the neighboring peoples. Because freedom was the highest of ideals, however, it was to be enjoyed only by those of highest social status. The common classes in Greek society were to serve the ruling class, and the aristocracy of the conquered nations had the privilege of replenishing the dwindling Greek treasury.

Our Jewish foundation story provides the same first lesson: Adonai favors the Israelites over the Egyptians. Just before inflicting the ten plagues upon Egypt, God tells Moses: "The Egyptians shall know that I am Adonai, when I stretch out my hand over Egypt and bring out the Israelites from their midst" (Exodus 7:5). The second lesson is also echoed in the Exodus-Sinai narrative: our ancestors, too, felt that God had given them a destiny of freedom.

But here is where our foundation story diverges radically. No less than thirty-six times the Torah records the following teaching: we are forbidden to oppress the stranger, the orphan, and the poor, "for you know the feelings of the stranger, having yourselves been strangers in the land of

Egypt" (e.g., Exodus 23:9). Our historical experience taught us not to *victimize* but to *empathize*. For the Israelites, freedom is the right of all peoples and all classes, because every human being is created in the image of God.

According to Velikovsky, this teaching of empathy is what distinguished ancient Israel from other peoples of the time. The foundation story of Israel was the only one that applies its message not just to Jews but to all of humankind:

> The Jewish people did not obtain all of its "supremacy" in that one day at the Mountain of Lawgiving; this people did not receive the message of monotheism as a gift. It struggled for it; and step by step ... from the furnace of affliction of Egypt, from the deliverance at the Red Sea amid the sky-high tides ... from the internal struggle, from the search for God and for justice between man and man, from the desperate and heroic struggle for national existence on its narrow strip of land against the overwhelming empires of Assyria and Egypt, it became a nation chosen to bring a message of the brotherhood of man to all the peoples of the world.[4]

That lesson became incorporated into the cycle of Jewish festivals. On Shabbat, for example, every member of the household is to rest, including the servants, because "you were a slave in the land of Egypt" (Deuteronomy 5:15). As Jews observe the particularist rituals of lighting Shabbat candles, singing the *Kiddush*, and saying the *Motzi*, we also affirm the universal values of freedom and justice for all.

In more recent times, Jewish immigrants to the New World brought that lesson of empathy with them. As they settled into the towns and cities of North America, for example, they built synagogues, schools, and cemeteries to serve their own people. But they also created hospitals and charitable organizations that were designed to serve anyone who needed them, regardless of race or religion. They perceived their role as twofold: to become productive citizens of their new society, but also to serve as watchdogs of that society to ensure that our universal values would be extended to every resident.

This brings us full circle back to Hillel's Golden Rule. There is a second part to it, which is often overlooked. So let's take a look at his entire summary of Judaism: "What is hateful to you, do not do to another. *That is the whole Torah; the rest is commentary. Go and learn it.*" That final statement holds the story of the Jewish People: a story of overcoming tyranny to gain freedom, a story of empathy that extends our pursuit of freedom to all the peoples of the world.

In the Coen Brothers' movie *The Big Lubowsky*, one of the characters, the Dude, invites his friend Walter to go bowling on Saturday. Walter replies, "I don't roll on Shabbes." Walter converted to Judaism when he married his wife Cynthia but, as the Dude points out, has been divorced for more than five years. "You're living in the past," the Dude tells him. Then Walter delivers the punch line: "Three thousand years of beautiful tradition, from Moses to Sandy Koufax. You're damn right I live in the past!"

The Jewish story of the past delivers a message that the world still needs to hear.

A "Light unto the Nations" or a "People Who Dwell Alone"?

Rabbi Shoshana Boyd Gelfand

Each August, I set off on my annual pilgrimage to Cheltenham, England, to attend Greenbelt Festival, a kind of Christian version of *Limmud*, where twenty thousand Christians spend a weekend celebrating Christian music, faith, and justice. It is a rather unusual place for a Jew to find herself. So why do I go? In part, I believe it is important to accept interfaith invitations; but in part also, I believe Greenbelt and I have something to offer one another.

Greenbelt both inspires and disturbs me: what inspires is the sight of twenty thousand co-religionists taking communion together and seeking to access the divine; what disturbs is the way Israel is sometimes portrayed and the misunderstanding of Jews as simply a faith as opposed to a people. Regardless, I always return from Greenbelt with new insight into Jewish identity and the Jewish mission. Having spent this time with professing Christians, I invariably wonder what the ideal relationship is between us: Is the Jewish mission to be a "light unto the nations" (Isaiah 49:6), or are

---

Rabbi Shoshana Boyd Gelfand received her rabbinic ordination in 1993 at The Jewish Theological Seminary in New York. She has served as chief executive of the United Kingdom Movement for Reform Judaism and prior to that was vice president of the Wexner Heritage Foundation in New York. Currently she is director of JHub, an operating program of the London-based Pears Foundation. She contributed to *All These Vows*—Kol Nidre, *We Have Sinned: Sin and Confession in Judaism*—Ashamnu *and* Al Chet, and *May God Remember: Memory and Memorializing in Judaism*—Yizkor (all Jewish Lights).

we actually a "people who dwell alone" (Numbers 23:9)? What universal themes arise authentically from Jewish tradition, and where does Judaism unabashedly speak only to members of the tribe? What is the ideal balance between the two?

No educated person can deny that both are present. Our liturgy, our scripture, our rituals, our holidays, and our ethical literature all straddle the tension that governs the universalism-particularism divide. Halakhah (Jewish law) establishes Jewish relationships with the outside world of people other than ourselves, but it also emphasizes Jewish distinctiveness—the inherent difference between Israel and the nations (social distinctions), Shabbat and the workweek (temporal distinctions), light and darkness (natural distinctions).

Halakhah is primarily a matter of tribal talk, however: measures of behavior addressed to Jews alone and the boundaries that set us apart. Boundaries establish identity. Even for those who don't consider halakhah to be literally commanded by God, the halakhic focus on particularism connects us to Jewish uniqueness. Author Thomas Friedman in his book *The Lexus and the Olive Tree* describes the human need for specific religious or national allegiance by using the metaphor of the olive tree: local, deep, and ancient.

> Olive trees are important. They represent everything that roots us, anchors us, identifies us, and locates us in this world—whether it be belonging to a family, a community, a tribe, a nation, a religion or, most of all, a place called home. Olive trees are what give us the warmth of family, the joy of individuality, the intimacy of personal rituals, the depth of private relationships, as well as the confidence and security to reach out and encounter others. We fight so intensely at times over our olive trees because, at their best, they provide the feelings of self-esteem and belonging that are as essential for human survival as food in the belly.[1]

The "olive trees" of halakhah are balanced, however, by myriad occasions in scripture and the liturgy that focus on universal themes. The prophets regularly paint an idealized picture of universal peace and harmony where all nations recognize God as the ruler of the universe. Amos explicitly likens Israel to other nations:

> To Me, O Israelites, you are
> Just like the Ethiopians
>   —declares the Lord.
> True, I brought Israel up
> From the land of Egypt,
> But also the Philistines from Caphtor
> And the Arameans from Kir. (Amos 9:7)

Jewish liturgy sometimes juxtaposes universal and particular themes within the very same prayer, as in *Uv'khen*, a centerpiece of this book. It rapidly alternates between a universalist vision ("So that all creatures will revere you") and a particular one ("Happiness in your land, joy in your city, and blossoming strength in David your servant")—and then back again to universalism (in the prayer following, *V'ye'etayu*, and "everyone will arrive to serve You and praise your glorious name").

Uv'khen is not the only place in the Jewish liturgy to express both sides of the dilemma within the same prayer. Perhaps the best-known example is Friday night *Kiddush*, which includes the phrases *zikaron l'ma'aseh v'reshit* ("a memorial to the works of creation") and *zekher litziat mitzrayim* ("a remembrance of the Exodus from Egypt"). *Kiddush* articulates both the universal theme of creation and the particular theme of Exodus as the rationale for Shabbat, ensuring that we have both a universal and a particular rationale for this weekly affirmation of Jewish identity.

The larger Jewish holiday cycle provides a further opportunity to communicate this dialectic. Every given year alternates between "particular-focused holidays" and "universal-focused holidays," ensuring that we have at least one intensive weeklong immersion in each. The two seven-day holidays that anchor the year are Pesach and Sukkot, beginning, respectively, on the fifteenth day of Nisan and Tishrei, exactly six months apart. Pesach is almost wholly particularist—it recounts the story of the Jewish People's birth. So inward looking is it that, traditionally, only Jews were allowed to partake of the paschal sacrifice. We nowadays like to emphasize its subtheme of the ultimate redemption of all humanity, but the primary message of Pesach is the redemption of Jews from Pharaoh and our special relationship with God.

Sukkot, however, exactly six months later, is the very antithesis. While it cannot be denied that certain themes in Sukkot pertain to the Jewish People (e.g., the booths where we lived while wandering in the desert), most of the Sukkot message is universal: offering sacrifices for each nation in the world; praying for rain for the entire world; inviting guests into the sukkah; and reciting the haftarah from Zechariah 14, which includes the following: "Adonai will be ruler over all the earth. On that day Adonai will be one and his name will be one" (Zechariah 14:9).

It would seem that the Rabbis of old designed our liturgy and our calendar to force us to oscillate between particularism and universalism. Whether through the recitation of Shabbat *Kiddush* or the annual journey from Pesach to Sukkot and back, the meta-message is clear: creation and Exodus are equally critical to Jewish consciousness.

Why, then, do so many Jews today overemphasize one at the expense of the other? Large parts of the contemporary Jewish community are almost completely cut off from engaging with the non-Jewish world. Living in mostly Jewish Israel or in a Jewish enclave in Brooklyn or Golders Green, they naturally focus on Jewish particularism—sometimes with such limited contact with non-Jews that they become a "people who dwell alone." While these Jewish communities often possess an enviable knowledge of Torah, a rich expression of Jewish tradition, and a wonderfully cohesive sense of community, their overfocus on Jewish particularity often makes them insular, lacking the ability to share Jewish wisdom and insight with the non-Jewish world.

Another set of Jews overfocus on the universal. Their Judaism amounts exclusively to "repairing the world" and being a "light unto the nations"—noble Jewish values, certainly, but denuded of their rootedness in Jewish tradition when touted in isolation from particularism. Again, I mean no criticism of the excellent work such organizations and people do; but by overfocusing on the universal, they overlook the parts of Jewish life that make *tikkun olam* distinctly Jewish (as opposed to simply "being a good person"). Without Shabbat, Torah, and covenant, we lose the unique path that we as Jews possess to be that light unto the nations.

These two groups—what I call the "Pesach-Jews" and the "Sukkot-Jews"—represent equally authentic poles of Jewish tradition, but they need each other to be complete. Outsiders, too, need to understand that neither one alone provides a proper portrait of what Jews truly are—we are neither simply "a light unto the nations" nor a "people who dwell alone." As just "a light unto the nations," we lose our distinct identity, are unable to articulate our unique gifts to the world, and will likely disappear as a people (with consequence to the world, not just to ourselves).

As just "a people who dwell alone," we sacrifice empathy with others and our larger purpose for existence, with no goal for that existence beyond just existence itself.

The tension between Jewish particularism and universalism is a necessary and indestructible polarity. It cannot (and should not) ever be "solved." We need, however, to recognize our tendency to gravitate to one of these poles, in part (perhaps) because of our unconscious discomfort with (or even fear of) the opposite one. Only by becoming aware of this tendency can we consciously aim at righting the balance—as our liturgy (*Uv'khen* or Friday night *Kiddush*) and the holiday cycle (Pesach and Sukkot) encourage us to do.

Part of the reason I cherish the diversity of *k'lal yisrael* is that different segments of the Jewish community navigate the particularist/universalist tension differently. There is no reason to strive for uniformity here. On the contrary, it is appropriate (and even desirable) to disagree about the level of permeability that Jews should want, the extent to which we should welcome or discourage converts, and the amount of energy we should expend on nurturing Jewish identity versus sharing the Jewish message with the non-Jewish world. Jewish groups and institutions will properly differ in their answers to these questions (e.g., Lubavitch Hasidim versus Satmar Hasidim, or synagogues versus institutions dedicated specifically to interfaith dialogue). What matters for us all is that we validate both Sukkot and Pesach as essential themes to visit during the course of a year. We likewise ought to see each Friday night as both creation and the Exodus. And even on a holiday such as Rosh Hashanah, when we celebrate the universal theme of "creation," we balance that with an acknowledgment of our particular relationship with God. The juxtaposition of both universal and particular themes in *Uv'khen* on Rosh Hashanah acknowledges that it is we as Jews who call for universal recognition of God.

☙❧

A Snowball That Cannot Melt

Rabbi Laura Geller

When Temple Emanuel of Beverly Hills was celebrating our seventy-fifth anniversary, we concluded our Erev Rosh Hashanah service with the old Reform anthem that I had grown up with: "All the world shall come to serve Thee." It seemed like an obvious way to celebrate the history of a congregation connected with the Reform Movement. Before we invited the congregation to sing, our cantor explained its history. Still, one congregant complained after services, "Why did we sing that? It sounded so ... goyish!"

What was it that sounded goyish? The formal English? The majestic music? No, what sounded goyish to him was the idea that eventually the whole world will serve the same God in the same way. "That's just not Jewish," he said. "I thought we believed that there were different spiritual paths that all lead to one God, and that our way is only one way—not better than the other ways, but right for us."

I admit that I also have problems with the triumphal theology of the hymn. For me the problem begins with the image of God as king that so permeates the Rosh Hashanah liturgy in its entirety. "All the World" just builds on that regal image. But like it or not, it is part of Jewish tradition, and I am, I suppose, stuck with it.

Rabbi Laura Geller, senior rabbi of Temple Emanuel of Beverly Hills, was one of the first women to be selected to lead a major metropolitan synagogue. She was twice named one of *Newsweek*'s 50 Most Influential Rabbis in America and was featured in the PBS documentary *Jewish Americans*. She is the author of many articles in books and journals, and was on the editorial board of *The Torah: A Women's Commentary*. She is a fellow of the Corporation of Brown University from where she graduated in 1971. Ordained by Hebrew Union College in 1976, she is the third woman in the Reform Movement to become a rabbi.

This triumphal assertion is the same theology we see in *Alenu*, which became a concluding prayer for every service by the fourteenth century, but was composed originally for the High Holy Day liturgy specifically, well over a millennium before. The message there too seems to be that Judaism will win out over all the other religious traditions in the world.

Apparently I am not the only one uncomfortable with *Alenu*. The multiple options for offering that prayer in our Reform Movement siddur, *Mishkan T'filah*, is an attempt to soften the triumphalism of Jewish uniqueness. But still, it is hard to know just what to make of *Alenu's* alternating messages of particularism and universalism.

The traditional version opens with a nod to universalism, "Let us now praise the sovereign of the universe," but quickly takes a particularistic turn as we "proclaim the greatness of the creator who has set us apart from the other families of the earth, giving us a destiny unique among the nations." It then reverts to universalism, acknowledging God as "the supreme sovereign, the Holy One of blessing" who "spread out the heavens and established the earth." Eventually, the prayer concludes, the entire world will be subject to God's sovereignty, idolatry will disappear, and the world will be perfected under the kingdom of God.

It is ironic that *tikkun olam*, the phrase that is widely used to signal universalism, originates here, as we pray that "the world be perfected [*l'taken olam*] under the rule of God, that all humanity invoke your name; turning all the wicked of the earth toward You." But the term means something quite different from the way it is used in contemporary Reform discourse. It doesn't mean "repairing the world *through social justice*." It means, instead, establishing the divine kingdom by eliminating any challenges to the exclusive sovereignty of God. *Our God.* It means rejecting the legitimacy of other religions, or at least those other religions that could be described as idolatrous. So it seems that particularism wins out.

Or does it? Rabbi Jill Jacobs argues that *Alenu* is universalistic, given its historical context. She cites its biblical inspiration in "the comparatively radical promise, in Isaiah 56:7, that '[God] will bring [the other nations] to my holy mountain and make them joyful in my house of prayer; their burnt offerings and their sacrifices shall be acceptable upon my altar, for my house shall be called a house of prayer for all peoples.'"

So which is it? Universal or particular? Does restoring the world to a perfected divine state entail that our way is adopted by everyone else, or do we really believe what Reform Judaism teaches: there is only one God, but there are many different paths that lead us to divinity.

This question is very personal for me. My close friend Sarah, raised as a nice Jewish girl from Long Island, has become a Buddhist. Not a Jewbu, a Jew who brings Buddhist teaching and spiritual practices into her Jewish religious life, but an actual Buddhist.

Sarah was always a sort of spiritual seeker. She was raised Jewish, celebrated Jewish holidays with family and friends, and went to synagogue for the High Holy Days. Her only child (at the time) became bar mitzvah in a Reform synagogue. I actually remember his *d'var torah*, which compared Judaism to a snowball, because the more it rolls down a mountain, the bigger it gets. He meant by that metaphor that each generation brings something new to Judaism, so Judaism gets stronger the longer it continues. He told us he was proud to carry on this tradition of his. Then, six months after his bar mitzvah, he was killed in an airplane crash on the way home from visiting his grandparents in Florida.

Sarah and her husband mourned for their child in the Jewish way, sought help in bereaved parents' groups, and met with a Jewish spiritual counselor who encouraged them to go on with their lives and adopt other children, which they did. Some years later, Sarah encountered Zen Buddhism when she visited a cousin on a Buddhist retreat. She began a practice of meditation and soon after became a regular member of a Zen *sanga* (community), spending most Sundays with that community and participating in regular long retreats. The *roshi* (teacher) of her Zen center is an important spiritual teacher for her, challenging her to continue deepening her spiritual life through meditation, learning, and service to the larger community. Recently, Sarah chose to publicly declare herself Buddhist through the precept-taking ceremony called *jukai*. *Jukai* means "receiving the precepts," passed down from teacher to student. In taking the precepts you not only formally become a Buddhist, but you also take on a Buddhist name and a new lineage that connects you through your teachers to the Buddha.

I too have learned a great deal from Buddhist teaching, through the Institute for Jewish Spirituality (IJS). I learned from my teachers there how to meditate. I discovered the power of silence as well as the power of intense prayer. I discovered a new way to imagine God through Hasidic texts that speak about divinity as the power that connects everything to everything else. Buddhism uses different metaphors, but when Sarah and

I talk about spirituality, it feels to me that we are talking about the same experience.

So why is Sarah's choice so hard for me? Sarah assures me she is still Jewish. She goes to a Passover seder. She lights Hanukkah candles and makes latkes. She doesn't think of Buddhism as a religion. And yet, just as a convert to Judaism would, Sarah has taken on a new name and a new lineage. While she remains, in her mind, culturally Jewish, the Jewish spiritual path is no longer her lineage.

Sarah's choice makes me sad. Everything Sarah has found in Buddhism is in Judaism, too. I notice that I often want to tell her that the insights she learns from her *roshi* are right there in Jewish texts; that meditation, chanting, movement, and mindfulness are also part of her Jewish heritage, as is her "Buddhist" accent on character refinement through traits like gratitude, forgiveness, and equanimity. But this is not about "telling" someone else to follow the Jewish path. Either you resonate with it or you don't.

The Jewish spiritual path never resonated for her. Part of what turned her off were the High Holy Day images of God as king and the triumphalism that undergirds the metaphor. For that and so many other reasons, she didn't find what she was looking for in Jewish prayer and study, and she never found the kind of community within Jewish circles that she discovered at her Zen center. That makes me sad. Some of my sadness is that someone like her, with her energy, passion, clarity, and mindfulness, could bring so much to our Jewish community. But the even deeper sadness is the truth that if Jews choose a non-Jewish spiritual path, that snowball her son described at his bar mitzvah will melt sometime in the future, and the particular unique Jewish lineage and path will someday disappear.

For me, the particular Jewish path—the longest ongoing book club in the world; the Jewish conversation over ancient and contemporary texts that transcends time, place, and language; and the values that emerge out of that conversation that challenge us to repair the world—is the way I access the universal. It is the treasure map that helps me discover the treasure.

I am not just an individual soul seeking enlightenment but also a person in relationship to other people—first my family, then my people, then the larger community and world. I learn how to love humanity by first loving particular people. The universal values that make a claim on me come from a particular place; I see the world through a particular lens, history, spiritual path, lineage, and culture. Sarah has discovered those universal values through a different particular lens. She is using a different map.

Universalism or particularism? Maybe that is not really the question. The question for me is what particular path leads us to the universal. On Rosh Hashanah we celebrate the creation of the world. But we don't read the story of creation; instead, we read the story of one family—our family, our lineage. We are reminded through the particularism of the prayer, the rituals, the teaching, and the spiritual practices of *t'shuvah*, *t'fillah*, and *tz'dakah* of the power of our particular path to the universal.

Sarah's journey is a challenge to me and to other synagogue leaders. It forces me to ask: what should we be doing to better help our communities discover the spiritual practices, the teachings, and the openness to divinity that will not only uncover what is universal but will also keep that snowball getting bigger?

ᏩᎳᎵᎧ

Laughing Islands, Dancing Prayer Books

Rabbi Edwin Goldberg, DHL

When I was young, I attended High Holy Day services with my family in Kansas City at The Temple. I remember always being happy at the end of the Rosh Hashanah service (or perhaps it was also on Shabbat) and not because the service was over. I felt joy because the closing song was so peppy. "All the World Shall Come to Serve Thee" we would sing, and in my juvenile mind, I always pictured dancing, twirling prayer books. The lasting memory was one of glee.

As I now know, "All the World Shall Come to Serve Thee" was a Jewish hymn composed by Abraham Binder based on a text by Israel Zangwill and itself was based on a medieval *piyyut* from the Rosh Hashanah liturgy, *V'ye'etayu*—"And Everyone Will Arrive ... to Present You with a Royal Crown."

> All the world shall come to serve Thee,
> And bless Thy glorious Name,
> And Thy righteousness triumphant
> The islands shall acclaim....

Rabbi Edwin Goldberg, DHL, serves as coordinator of the Central Conference of American Rabbis (CCAR) editorial committee on the forthcoming CCAR *machzor*. He has a doctorate in Hebrew letters from Hebrew Union College–Jewish Institute of Religion and is the senior rabbi at Temple Sholom of Chicago. He is author of *Saying No and Letting Go: Jewish Wisdom on Making Room for What Matters Most* (Jewish Lights). He contributed to *We Have Sinned: Sin and Confession in Judaism—Ashamnu and Al Chet* and *May God Remember: Memory and Memorializing in Judaism—Yizkor* (both Jewish Lights).

> With the coming of Thy kingdom
> The hills shall break into song,
> And the islands laugh exultant,
> That they to God belong.
> And all their congregations,
> So loud Thy praise shall sing,
> That the uttermost peoples hearing,
> Shall hail Thee crowned King.

Reviewing this song as an adult, I am struck most by the image of the laughing islands. Why do islands laugh? I assume that the reason the author of the *piyyut* liked the image was its reference to Isaiah 42, which speaks of islands—peoples, presumably, who heretofore have not followed the laws of civilized humanity—who now turn to acknowledging God. Acknowledging, yes; but why laughing? All I know is that I want to live in a world of laughing islands—and dancing prayer books!

The notion of the entire world coming together is a happy one, as long as we are uniting for a noble purpose. Those of us who enjoyed watching *Star Trek* on TV liked the idea of the world uniting to peacefully explore other planets. It is diagnostic of a scary and uncertain world that the new movie series of *Star Trek* depicts a far darker time. With nuclear and chemical weapons increasingly in our worry zone, the future of the world can seem pretty dark. In contrast, breezy and relaxing islands beckon us with an enticing invitation to relinquish our fears.

Back to those laughing islands, then. What is the source of the joy, of the laughter? Perhaps it is the laughter of absurdity! We cannot help but laugh at the recognition that we lowly humans—Jews no less—get to crown the creator and ruler of the universe.

What does this mean?

Rabbi Joseph B. Soloveitchik, as quoted in Rabbi Jonathan Sacks's recently published Rosh Hashanah *machzor*, used to tell the following story about his childhood in Chaslavitch:

> Our teacher, who was a Chabad Hasid, said to us: "Do you know what Rosh Hashana is? The Rebbe, the Tzemah Tzedek, would call the night of Rosh Hashana Karanatzia [Coronation Night]." Then he would ask the children, "Do you know whom we will be crowning?" Once I replied, "Czar Nicholas" [Nicholas II, the last emperor

of Russia]. The teacher responded: "Nicholas? He was crowned years ago. Why do we need to crown him again? Besides, he is not the real king. No, tonight, my dear children, we crown God.

"And do you know who places the crown on his head?" the teacher continued. "Yankel the tailor, Berel the shoemaker, Zalman the water-carrier, Yossel the painter, Dovid the butcher...."[1]

How wonderfully democratic is our vision of the world! The tailor, shoemaker, and butcher get to crown God, as it were. It is not just the rabbis and scholars who matter but the ordinary people as well. All get to crown God, not just the elite. In other words, we are important to God even as God is important to us.

The midrash quotes Isaiah:

> "You are my witnesses ... that I am God; before Me there was no God formed, neither shall there be any after Me" (Isaiah 43:10). Rabbi Shimon bar Yochai explains: "If you are my witnesses, then I am God, the first One, neither shall any be after Me. But if you are not my witnesses, I am not, as it were, God." (*Pesikta D'rav Kahana* 12:6)

God needs us, as we need God. The idea is radical and spiritual. It's also absurd. So we laugh and dance and celebrate that we live in a world where God is dependent upon us.

We live in an era when hope seems so difficult. Gone for many of us is the ease of believing automatically in a higher power, or at least one that can affect our lives and effect a better world. And yet, our Jewish heritage has always counseled at least "hoping for hope," not giving up on hope even when hope seems so difficult to maintain. Our world is far from a place where humanity works together for noble purposes. Nevertheless, the islands laugh and so should we, for in the long scheme of things, there is much to celebrate. If we are not yet where we have to be, at least we are moving in the right direction. Yes, millions go without enough food and medication, and violence continues to plague us. But continuing technological and medicinal breakthroughs can yet lead humanity toward light and righteousness, if we only practice the hope that allows us to do our part in this effort.

In a world where it is hard to believe in God altogether, much less a God who is some sort of regal ruler, what does it mean to crown God king? I choose a metaphorical path toward hope: we crown God not the way our ancestors must have imagined it—by bowing down as if declaring, "We are not worthy." We crown God when we insist on honoring the highest values that we would associate with God. We choose God when we practice kindness, act with compassion, and fight against injustice. Rosh Hashanah, then, becomes God's day when we recognize we are responsible for making the world a better place.

Back in the days before the Civil War, some visitors from the North were watching a company of slaves in New Orleans shuffling wearily along the dock. One of them, in striking contrast with the others, held his head erect and, with an unbroken spirit, strode among the others with the dignified bearing of a conqueror.

Someone asked, "Who is he? Is he the straw boss or the owner of the slaves?"

"No," came the answer. "That fellow can't get it out of his head that he is the son of a king!"

And so he was. He had been caught and dragged into slavery as a small child but had already been taught that he was no ordinary person: he was the son of a king. And now, after half a lifetime of hardship and abuse that had broken the spirit of others, he was still the son of a king!

The tragedy of our lives is not that we think too much of ourselves but that we grow up thinking too little. If we knew who we really were, we would not waste so much time pursuing concerns of little consequence. We would not degrade ourselves with misplaced ambitions and unworthy actions. We would not shrink back from nobility on the grounds that we are too paltry to matter. We would not be afraid of hope.

The midrash envisions the angels asking, "When is Rosh Hashanah? When does the New Year begin?" The answer is not found on the calendar but in our deeds: when we recognize the humanity and the divinity within every human being and act accordingly.

In many ways, Reform Judaism has moved beyond "All the World Shall Come to Serve Thee"—that is, we rarely sing English hymns anymore, and the classical English of the poem is not what we are used to. But the message of this old standby remains important: Jews of all stripes would do well to remember that we are here to make the world a better place. We serve God by daring still to hope for a world that will get better, because we believe we are descendants of God, the One our tradition calls the king of kings, and therefore able to make a difference.

Another "King," Martin Luther King Jr., once declared, "The arc of history moves slowly, but it bends toward justice." Our task, in partnership with God, is to bend it toward justice, to hope that our mission will succeed, and then (like the islands) to rejoice that we ordinary human beings have a mission that is so sacred.

"All the World" may not be sung as often as it was, but its message could not be more timely. So I say, "Let the prayer books dance and the islands laugh, for we are summoned to holiness. We are important to God, and the world needs us now more than ever."

ᏟᎾᏘᎭᎧ

"One True Religion" or "Any Number Can Play"?

Dr. Joel M. Hoffman

What would it actually look like for the entire world to serve the Jewish God? And would everyone have to be Jewish to do it?

There's a simple answer, which strikes me as both obvious and wrong: the only way to serve God is by doing what Jews do. Then, if serving God means practicing Judaism to the exclusion of other religions, the conversation about whether only Jews can do it comes down to details of what it means to be Jewish. But this approach—call it colloquially the "One True Religion" answer—offers a pretty narrow understanding of serving God.

At the other extreme is another simplistic answer, which we might call "Any Number Can Play." It asserts that Judaism is no better and no worse than any other religion.

Dr. Joel M. Hoffman lectures around the globe on popular and scholarly topics spanning history, Hebrew, prayer, and Jewish continuity. He has served on the faculties of Brandeis University in Waltham, Massachusetts, and Hebrew Union College–Jewish Institute of Religion in New York. He is author of *And God Said: How Translations Conceal the Bible's Original Meaning* and *In the Beginning: A Short History of the Hebrew Language*, and has written for the international *Jerusalem Post*. He contributed to all ten volumes of the *My People's Prayer Book: Traditional Prayers, Modern Commentaries* series, winner of the National Jewish Book Award; to *My People's Passover Haggadah: Traditional Texts, Modern Commentaries*; and to *Who by Fire, Who by Water*—Un'taneh Tokef, *We Have Sinned: Sin and Confession in Judaism*—Ashamnu *and* Al Chet, and *May God Remember: Memory and Memorializing in Judaism*—Yizkor (all Jewish Lights).

Between One True Religion and Any Number Can Play, though, I find a nuanced approach that distinguishes between what God wants and the way we achieve it.

By analogy, we might consider traffic laws. Drivers in the United States keep to the right, while drivers in the United Kingdom do the opposite. The "One True Religion" of driving would assert that only the United States or the United Kingdom system is valid, so either Americans or Brits should immediately start driving on the other side of the road. The "Any Number Can Play" theory would see no advantage to either system and let people drive on whichever side of the road pleases them. But neither of these naive responses captures the purpose of having a preferred side of the road on which to drive: we don't want people crashing into each other.

Similarly, simply to ask whether everyone should or should not practice Judaism is to skip over the fundamental question of why we have Judaism. And here I think a powerful and surprising answer presents itself.

Monotheism was only one of the Jews' inventions three thousand years ago, as they built the great Temple, implemented sacrifice, prescribed religious observances, and otherwise set about creating Judaism. Another was the alphabet, which made widespread literacy possible (and which may even have made the preservation of Judaism possible). A third was the Sabbath, a predecessor of the weekend.

But for me, a fourth invention really lies at the core of Judaism, and that is the unwavering belief that every human has inherent equal value. This is why most of the Torah's laws of behavior apply to everyone.

Leviticus 19:15 specifically demands that neither the rich nor the poor be granted favoritism, just as Numbers 35:31 denies the rich any possibility of buying their way out of a death sentence. Even "slaves" were paid and eventually freed. And everyone, from the loftiest tribal elders down to the lowliest menial servants, gathered as equals (in Deuteronomy 29) to enter God's covenant.

Similarly, the poor were given food and otherwise looked after, as (for example) in Leviticus 19:9–10, which demands that farmers leave the corners of their fields unharvested and that vintners leave some grapes on the vine, so that the poor will have food and drink.

And the Ten Commandments boldly assert that it is simply wrong to harm one's fellow, a sentiment that is repeated and reinforced often in the Torah.

Many of these Jewish innovations are now deeply ingrained in modern Western civilization. Even the president of the United States is subject to its laws (which is why President Nixon could be removed from office), just as even the wealthiest U.S. citizens are not permitted to murder (which is why bribery is illegal). Yet in many parts of the world—much of South America, large swaths of the Middle and Far East, and nearly all of Africa—the rich and powerful do as they please, knowing that they are exempt from the laws that govern less prosperous people.

In those decidedly non-Jewish nations, the rich are the masters, doing what they want and taking what they want, while the poor function substantially like other property that the rich own. One way to express that multitiered legal and moral system is to say that the poor serve the rich.

And one way to express its Jewish antithesis, the Jewish insistence on equality, is to say that everyone serves God.

In this respect, serving God has very little to do with what service actually looks like, and has everything to do with who does it, namely, everyone.

This kind of equality has a direct benefit, an indirect benefit, a vision, and a promise.

The direct benefit is that everyone is treated with dignity during their time here on earth. Everyone born into the legacy of equality knows that they will share in life's bounty and joy.

The indirect benefit is that more people are available to augment that very bounty and joy. To see how, we might consider a poor person who has a really good idea about how to make more food. In cultures that categorize people into strict castes or that otherwise limit human advancement, the poor person's idea will never be noticed by society, much less implemented, and no one will benefit from it. By contrast, in a culture of equality, the poor person's idea will help everyone thrive. Or to look at things the other way around, societies better succeed when they are better able to take advantage of all of their members' potential.

And this brings us to the vision: Taken by itself, it is neither inherently positive nor inherently negative to let everyone shape society, because people might in principle exert their influence for the better or for the worse. The vision is that people will rise to the occasion and work for the betterment of God's world. The vision is that people will behave righteously.

And this is where the promise comes into play: The promise is to help people become their better selves, primarily by educating them about what is right and wrong. We know that two-year-olds will hit each other as they try to get what they want. But we recognize our obligation to teach them not to keep acting that way as they grow older.

The more we keep the promise, the more the dream succeeds and, with it, the more people and the society in which they live prosper, all of which is to say that everyone is better off when everyone serves God.

6∞9

Crowning "the Un-king" King

Rabbi Elie Kaunfer, DHL

We often think of Rosh Hashanah as the Day of Judgment, a solemn undertaking suffused with repentance and introspection. But another side to Rosh Hashanah is evident in the poems and texts of the third blessing of the *Amidah*: on Rosh Hashanah, God is crowned king.

This itself is a radical theological notion. After all, God—the eternal ruler of the universe—should not need to be given a crown. And yet, that is exactly what we emphasize in the poem *V'ye'etayu* when we proclaim, in the last stanza, "They will present You with a royal crown." In some melodies, this phrase is recited repeatedly, thus emphasizing the coronation image even more acutely.

The concept of crowning God is based on the midrashic notion that in order to be ruler, God actually needs people to rule over. In the words of *Pirkei D'rabbi Eliezer*, "Master of the universe: If there is no army for the king, and no camp for the king, over what is he king?"[1] Rosh Hashanah is the day in which this crowning happens, because it is the anniversary of the creation of humans. On that day, according to the Talmud, God began to rule.[2] It therefore makes sense that on Rosh Hashanah we yearn for the day in which all of humanity proclaims God to be king.

Rabbi Elie Kaunfer, DHL, is cofounder and executive director of Mechon Hadar (www.mechonhadar.org). He holds a doctorate in liturgy and is the author of *Empowered Judaism: What Independent Minyanim Can Teach Us about Building Vibrant Jewish Communities.* He is a contributor to *Who by Fire, Who by Water*—Un'taneh Tokef, *All These Vows*—Kol Nidre, and *We Have Sinned: Sin and Confession in Judaism*—Ashamnu *and* Al Chet (all Jewish Lights). *Newsweek* named him one of fifty top rabbis in America.

Like most messianic hopes in Judaism, this one, too, is a desire to return to an original state. Adam, not Abraham, was the first to call God king.[3] And, indeed, in *V'ye'etayu*, we refer to God's kingship over *all* creatures no less than four times—and an additional two times in the stanzas of *U'v'khen* that come immediately before. On Rosh Hashanah, we pray for God's kingship to be restored "over all his creatures" (*al kol ma'asekha*).

Yet many contemporary worshipers chafe at the metaphor of God as king. The image of a king simply doesn't inspire religious feelings in them. Especially in American culture, where kings symbolize the ruler against whom we collectively rebelled, the metaphor meets with much resistance. It is not unusual to hear the protest, "If God is a king, with all the implications of that word, then count me out."

The irony is that the authors of the liturgy were similarly turned off by the image of a king. The Rabbis, over and over again, set up a clear distinction between a "flesh and blood" king and the kingship of God. In short, God, the supreme king, is the *opposite* of everything we know about kings. If you don't like kings, you are in good company. The God of Rabbinic literature is the "un-king" king.

Let's investigate a few examples of this phenomenon in Rabbinic midrash.

A King Who Hears All

"One who hears prayer—all flesh shall come to You" (Psalm 65:3).

... A flesh-and-blood king can hear two or three people, but not all of them. God is not so. Rather—all pray, and God hears their prayer as one.

A flesh-and-blood person: his ears are filled from hearing and his eyes are filled from seeing. But God's eyes are not filled and ears are not filled. This is the meaning of "hears prayer." (*Midrash T'hillim* 65:2, ed. Buber, p. 156b)

God is the ultimate listener. It is never possible to overwhelm God with too many people attempting to form a relationship simultaneously. Imagine a ruler who had infinite capacity to connect one-on-one with everyone who wanted to speak with him. This is the opposite of our notion of king, who is cloistered, protected, and, being human, unable to engage with throngs of people individually at once.

A King Who Does Not Discriminate

> A king of flesh and blood: if a person disfigured with a burn mark or a person who is poor asks after the king's welfare, the king considers it a degradation and does not respond.
>
> But God is not so. All are accepted by God, who says, "Praise me! It is pleasing [*tov*] to Me." As it says: "It is good [*tov*] to sing to our God" (Psalm 147:1). (*Midrash T'hillim* 147:2, ed. Buber, p. 269a)

Not only does God distinguish God's kingship by listening to multiple people at once, but also God does not make distinctions based on outward appearances. A human king is defined by the people he interacts with. It is inconceivable that poor people would have a regular audience with a king. But God is the un-king: all people, regardless of their physical appearance or social status, can connect with God.

Humans Influence Royal Decrees

> It is the way of the world that a flesh-and-blood king makes a decree; if his underlings want to cancel it, they cannot; willingly or unwillingly, they uphold the decrees of the king. But the king: if he wants to uphold it, it is upheld; if he wants to cancel it, it is canceled.
>
> God is not so: Whatever his Sanhedrin below declares, God upholds.
>
> When? On Rosh Hashanah. When the Sanhedrin sits and says, "We declare Rosh Hashanah to be on Monday or Tuesday," immediately God convenes the upper Sanhedrin of ministering angels and says to them, "Go down and see what decree the lower court has agreed upon." [In antiquity, prior to the dissemination of an accurate mathematically based calendar, the days when Rosh Hashanah fell had to be declared each year, based on witnesses who

observed the actual occurrence of the new moon. Here, the court is assumed to have declared it to be a Monday or Tuesday, for example.]

They respond, "Master of the universe: they concluded that Rosh Hashanah should be on such and such a day." Immediately God sits in judgment on his world.

This is quite an astonishing contrast to the royal law of making a human monarch. In actual earthy palaces, a king's ministers cannot alter laws; only kings can. But God works the opposite way: God consults with the "lower court" before making a decree about when the Day of Judgment will take place.

A King Who Has No Need of Royal Trappings

"Who is the king of glory?" (Psalm 24:10a). The One who gives glory to those who fear Him, namely, *Adonai tz'va'ot* (Psalm 24:10b).

How?

With a flesh-and-blood king, others cannot sit on his throne. But God sat King Solomon on his throne, as it says: "Solomon sat on the throne of Adonai" (1 Chronicles 29:23).

With a flesh-and-blood king, others cannot ride his chariot. But God caused Elijah to ride his horse—since storms and whirlwinds are his horse. As it says: "The way of Adonai is in the whirlwind and the storm" (Nahum 1:3); and it says: "Elijah rose in the storm" (2 Kings 2:11).

With a flesh-and-blood king, others cannot use his scepter. But Moses used the scepter of God, as it says: "Moses took the staff of God in his hand" (Exodus 4:20).

With a flesh-and-blood king, others do not wear his crown. But God gives his crown to the anointed king (messiah). God's crown is gold, as it says: "His head is as the most fine gold" (Song of Songs 5:11); and it is written: "You set a crown of fine gold on his head" (Psalm 21:4).

With a flesh-and-blood king, others do not wear his clothing. But Israel wore the clothing of God, as it says: "God gave Israel strength" (Psalm 29:11).

A flesh-and-blood king is not called by his name, like Caesar Augustus Basileus. And if a person calls him by one of those names, his life is forfeit. But God said to Moses: I made you as I am to Pharaoh ... as it is written: "Behold I have made you like a God to Pharaoh" (Exodus 7:1).

This is a king who shares his glory with those who fear Him. (*Yalkut Shimoni* to Psalms, #700)

This is perhaps the most daring text of all. Here, all the physical trappings of kingship—throne, scepter, crown, clothing, title—are not exclusive to the true king. On the contrary, God uses those symbols of power to build connection and relationship, as opposed to creating distance and otherness. The king we are meant to pray to is the king who recognizes the limitations of symbols of power and has no use for them.

Perhaps the most familiar use of royal imagery comes in the well-known *Avinu Malkenu* ("Our father, our king")—an odd mix of metaphor (cf. Talmud, Ta'anit 25b). It has always struck me as odd to combine these two descriptions. There is nothing so distancing as a king and nothing more personal than a father. How is it possible to have the relationship of both father and king with the same person? Only the distinctively Rabbinic understanding of God's kingship clarifies this apparent metaphoric mismatch. As divine king, God is the opposite of our associations of an earthly king, and, therefore, very much like a parent, who has deep emotional connections and a desire to build relationship.

It is perhaps only in this light that we can imagine a world in which all peoples on earth recognize God as the true (un-)king.

෴

They Are Us: *Uv'khen* and *T'shuvah*

Rabbi Noa Kushner

The three paragraphs of *Uv'khen* read like a religious power fantasy written by people with big dreams but little or no power to achieve them. Why? Because the theme of *Uv'khen*—a worldwide acknowledgment and fear of our God—betrays the fact that this universal agreement was not the case. Otherwise, why write the prayer? If we had been powerful enough to dominate the religious marketplace, the prayer would have been unnecessary. *Uv'khen* is a prayer that aspires to total unanimity in world belief, a goal that would make any fund-raiser proud: it demands nothing less than 100 percent participation.

To consider *Uv'khen* only a prayer for religious popularity, however, is to sell the prayer short. While there is undoubtedly an emphasis on humanity "collected together as one," this solidarity is a means "to do [God's] will with a whole heart." Yes, we pray that our God will have top billing, but only to bring righteousness to the world.

When this revolution occurs, not only will the upright rejoice, but "injustice will shut its mouth." Goodness will be so universally self-evident that wickedness, without a single place in which to take root, "will vanish like smoke."

Therefore, while our first impression of *Uv'khen* is that it seeks our God's world domination, as we look further we see that its actual theme is a desire for good to flourish—universally, unquestionably,

---

Rabbi Noa Kushner is founding rabbi of The Kitchen. One part indie Shabbat community, one part San Francisco experiment, and one part tool kit for DIY Jewish practice, The Kitchen works to build a new resonant approach to religious life. She contributed to *Who by Fire, Who by Water—Un'taneh Tokef, All These Vows—Kol Nidre*, and *We Have Sinned: Sin and Confession in Judaism—Ashamnu and Al Chet* (all Jewish Lights).

and completely. It is a vision of worldwide *tz'dakah* and *chesed*—
"righteousness" and "loving-kindness." We might disagree with the non-
pluralistic language and prefer a formula that admits to the validity of all
the world's great religions, but it is hard to argue with the prayer's final
goal of universal goodness.

Most of the liturgy specific to the High Holy Days—the confessions, for example—are personal pleas (albeit framed in communal
terms). "We have sinned" means that *each* of us has sinned. To be sure, we
apologize *together* for these individual transgressions, but we do not mean
to say that we have sinned collectively as a community (even though that
may also be true). The High Holy Days, therefore, play a neat liturgical
trick: it is arguably the most communal day of the year (certainly more
people show up than at any other time) but also the most personal. In
the large community setting, many people go through moments of deep
personal introspection.

By contrast, in *Uv'khen*, as in much of the general *Amidah* (the
larger unit in which *Uv'khen* is inserted), we speak completely collectively. What does it mean, in the context of our personal High Holy Day
introspections, for us to now pray for the goodness of the whole world?

Could it be that *Uv'khen*, a part of the service that is often mumbled
or rushed through without comment, was written to help us understand
that our personal *t'shuvah* is only a part of a larger, more epic project? That
recovering our *sh'lichut* (our "agency" as playing a God-given role on this
earth) is only the beginning? In other words, how would it change our
grasp of the hard slog of *t'shuvah*—of looking within, admitting where
we went wrong, and approaching others and God to make it right—if we
believed that this personal work came with ultimate significance, not just
for our own lives but also for humanity?

Uv'khen offers just this larger context for our High Holy Day soul
searching. Not only do we need to make *t'shuvah* to repair a dysfunctional
relationship with another person or to change a destructive habit within
ourselves, but we also need to make *t'shuvah* to carry "God's will with a
whole heart" into the world. Without our individual acts of *t'shuvah*, how
else will righteousness ever triumph over injustice?

With this reading, it seems reasonable to reconsider the identity of
the "others" addressed in the beginning of the prayer: the ones who would
do well to place fear of God front and center, the ones who could stand
to brush up on their worship skills. They are neither heathens practicing

other religions nor recalcitrant infidels; they are us. The many uses of the word *kol,* "all," in the prayer refer us back to ourselves.

"Instill fear of You in *all* of your creatures, dread in *all* that You have made, so your works will revere You, and *all* that You have made will bow down before You." Fear, awe, and reverence are essential to engage in serious *t'shuvah,* and so to bring righteousness to the world.

In the beginning, we read this prayer as a plea to God to make outsiders see things our way. Now we understand that it puts the burden on us, on our acts of *t'shuvah,* to make a world where righteousness can flourish. Seen in this light, our *t'shuvah* is nothing less than a battle for the universal good of the world; the stakes are higher than simply our own well-being.

"Your hand [is] strong and your grasp mighty." The image of the divine hand is clearly metaphoric, but there is no doubt that God needs our very real human hands to realize the dream of greater righteousness. *T'shuvah* is but one of many ways we bring the "hands" of God, the mighty grasp, to life and to the world.

Likewise, while our hands can help bring righteousness, our hands can also destroy. If we seek a day when "injustice will have nothing more to say, no voice," and if we recognize that it is our personal actions—our hands, our *t'shuvah,* our words—that will bring this day, then we must also acknowledge that it is our failings that help hold this day back. If the rule of arrogance and malice is to be swept from the earth, then the *Uv'khen* reminds us that not only will we have to help do the sweeping, but we will also have to rid ourselves of our own arrogance and malice.

The world's problems can seem far beyond our abilities to create solutions. But *Uv'khen* insists that we have more power than we think. There exists an unbreakable connection between our personal lives and the state of the world. Peace does not mean converting others to our way of seeing things. It means converting our own personal *t'shuvah* into a communal effort to bring greater goodness for all. That is the messianic day that *Uv'khen* dares us to hope for, the day when "God will be one and God's name will be one."

○∭∞

Iftar in the Synagogue

JEWISH-MUSLIM RELATIONS, FROM THE PAGES OF THE *MACHZOR*

Rabbi Asher Lopatin

For many years, my synagogue, Anshe Sholom, celebrated with the Muslim community in Chicago during their Ramadan month of fasting by hosting one of the nightly break-fast meals called the *Iftar*. *Iftar* is from the same root as *haftarah* and *maftir*, meaning "end" or "conclude."

"*Iftar* in the Synagogue" became a regularized time when Orthodox observant Jews could join Muslims engaged in their Islamic rituals. We even had a Jewish afternoon service (*Minchah*) in the sanctuary, followed by Muslim *Salat*, which needed to be in the gym so that worshipers could have room to bow on the floor; the food after the services, of course, was both kosher and halal. For some years, Ramadan coincided with the Jewish month of Tishrei, but whether it fell around the High Holy Days or not, I believe "*Iftar* in the Synagogue" was inspired directly by the vision of the High Holy Day *machzor*, especially *Uv'khen*, which comes within the *K'dushah*, the third blessing of the *Amidah,* which celebrates God's sanctity. The *K'dushah* proclaims a time when, ultimately, God will rule "on Mount Zion, the abode of your [God's] majesty, and in Jerusalem,

Rabbi Asher Lopatin is the president of Yeshivat Chovevei Torah Rabbinical School, an Orthodox rabbinical school that teaches an inclusive, open, and inquisitive Torah. He is the former rabbi of Anshe Sholom B'nai Israel Congregation, a modern Orthodox synagogue in Chicago, and is a founding rabbi of the multidenominational Chicago Jewish Day School. He contributed to *Who by Fire, Who by Water—Un'taneh Tokef* (Jewish Lights).

your [God's] holy city." This bold assertion symbolizes our faith in God's holiness, which encompasses all the world. "Blessed are You," we say, as the blessing concludes, "the holy king" (*hamelekh hakadosh*).

On the High Holy Days, as on other days, this liturgical proclamation of God's holiness focuses on God from the perspective of Jewish tradition, specifically. But the High Holy Day version differs, because it quickly lifts us above Jewish particularism and takes us on a beautiful poetic journey across the world and universe to teach us that *all* of God's creations, not just ourselves, sing God's praises and sanctify God's holy name. The trip begins with *V'khol Ma'aminim* ("Everyone Believes")— not just Jews, that is, but potentially, and sometimes even actually, the entire world realizes God's greatness. The blessing of God's holiness then expands into a universal version beginning with several *Uv'khen*s, "And so ...," which imagine all creatures bowing in awe before God. Yet these same paragraphs swing back to Israel—the people and the Land—and to the Holy City of Jerusalem, calling for God to make them respected and blessed. So we have a movement back and forth from particular to universal and back again to particular, but ending with the recognition that God is holy, beyond any particular people or place.

It is this dance, from particular to universal and back again, that inspired Anshe Sholom to have "*Iftar* in the Synagogue" and that sets a blueprint for Jews and Muslims—and any diverse communities—to share each other's joyous moments and rich cultures, while maintaining their individual identities, and actually growing in the understanding of what makes them special and unique.

We grow as a people precisely through this pattern of *Uv'khen*: We first look in at our own particular relationship with God and the world; we then look out at the world to see how God is everywhere; we then look back in again with even greater comprehension of our own uniqueness.

The great nineteenth-century thinker and halakhic authority Rav Naftali Tzvi Yehuda Berlin, who was sequestered for most of his life as the leader of the Lithuanian yeshivah of Volozyn, wrote constantly about the importance of looking at the wisdom of those outside of the tradition of Torah, in order to understand the Torah itself. Without a universal outlook—without "Everyone believes"—the Jewish People will never be able to decipher the Torah that was given to us in its entirety on Mount Sinai. How paradoxical! To fully comprehend God's revelation to the Jewish People in particular, it is necessary to see God's connection to others. So for us to grasp even the slightest sense of God's holiness, it cannot be only about Jerusalem, the Holy Land of Israel, or even the entire people of Israel; we need to bring the world that God created into the conversation.

On the one hand, then, the particularist relationship we have with God depends on our openness to the universal presence of God among all peoples; on the other hand, however, the High Holy Day message of the creation of the universe and of all humankind will get lost if we forget who we, in particular, are.

One of the amazing things about the *Iftar* was that it attracted more than just the "regulars" in our community—those who came to synagogue as a matter of course. Among the attendees were people who rarely came at all, people who were not even traditionally observant. This was a chance to meet Muslims and see them doing the *Salat*. By witnessing the pride they felt in their own traditions, we could better appreciate our own passion for Judaism; it was this heightened respect that each of us felt for our own faiths and practices that enabled us to come together in such a spirited way. In other words, it was a commitment to internal Judaism— to the holiness of Zion, the Land, the Jewish People, and the Torah—that enabled us and our synagogue to open up and welcome Muslims fasting on Ramadan and then to share our kosher and halal meals together. Jews we rarely saw otherwise were attracted to the event—and to the Jewish *Minchah* service and a discussion of Jewish ritual—because it celebrated the universal God, who is worshiped and sanctified by Muslims and Jews alike.

The prayers of the High Holy Days, in their back and forth between an inner and an outer focus, describe perfectly the layers of that shared *Iftar* moment in the synagogue, where the universal and the particular mixed so beautifully together. Muslims could help Jews understand the beauty of their own rituals, because they were already so deeply committed to them. Similarly, from the Jewish perspective, our own pride in Jewish ritual—*Minchah,* the *Birkat Hamazon* (the prayer after the meal), and the synagogue itself—gave us the confidence to reach outside and celebrate with the others the fact of our own uniqueness, so essential to God's creation.

Even the modern State of Israel fulfills some of this vision of the High Holy Day prayers. On the one hand, the return of the Jewish People to our land and the establishment of a Jewish state upon it is the height of particularism, celebrated in the prayers that God is made holy by returning with the Jewish People to Zion. On the other hand, since its inception, the State of Israel and its citizens have strived to help the outside world in many ways: agriculturally, through agrarian consultation in third-world nations; technologically, through innovative breakthroughs in medicine, computers, and even software that gets us to work without traffic (Waze); and culturally, especially in the Israeli movie industry, which struggles with issues of Jew and Arab inhabiting the same land. Israel at its best is a celebration of particularistic Judaism, while understanding that Zion, Jerusalem, and the Holy Land lack meaning if our very particularism is unconnected with the world beyond—if, that is, we do not make a difference in the world while, at the same time, learning from the world how to make Israel a better place.

So let us celebrate on the High Holy Days a holy God who pushes us to be passionate about who we are, to be committed to the Torah of Israel and to the destiny of the Jewish People; but at the same time, a God who is made holy by the entire world and an Israel that shines and understands itself best by looking outward and making the universal an inherent part of what Judaism and the Torah are about.

Words—especially words of prayer—are powerful, but if they are to come to life, we must put them into action. We are called upon, then, especially as we rise from prayer on Rosh Hashanah and Yom Kippur, to move back and forth between the particular and the universal in our lives. The vision of the High Holy Day *machzor* requires them both.

⟨ᴍᴍᴑ⟩

The Acidic Masters

Catherine Madsen

"This I shall do by printing in the infernal method, by
corrosives."
—WILLIAM BLAKE, "THE MARRIAGE OF HEAVEN AND HELL"

In my family, thinking never meant systematic rational consideration
with an exam at the end. We were readers and writers and storytellers;
for us thinking meant finding a new book, going off the rails about it for a
while, carrying its central idea around protectively and a little desperately
like a dog with a new squeak toy. What that meant for me religiously as
I grew up (and we didn't practice religion then, but we couldn't leave it
alone in art and music and poetry) was that I could find my religion for
myself: first a solitary and improvised paganism, then Christianity (my
family's default), and then a semi-organized neopaganism that I labored
to take seriously. But I was never quite in search of religion as most people
understood it; I was in search of the intellectual mainspring of my life.
I didn't quite want security, which seems to be what many people want
from religion—a like-minded social group, a shared cosmological myth,
and an airtight moral system. I wanted the wound to the conscience.

I got it on Christmas Eve of 1983 from Cynthia Ozick. As the
most intelligent and intransigent voice in Susannah Heschel's anthology
On Being a Jewish Feminist—which I took up that evening in search of

---

Catherine Madsen is the author of *The Bones Reassemble: Reconstituting
Liturgical Speech; In Medias Res: Liturgy for the Estranged*; and a novel, *A
Portable Egypt*. She is librettist for Robert Stern's oratorio "Shofar" (on
the CD *Awakenings*, Navona Records NV5878), and bibliographer at the
Yiddish Book Center. She contributed to *Who by Fire, Who by Water*—
Un'taneh Tokef, *All These Vows*—Kol Nidre, *We Have Sinned: Sin and
Confession in Judaism*—Ashamnu *and* Al Chet, and *May God Remember:
Memory and Memorializing in Judaism*—Yizkor (all Jewish Lights).

something non-Christian to read—Ozick spoke commandingly. In the essay "Notes Toward Finding the Right Question" she shot to pieces all the feminist assumptions about God-language that were in the air at the time. I had already read some of her stories, starting with "The Pagan Rabbi," and knew her formidable skill at backing the reader into a corner. She presented Jewish existence at its most uncompromising and least attractive, and then insisted that for Jews there was no escape from it. She left the non-Jew no moral ground to stand on, and then mocked at converts—Lucy in "Levitation," who misses Jesus, and from whom the room goes spinning away as her husband and their Jewish guests listen to a refugee's tale of a Nazi massacre, while she thinks pitilessly how morbid they are and daydreams of a chthonic pagan dance.

I thought Ozick was wrong about paganism—my own was the austere northern variety, not Lucy's orgiastic Mediterranean one; I thought she was wrong about converts; I knew female God-language didn't always imply polytheism and fertility rites; but none of that mattered, because she could write all the other contributors under the table. When I went on to read her essays in *Art and Ardor* I thought she was wrong about the idolatrous nature of the imagination, and that didn't matter either. Who was I, after all, to say she was wrong? At thirteen, obsessed with *The Lord of the Rings*, I had read Tolkien's essay "On Fairy-Stories" and discovered his notion of storytelling as sub-creation, something we do as a by-product of being made in the image of God. That had made sense to me, but who was I to dispute Ozick's severe Jewish formula with an expansive and forgiving Catholic one? Who was I to suppose that my own innocent, protected post-Protestant upbringing entitled me to an opinion? Behind Ozick's relentless logic and accusatory tone lay centuries of pain, which had erupted into a terrible convulsion just before my life began. Reading her I felt the shattering anguish of being a Christian, or even a pagan, in relation to Jews.

One can't write—from a midwestern zip code, no less—to a crabbed and complex and highly ironized writer, pleading "But what is a goy of conscience to *do*?" Instead I went off the rails about Jewish thought: the imperatives of Levinas, the intellectual high-wire act of Allen Mandelbaum's *Chelmaxioms*, Lionel Trilling's criticism, Canetti's aphorisms, Leonard Baskin's prints. Doubtless it was the mistake of the autodidact to fall in love with a kind of undifferentiated Jewishness, so that Ozick, Harold Bloom, Primo Levi, Edmond Jabès, Walter Kaufmann,

Leo Baeck, Leo Steinberg, Milton Steinberg, George Steiner, and for a while even Michael Lerner—whose first book *Surplus Powerlessness* finished the job Walter Kaufmann had started with his inelegant term "humbition" and pried me loose from my dead-end library job—all sang to the same frequency. There was a flavor, a *tam*: it was like learning to pick out the taste of turmeric or cilantro in Indian food. I quit my job, left the Midwest, went to graduate school, converted to Judaism, had an abortive career as an adjunct writing instructor, and finally landed in a Sisyphean job at the Yiddish Book Center, all because there is a critical difference between the potential and the actual, because what matters is not our beliefs but our deeds, because I had learned the word *hineni*.

Judaism can exert a powerful attraction on the autodidact; its traditions of bookishness, open-ended debate, multilingual punning, and the mortal necessity of honing your intelligence to the sharpest possible edge all hold a strong appeal for the isolated and lonely mind. I was drawn to the notion of *hevdelim*, distinctions, in a world that seemed to encourage elisions and reconciliations. I was drawn to the tradition of Talmudic debate, in which all the opinions were saved for future reference and no one was burned at the stake. Headiest of all was the thought of Judaism as a form of refusal: the rejection of idols, the (eventual) disillusion with ideologies, the persistent No—which Emily Dickinson once called "the wildest word we consign to language"—to every system of easy affirmation the world could devise. Of course these habits of thought can serve as templates outside the Jewish sphere—the "hermeneutic of suspicion" now in general academic use is one instance—but I wanted to go straight to the source, where you could have all that *and* the Psalms. Judaism, Jewishness, Jewish history, was both a vessel of religious ardor and a vaccine against self-deception.

But it's easy to make the other mistake of the autodidact, to think anyone else will care about these matters in quite the same way. One can't assume that people brought up in a tradition—even its institutional leaders—will necessarily be excited by its most demanding strains of thought, or have any enthusiasm, even as People of the Book, for intellectual heavy lifting. Having converted, where was I actually to find the things that had drawn me with such compulsion? Had I found them already, to the extent that they were findable? Were the particularities that drew me—so unmistakably Jewish to my newly sensitized radar—simply unremarkable and unimportant in Jewish daily life? Was it only the *apikorsim* who, in their flight from orthodoxy and into the university, had presented Jewish habits of thought so compellingly, by sneaking them into art and anthropology and philosophy and psychology and lit. crit.?

Orthodoxy, at least from my vantage point, seemed to be consumed with the details of practice to the neglect of thought, maybe especially where women were concerned (unless you were Nechama Leibowitz or Avivah Zornberg). Liberal Jewish "educators," as they called themselves, didn't do well with habits of thought either—not in their official statements, at any rate—preoccupied as they were with devising ploys and expedients to keep marginal Jews from wandering away. (Christianity, I observed, devotes endless energy to bringing people in; Judaism is always desperate to keep them from getting out. Why? How far can they go?) I went on to make transforming friendships with very intelligent and very honest and very good people, but I have found no shortage of self-deception in Jewish life; perhaps I deceived myself in thinking I could most honor it by joining it. I'm not sure how well I have been able to honor it from the inside: what began as a moral pressure, and had consequence, has ended mainly as a time pressure.

In a sense—though, God knows, only in a sense—modernity made everyone Jewish: mobile, insecure, critical and self-critical. A *shiksa luftmensch* with a wounded conscience and a helpless attraction to davvening can fit into the liberal Jewish scene fairly easily. Yet it's clearly a very different thing to be a conscript in the struggle with God than to be desperate to join it. Learning to davven after reading Ozick and Steiner and Levinas, in shame and aspiration and longing, is nothing like being dropped off at Hebrew school week after week to be thoroughly bored, or having Buber and Heschel dangled in front of you as bait with the inevitable nice Jewish boy or girl on the other end. For me Judaism is an allegiance, chosen as an adult with what I hoped was my full intellectual force; for born Jews it's often a puzzling inheritance, forced on them as a familial duty with one hand while being withheld as intellectual sustenance with the other. No wonder born Jews in America so often define Jewishness by food and stand-up comedy and movies and graphic novels—all those particulars that bind people together through familiarity and pleasure without making any moral demands. Nobody has given them a coherent sense of what else it means to be Jewish. This is where the room goes spinning away from me, not when born Jews start talking about their suffering but when they start talking about their identity.

I have no problem with liturgical assertions like "all shall call upon your name"; everyone has access to the soul of the universe (call it God or whatever you want) with or without religious membership. There may even come a day when we all know it at the same time. I have no problem with the assertion of chosenness: do we fault the Inuit and other indigenous nations for calling themselves "the real people"? Such language represents an aspiration and a standard, a means of remaining not only a cohesive group but a responsive and responsible one. What I cannot get my mind around is particularity without substance, particularity that maintains itself for no definite purpose and is not quite sure it wants any purpose beyond maintaining itself. I wouldn't deny anyone's right to be aimless, but neither the minutiae of observance on the one hand nor the trivia of pop culture on the other were aim enough for the writers who drew me to Judaism. Call them the acidic masters: writing from an excess of intelligence and moral energy, they dissolved illusions, scorned ulterior motives, and conveyed a *ko'ach*—a life-force—that was principled, indelibly Jewish, and infinitely desirable.

෴

Word and World

FROM FAITH TO ACTION

Ruth Messinger and Lisa Exler

O n the High Holy Days, we celebrate the creation of the world and reflect on our role in its ongoing maintenance. But do we really mean what we celebrate? One way to answer that question is to look carefully at one particular moment in the service: when the ark is opened and we rise for the spirited and familiar melody for *V'khol Ma'aminim* ("Everyone Believes"). Singing this communal proclamation of our faith in the omnipotence, justice, and kindness of God allows us to examine whether the world we are building is consistent with the justice and righteousness that the words demand—whether, that is, world and word match.

V'khol Ma'aminim is a series of couplets that all follow the same structure: a *statement about God* followed by a collective affirmation of *faith in God*. Most congregations, however, sing the prayer with the structure reversed—first with the collective affirmation ("Everyone believes") and only then the declaration of a particular divine attribute that is the object of the belief.

The difference between the original structure of the poem and the way in which it is usually sung highlights a fundamental question about the relationship between faith, certainty, and doubt: what comes first, knowledge of God or faith in God? The original structure implies that

Ruth Messinger is the president of American Jewish World Service (AJWS). She contributed to *Who by Fire, Who by Water*—Un'taneh Tokef, *All These Vows*—Kol Nidre, and *We Have Sinned: Sin and Confession in Judaism*—Ashamnu *and* Al Chet (all Jewish Lights).

Lisa Exler is a senior program officer in the experiential education department at American Jewish World Service (AJWS). She contributed to *We Have Sinned: Sin and Confession in Judaism*—Ashamnu *and* Al Chet (Jewish Lights).

knowledge comes first—by recognizing an awe-inspiring attribute of God, we are inspired to have faith. But in the way the prayer is usually sung, it is as if the very act of proclaiming our faith forces the declaration about God to be true; we are convincing ourselves of our belief by proclaiming it.

Jewish text and tradition support this understanding that faith is not just an assertion of some self-evident truth; rather, it is a dynamic response to something far less tangible and definitive. Faith derives not only from awe, but also from doubt, uncertainty, and the unknown.

The first time the verb "to believe" or "to have faith" appears in the Torah is in relation to Abraham—no surprise, perhaps, as Abraham is known for his dramatic demonstrations of faith in God: he leaves his birthplace to set out on a journey to an unknown destination and is even willing to comply with God's command to sacrifice his beloved son Isaac.

But strikingly, it is not in connection with either of these dramatic decisions that Abraham is described as "believing." Instead, the description comes at the end of a tense dialogue with God in which Abraham expresses confusion and doubt about God's promise that he will father a great nation.[1] When God assures Abraham of God's protection and reward, Abraham challenges God: "What can You give me, seeing that I shall die childless, and the one in charge of my household is [my servant] Eliezer of Damascus? Since You have granted me no offspring, my steward will be my heir" (Genesis 15:2–3).

Nahum Sarna, in his commentary on Genesis, describes Abraham's state of mind in this moment:

> For the first time Abram speaks to God. In unquestioning obedience to the divine command, he had broken his ties with his family and become a wanderer in a strange land. His life had been repeatedly in danger. The years had rolled by and the promises of progeny had not materialized. Through it all Abram maintained his silence. Now the measure of recurring disappointment and prolonged frustration has reached its limit. The bonds of restraint are broken, and the patriarch bares the bitterness of his soul in a brief, poignant outburst bordering on utter despair.[2]

Abraham is distraught, angry, and plagued by doubt about whether God will fulfill the promise or not. This hardly sounds like a man who trusts in God. God responds to Abraham's doubt by reassuring him that his offspring will be as numerous as the stars, and the scene concludes with an assertion of Abraham's faith, "and Abraham believed in God" (Genesis 15:6).

Abraham's faith in God and God's promise comes without any supporting evidence. God verbally reiterates the promise of descendants, but Sarah is still far from being pregnant. The facts on the ground have not changed, but nevertheless, Abraham believes.

Sarna's interpretation affirms an understanding of faith that exists alongside doubt: "The scene that opens with fear and depression closes with a firm statement that Abram remains steadfast in his faith in God. The promises must be realized, even in the face of a seemingly recalcitrant reality."[3]

As we sing *V'khol Ma'aminim*, a prayer described by Chief Rabbi Lord Jonathan Sacks as a "sustained declaration of faith in divine justice and compassion,"[4] we too are faced with a "seemingly recalcitrant reality." Many of its declarations about God do not ring true in our experience. We say, "Everyone believes [God] is good to everyone," yet so many people in the world seem not to benefit from God's goodness. We say, "Everyone believes [God] answers silent prayers," yet the world is full of those who suffer and whose prayers go unanswered. We say, "Everyone believes [God] is a righteous judge," but our world often seems so lacking in justice. What is the use of stating our belief in a just God and a just world when the gulf between rich and poor increases every day and people's human rights are regularly and systematically violated?

This prayer may not convince us of a reality we don't perceive, but it should inspire us to act in order to achieve that reality.[5] In his Nobel Prize acceptance speech, Dr. Martin Luther King Jr. articulated the connection between his abiding belief in justice and his compelling courage to act.

Indeed, King's repetition of "I believe" in this speech echoes the refrain of *V'khol Ma'aminim*:

> I believe that unarmed truth and unconditional love will have the final word in reality. This is why right temporarily defeated is stronger than evil triumphant. I believe that even amid today's mortar bursts and whining bullets, there is still hope for a brighter tomorrow. I believe that wounded justice, lying prostrate on the blood-flowing streets of our nations, can be lifted from this dust of shame to reign supreme among the children of men. I have the

audacity to believe that peoples everywhere can have three meals a day for their bodies, education and culture for their minds, and dignity, equality and freedom for their spirits....

This faith can give us courage to face the uncertainties of the future. It will give our tired feet new strength as we continue our forward stride toward the city of freedom.[6]

King's belief in justice motivated his activism to attain it; so, too, should our collective belief in justice lead us to the collective pursuit of it. When we sing *V'khol Ma'aminim* and articulate our belief in a just world, we should be asking ourselves and each other, "What actions are we taking to make sure that justice really arrives, so that word and world (the prayer and the reality on the ground) are somehow consistent?"

Rabbi Joseph B. Soloveitchik understood human beings to be God's partners in the creation and perfection of the world. He wrote, "Just as the Almighty constantly refined and improved the realm of existence during the six days of creation, so must man complete that creation and transform the domain of chaos and void into a perfect and beautiful reality."[7]

On Rosh Hashanah, when we celebrate the creation of the world and of humanity, we are expected to embrace our role as partners in creation and to work with "the holder of the scales of justice" to bring about a world that is truly just.

⌒⌇⌇⌇⌇⌒

"So Loud Your Praise Shall Sing"

Rabbi Charles H. Middleburgh, PhD

When I was an undergraduate at University College London in the 1970s, studying ancient and medieval Hebrew with Aramaic and Syriac, I was fortunate to be taught by Professor Raphael Loewe, *zikhrono liv'rakhah*. Loewe, scion of an illustrious family (his grandfather had been Sir Moses Montefiore's private secretary) and a decorated war hero, became a dear friend, mentor, and guide until his death in 2011 at the age of ninety-two. Loewe's specialty, however, and his passion, was poetry, quintessentially the medieval Hebrew poetry of the Golden Age of Spain. I shall always be grateful for his tutelage in the subject, which has remained my interest as well, to this very day.

Loewe was not just a teacher of poetry; he was a poet himself—a translator of the greats of Muslim Spain into rhyming English; a writer of original poetry in English, Greek, Latin, and Hebrew; and a translator into Hebrew from other languages (his version of Gray's *Elegy in a Country Churchyard* is the apotheosis of his genius).[1]

What made medieval Hebrew poetry so fascinating was Loewe's ability to tease out allusions to or quotations from Rabbinic and biblical literature; it was he also who sparked my fascination with words, their meanings, and the rich scope for their interpretation. I was introduced,

Rabbi Charles H. Middleburgh, PhD, is the director of studies at Leo Baeck College in London, where he has taught since 1984. He is coeditor with Rabbi Andrew Goldstein, PhD, of the Liberal Judaism *Machzor Ruach Chadashah* and the anthologies *High and Holy Days: A Book of Jewish Wisdom* and *A Jewish Book of Comfort*. He contributed to *Who by Fire, Who by Water*—Un'taneh Tokef, *All These Vows*—Kol Nidre, *We Have Sinned: Sin and Confession in Judaism*—Ashamnu *and* Al Chet, and *May God Remember: Memory and Memorializing in Judaism*—Yizkor (all Jewish Lights).

213

for example, to Solomon ibn Gabirol's great lament on the murder of his patron, Yekutiel, the former vizier of Saragossa, a poem that remains a benchmark for the synergy between the surface language in which a poem is composed and its quoted allusions that add layers and layers of meaning to an ostensibly straightforward text.[2]

It was Loewe who sprang immediately to mind when I was asked to contribute to this fifth volume of Prayers of Awe, focusing on the *Uv'khen* passages of the High Holy Days and the accompanying *piyyut V'ye'etayu*, sung in Liberal and some Reform congregations in the United Kingdom after the last set of shofar calls have been sounded on Rosh Hashanah.

The three paragraphs, each beginning with the word *uv'khen*, do a reasonably stylish slalom between universalism and particularism, and their content is wholly appropriate for the High Holy Days, speaking of the majesty of God, the organic relationship between God and humanity, and the coming of a halcyon time of freedom, stability, peace, and the rule of God.

One word, particularly, in the *Uv'khen* paragraphs has always fascinated me: *shilton*. Traditional liturgies usually say *shaltan*, but Goldschmidt's scientific text lists *shilton* as an alternative, and *shilton* (which is grammatically preferable) is generally what one finds in non-Orthodox liturgies—not just our own Liberal and Reform *machzorim* of Great Britain but also Reform, Conservative, and Reconstructionist texts in North America, for example.[3] Whatever microscopically fine distinction may be drawn between the two words, however, they are just different forms of a noun deriving from the root *shin lamed tet*: "to have power over" or "to be in authority," in application to God or a benign human monarch; but also "to domineer" or "to tyrannize" in the case of a less benevolent ruler. The context of *uv'khen* definitely applies it to God, but its biblical origins set it in a more human context.

I say "biblical origins," but the word is not found commonly from the biblical era. Outside the Bible, a scrap of the apocryphal work Ben Sirach (4:7) found at Masada has the word written on it, and in the Hebrew Bible itself, we find it used in just one single book, Kohelet (Ecclesiastes), which scholars believe to be one of the latest of all the books in the biblical canon.[4]

Loewe would have said that the word cannot be considered without taking note of the biblical context in which it occurs, in this case, Kohelet's accent on the harsh realism about human life in all its aspects. It is Kohelet who gives us such famous aphorisms as "Vanity of vanities, all is vanity," "There is nothing new under the sun," and "That which is, has already been, and that which is to be has already been." For Kohelet, life is tough and regularly unfair; living an ethical and moral existence is no certain guarantee of enjoying the fruits of one's virtue.

Some label Kohelet a cynic; others (myself included), a realist. Either way, one cannot avoid the conclusion that whoever framed this prayer for our High Hoy Day service—it occurs first in *Seder Rav Amram* (eighth century)—must have done so with its biblical origins in mind; of this, more later.

Against this must be set the anonymous medieval *piyyut V'ye'etayu*, first found in *Machzor Vitry* (tenth to eleventh century) and commencing with another intriguing word.

In the synagogue of my youth, this *piyyut* was sung in the English translation of Israel Zangwill to a tune written by the great Victorian composer Sir Arthur Sullivan, cocreator of some of the most loved musical dramas of the nineteenth and twentieth centuries[5] and framer of the Christmas carol "It Came Upon the Midnight Clear."[6] It was not until the 1990s that I first heard it sung in its original Hebrew, to a challenging but wonderful *niggun*, though whether it is widely sung today I do not know.

What I do know is the extent to which the very first word of the *piyyut* has proved for me a source of enormous fascination. Having traced the origin of *shilton* to Kohelet, we should now look at the word *v'ye'etayu*, which has its own, quite contrasting, lesson for us.

V'ye'etayu is derived from a root *alef tav heh*, meaning "to come," and while not altogether uncommon in the Hebrew Bible, it is nowhere near as frequently used as is its synonym *bet vav alef*. So the discovery of a verse in the *Tanakh* where the same word is used sets up an interesting contextual connection. In Psalm 68:32 we read, *Ye'etayu chashmanim minimitzrayim, kush taritz yadav lelohim*, "Tribute bearers shall come from Egypt; Cush shall hasten its gifts to God." My translation follows the JPS *Tanakh*, which renders the first word *chashmanim* "tribute bearers"; the classic Brown-Driver-Briggs *Biblical Aramaic and Hebrew Dictionary*[7] prefers "ambassadors," and the King James Bible has "princes." In any case, a picture emerges of representatives from all nations bringing gifts to God, in preparation for the following verse (68:33), which proclaims, "Sing to God, you nations of the earth, sing praises to Adonai."

These psalm verses anticipate a time when the universal sovereignty of the God of Israel will be acknowledged by all the nations of the earth, a sentiment that is clearly echoed in the first and third *Uv'khen* paragraphs about humanity uniting in worship of God.

By choosing the word *v'ye'etayu*—merely adding a *vav* to the opening word of Psalm 68:32—the anonymous author of this splendid *piyyut* is making his underlying message explicitly clear. The word *ye'etayu*, not a random but a very deliberate choice, expresses with great power the idea that our *t'shuvah* must be of a nature and quality not just to bring *near* this messianic time, but actually to bring it *on*!

All of which is fine and dandy for the wave of emotion that characterizes the High Holy Days, when God's ultimate rule may actually seem attainable ... but then that strange word *shilton* comes awkwardly back into the picture. In contrast to the heady optimism of *v'ye'etayu*, we have *shilton*'s resonating echoes from Kohelet—a message that strikes me as being much more realistic, and much more relevant.

The inference from *shilton* is not just that there is a major difference between divine and human rule, but that there is the potential for both to go catastrophically wrong, the former because of its frequent abuse by the men (it is usually men) who think they are agents of God on earth, the latter because of the awful human potential for cruelty, barbarity, and the persecution of the weak and vulnerable, catalogued time and time again throughout history.

In this light we can view the *Uv'khen* and *V'ye'etayu* passages as having two messages, either one of which we may choose to identify with. The "soft" message (from *V'ye'etayu*) is all about striving to bring on the messianic age, a laudable but (in my view) somewhat unrealistic endeavor. The "hard" message (from *shilton*) is less triumphal and more balanced, although also wholly in keeping with the spirit of the *Yamim Nora'im* ("Days of Awe"): namely, that even if we cannot promise the "coming of the kingdom," we can at least exercise integrity in our relationships with others, especially if they are relationships between unequal parties; and that those in a position of power must be especially wary of making inappropriate use of their authority; but the sting in the tail is Kohelet's pragmatic warning that in the end, no matter what we try, it will probably end in disappointment and tears.

All may, in the end, be vanity, but the nobility of the High Holy Day message is that we nonetheless must act as if it isn't. Throughout the year that the High Holy Days inaugurate, we commit ourselves to living as honorably and as constructively as we can.

A Synthesis of Hope

Rabbi Jay Henry Moses

For a people credited with bringing the concept of monotheism to the world, Jews are remarkably inconsistent with our language and ideas about the divine. The God of Israel, singular and unique though this God may be, is awfully hard to pin down. There is not even any Jewish word for "theology"; the systematized study (Greek: *logos*) of God (Greek: *theo*) has no Hebrew equivalent. This is no accident; Jewish sages and scholars of every generation have opted for diverse imagery over dogmatic consistency.

This manifold portrayal of God is evident from a cursory reading of the Bible itself (and spelled out magnificently in Jack Miles's extraordinary book *God: A Biography*). But the diversity of God images is displayed even more vividly in the liturgy, where we read of a God who is both immanent and transcendent, vengeful and forgiving, personal and abstract. The God we encounter there is creator and judge of the entire universe, but also, simultaneously, intimate friend and protector in a covenant with this tiny people known as Israel.

Jewish daily and weekly liturgy already illustrates this variety of God imagery, but on the *Yamim Nora'im* ("Days of Awe," the High Holy Days), these polarities are particularly stark, since these holidays have long been climactic public experiences, designed to articulate the key themes of Jewish theology in a maximally dramatic way.

Rabbi Jay Henry Moses is director of the Wexner Heritage Program at the Wexner Foundation. Previously, he served for five years as associate rabbi at Temple Sholom of Chicago. Rabbi Moses has taught at Hebrew Union College–Jewish Institute of Religion, the Jewish Community Center in Manhattan and its Makom: Center for Mindfulness, and in many other adult education settings. He contributed to *We Have Sinned: Sin and Confession in Judaism*—Ashamnu *and* Al Chet *and* May God Remember: Memory and Memorializing in Judaism—Yizkor (both Jewish Lights).

On Rosh Hashanah and Yom Kippur, our key concerns are life and death, sin and forgiveness—the existential questions that animate every human soul, Jewish and non-Jewish alike. Yet just as often the language of our High Holy Day prayers reflects the parochial concerns of the Jewish People, especially with regard to the ultimate redemption and salvation for which we pray. This is where questions cease being purely academic and gain some teeth: is the glorious vision of eternity spelled out on Rosh Hashanah the exclusive purview of the Jewish People, or is the world of our dreams to be shared by all humanity?

The liturgy featured in this volume illustrates the tension. Our introductory poem (V'khol Ma'aminim) moves directly from calling God the one who "remembers the covenant" (verse 7) to acknowledging the one who "allocates life to every living being" (verse 8). The Uv'khen additions to every Amidah ask God to "instill fear of You in all of your creatures" (verse 1); but also, just a moment later, to "install honor in your people" (verse 6), referring clearly to Israel.

These apparently contradictory images, so confusingly interwoven, are actually not dichotomies at all, but dialectics, deliberately intertwined. By poetically juxtaposing images of a God who is universal (absent any special reference to the Jewish People) with images of a God who is intimately and preferentially inclined toward that very people, the machzor points us toward a deeper truth.

This truth is embedded at the very heart of the Jewish tradition. The great medieval biblical commentator Rashi famously asks why the Torah begins with the creation of the world and not with the first laws that pertain to specifically Jewish practice. Among the answers to this question is that the subsequent claims of the Jewish People, both historically and theologically, require that the God with whom we are in covenant is the God of the entire universe—not just one god among many.

This is the God of Genesis: transcendent and abstract, the ground and cause of the cosmos, the God of creation. But there is also the God of Exodus, the God who hears the cry of the Israelites in bondage in Egypt and personally liberates them "with a mighty hand and an outstretched arm." The climactic event of Exodus is the giving of the law at Sinai, where God chooses this one tiny, beleaguered people for a relationship that will entail special responsibilities and privileges. This is the God of covenant—involved in and concerned with the affairs of one extended family known as the Israelites.

Both divine images occur regularly and in rapid succession in the texts of the *machzor,* particularly in the representative section of the liturgy reproduced here. What is the effect of simultaneously invoking the God of Genesis and the God of Exodus, the God of creation and the God of covenant?

The *Yamim Nora'im* are designed to take the worshiper on a journey, spelling out the arc of a single human life and of humanity as a whole. It begins on Rosh Hashanah, invoking God as the universal creator of the world—a God who exercises dominion over all. God is the judge of the universe, enthroned on high, *yode'a yetzer kol y'tzurim,* knowing "the cravings of every creature," in the words of our opening *piyyut* (verse 10).

The journey ends at *N'ilah,* the concluding service for Yom Kippur, when the gates of repentance slowly swing shut, while each worshiper individually begs for mercy. Having orchestrated a brush with mortality through fasting, we close the day pleading for personal life and redemption, promising—as the Jewish People now, not as universal human beings—to uphold the covenant more faithfully in the year to come.

There is method to this liturgical madness—a reason behind editorial and theological unclarity in the *machzor.* The ultimate vision toward which Judaism points is precisely the synthesis of the universal God of creation and the particular God of the covenant. *Mashiach,* the messiah, salvation, will arrive in the form of expanded consciousness; then, and only then, will all apparent contradictions be resolved.

Until then, human awareness is tragically stuck in the binary of black or white; we can only hold one image of God in our hearts and minds at any given time.

Sometimes our spiritual need in a given moment is to stand humbly before the transcendent creator of the universe. We are awed at the beauty of nature or terrified by its destructive power; overwhelmed with gratitude for the mysterious birth of a child or overcome by the injustice of the untimely death of a loved one.

At other times we need to situate ourselves within the story of the Jewish People. At the passing of the Torah from generation to generation during a bar/bat mitzvah, we brush up against eternity through our specifically Jewish covenantal relationship. When the miraculously reborn State of Israel is imperiled, we pray to a God who, we are certain, must pay special heed to the promise made to our ancestors long ago.

As the spiritual apex of the year, the *Yamim Nora'im* provide both of these images of God, not just intermittently, but dialectically—in evocative relationship with each other. Rosh Hashanah and Yom Kippur provide a vision for all humanity and for the people Israel. It is like a rehearsal for that time where our consciousness will expand and we will hold both images of God *simultaneously* in our minds and hearts.

All of humanity will do the same, for on that day, all of God's creation will be acutely aware of the ultimate purpose of existence; and at the same instant, they will be conscious of the unique role that they alone play in that universal and sacred drama, as individuals within a particular community. There will be no more conflict between people and no more competition among peoples. Any apparent contradiction between the God of Genesis and the God of Exodus will disappear. The dialectical tension between the two will resolve into a synthesis of deeper spiritual insight than any of us can even imagine now.

This ultimate vision of a resolution between the universal and the particular is both lofty in conception and distant in realization, but precisely on that account, it is apt for the High Holy Days. Each time our prayers veer back and forth from the cosmological and universal to the uniquely personal and Jewish, we are reminded that the sacred Jewish drama anticipates nothing less than a synthesis of hope.

◯◯◯

Melekh al Kol Ha'aretz

JUST HOW JEWISH IS ROSH HASHANAH, ANYWAY?

Rabbi Rachel Nussbaum

Rosh Hashanah is a very "Jewish" holiday, isn't it? Our non-Jewish friends and neighbors don't celebrate it, and we Jews who do mark it with Hebrew liturgy, apples dipped in honey, and hearing the shofar—all elements of Jewish particularity. The High Holy Days can also mean missing days of work or school—poignant reminder of difference, especially for school-aged children in a year when Rosh Hashanah falls at the very beginning of the academic year.

Obviously, Rosh Hashanah is deeply Jewish. But, unlike Hanukkah, Purim, or Passover, which revolve around historical narratives of the Jewish People, Rosh Hashanah celebrates the universal themes of the creation and governance of the world. So perhaps it is not so Jewish after all. Better put, we might say that Rosh Hashanah stands out among Jewish holidays for posing the most particular pathway toward a universal end.

One of the most frequently occurring words in the Rosh Hashanah liturgy is *melekh* ("ruler," "sovereign," or "king"), making God's rule a central theme of the day and, by extension, of the entire High Holy Day season. The symbols of Rosh Hashanah can be read through the lens of rulership as well: the shofar is blown as part of a divine coronation ceremony, and even the pomegranates with their crowns (the *rimonim* that decorate the Torah scrolls) remind us of God's sovereignty.

Rabbi Rachel Nussbaum is rabbi and executive director of the Kavana Cooperative in Seattle, Washington. She was ordained at The Jewish Theological Seminary of America and was recently awarded an Avi Chai Fellowship for her innovative approach to Jewish community building. She contributed to *Who by Fire, Who by Water*—Un'taneh Tokef (Jewish Lights).

For many individuals in my own congregation, however—and, I suspect, in others as well—the central *melekh* image is more hindrance than help. No doubt, this royal vocabulary was a natural fit for the Rabbis of antiquity who gave us our liturgy in the first place and for their rabbinic successors in medieval times, when the *machzor* as we know it was compiled. They saturated our literature and our liturgy with images of God as king, especially regarding Rosh Hashanah, when no one who opens up the prayer book can possibly avoid them. On Rosh Hashanah especially, then, we face the question of how to appropriate this language and theology of royalty for our time.

No pieces of the liturgy beg the question more than the *piyyutim* around which this volume is organized. In both *V'khol Ma'aminim* and *V'ye'etayu,* the language paints a repetitive picture of all of the inhabitants of the world declaring God's kingship, believing in God's sovereignty, and crowning God with the *keter m'lukhah,* a "crown of kingship."

Most of us know on an intellectual level that all the God-language of our prayer book is necessarily metaphorical—although, admittedly, it's easy to lose sight of this in the face of the liturgy's concrete images. But, with that metaphorical framework in mind, it's a little easier to flip the image and consider what this notion of God as king means for us on the human end of the relationship. By declaring God as king, reenacting a coronation ceremony, and bowing down to the ground in full prostration, we place ourselves in the role of subjects. This is not an entirely comfortable place to be, but the notion of seeing ourselves as subservient (in contrast to a divine ruler) is a powerful reminder of our humanity and our limitations. Sometimes, that is, talking about God is actually describing something about ourselves, because it is not the essence of God we are after so much as it is the divine-human relationship and what that relationship shows us about ourselves as the human actors in the cosmic drama that the liturgy is meant to evoke within us.

We can unpack the divine-king metaphor even further, however. The kings we know are always kings of something, never everything, so when we think about earthly kings, we are talking about a ruler of a particular group. The king's goal is to make his own kingdom prosper, often at the expense of other kingdoms; thus, earthly kings busy themselves with foreign affairs, wars, and treaties—think of Shakespeare's many histories, each one named after a king, and all of them a continuing saga of England at war. In contrast, the power of Rosh Hashanah's *melekh* metaphor comes from the fact that God is not just king of the Jews but "king of all the earth" (*melekh al kol ha'aretz*). This very claim features prominently in the Great *Alenu*, when we declare, *V'hayah Adonai l'melekh al kol ha'aretz* ("And God will be king over all the earth"), and bow all the way down to the ground as we articulate our universal vision for all of humanity to acknowledge God's sovereignty. The same thought occurs in the *Kiddush* for the day and in the *K'dushat Hayom* section of each Rosh Hashanah *Amidah* (the fourth benediction that celebrates the "holiness of the day").

The *piyyutim* in question here—*V'khol Ma'aminim* and *V'ye'etayu*—take the theme of God's kingship to its extreme with their repeated emphasis on this notion of "all" or "everyone" (*kol*): *everyone* believes [God] is ..."; "*everyone* will arrive to serve [God]." In the vision for redemption that we articulate on Rosh Hashanah, all the inhabitants of the world come to live under the rule of a single king. Or, to put it yet another way, we envision a time with a universal vision of the moral order: a single set of rules for engagement, a shared gravitational pull, just one set of expectations about how we treat the world and one another. Surprisingly, then, it turns out that our celebration of a particularly Jewish New Year results in an articulation of a very universal vision for all humanity.

When I started the Kavana Cooperative in Seattle in 2006, it was my hope that we could create a Jewish community with an outward orientation, a place where our Jewish particularity would be a springboard toward paying attention to themes of universal justice as they applied to the world around us. In truth, though, this element of the vision was among the most challenging to bring to fruition. For the first handful of years after Kavana was founded, my attempts to focus Kavana's energy on universal themes repeatedly fell flat, and I realized that I was trying to jump the gun and skip straight to the universal without first passing through the zone of the particular. Ultimately, I realized that in order to get to a place of honest engagement in the universal realm, we needed first to focus on building a strong sense of Jewish identity and Jewish community.

By Kavana's sixth year, the community finally felt mature enough to tackle issues of universal justice seriously. On the High Holy Days that year, I spoke about the Rosh Hashanah theme of God's kingship and how this notion of *malkhut* ("sovereignty") reorients the Jewish community, prompting us to aspire to lives that are informed by universal ethical commitments and a sense of justice for all the inhabitants of the world.

That year, Kavana launched a Fair Trade *Gelt* campaign. Our fledgling Social Justice Team had been thinking about a range of food justice issues, and when Hanukkah rolled around that year, it drew the community's attention to the terrible labor practices—including child slavery—rampant in the chocolate industry in West Africa. How, they challenged, on the very holiday that celebrates freedom from oppression, could we possibly consume Hanukkah *gelt* (the ubiquitous foil-wrapped chocolate coins in net baggies) whose cocoa beans might have been sourced at the expense of another human being's freedom? That first year, children and adults in our community had the opportunity to mold their own *gelt* using fair-trade chocolate, and we began talking about the issue within the Seattle community. The following year, Kavana partnered with a number of local and national Jewish organizations—University of Washington Hillel, Hazon, Rabbis for Human Rights (now T'ruah), Fair Trade Judaica—to create educational materials and broaden the campaign. The year after that, prompted in part by our phone calls, e-mails, and social media inquiries, several new fair-trade chocolatiers began manufacturing *gelt* for Hanukkah. And each year, more and more Jewish communities are pledging that the chocolate they purchase will all have been manufactured under fair labor practices.

Of course, the point is not so much the *gelt* alone as it is the lesson that what we consume should be an outgrowth of our deeply held values—in our case, the Jewish commitment to all human beings and to the world itself. Our particular Jewish celebrations of Hanukkah become an opportunity to demonstrate our commitment to universal values. This is the reason that our Jewish community on the western edge of North America is obligated to think about the well-being of children on cocoa plantations in western Africa. And this is but one example of how our particular Jewish identity orients us toward a vision of universal justice.

When we gather on Rosh Hashanah to recite the words "everyone believes" (*v'khol ma'aminim*) and "everyone will arrive to serve" (*v'ye'etayu khol l'ovdekha*), we are in essence reminding ourselves that if God is king of all the world, then people all over the world are equally God's subjects, in which case, we must be answerable to the same universal values as everyone else. Does that make Rosh Hashanah a Jewish holiday or a universal celebration of humanity and the world? It seems obvious to me that the answer is a resounding "both." The particular Jewish liturgy of our *machzor* reminds us that we inhabit a single system of universal justice and that our actions should make a difference for all the world.

Rosh Hashanah asks us to live as though there is a single king and a single set of rules for all humanity. The royalty-saturated liturgy should prompt us to build the kind of world that we, as universal subjects, are proud to inhabit!

CRNO

Let It Be!
Let It Be!
Let It Be!

Rabbi Jack Riemer

When I recite the three *Uv'khens*, I think of the refrain to the Beatles song: "Let it be, let it be, let it be." For that is what these prayers are: visions of the way the world should be; dreams of a time when the world will be united in the love of God; when the people of Israel, so much maligned, will finally have a bit of honor and respect; and when the righteous of the world will be able to rejoice at last.

Whoever wrote the first *Uv'khen* lived sometime in the early Middle Ages, after the conclusion of the Talmud, in all probability (sixth century), but before the very first Jewish prayer book we have, *Seder Rav Amram* (c. 860 CE). He lived before planes and cars, before telegrams and telephones. He probably never traveled more than a few hundred miles in any direction in his life.

And yet, this author, whoever he was, had the vision to imagine a world in which all humanity—more than just all humanity—all creation—would unite in the service of God and acknowledge the sovereignty of God over all the world.

Rabbi Jack Riemer, well-known author and speaker, has conducted many workshops and seminars to help people learn about the inspiring tradition of ethical wills and to prepare their own. As head of the National Rabbinic Network, a support system for rabbis across denominational lines, he gives sermon seminars to rabbis throughout the United States. He is editor of *The World of the High Holy Days* and *Wrestling with the Angel*, and coeditor of *So That Your Values Live On: Ethical Wills and How to Prepare Them* (Jewish Lights). He contributed to *May God Remember: Memory and Memorializing in Judaism—Yizkor* (Jewish Lights).

The First *Uv'khen*

The very first part of the vision prays that the world become *agudah achat*, "one group [of peoples] to do your [God's] will." Every time I come to that phrase I wince, because it reminds me of "one United Nations," and there is very little that the United Nations is united on these days. It has become a forum where the power blocs of the world jockey for supremacy and where the only thing on which the nations seem able to agree is shared contempt for Israel—hardly "God's will." More resolutions have been passed condemning Israel than on any other subject. Nations that are known for their brutality have been appointed to chair the Commission on Human Rights! This is hardly the United Nations that we dreamed of when the organization was first established.

And yet, we Jews still believe in the United Nations! Despite all the rejection we have received there, despite the fact that Israel is the only country that belongs to no geographical bloc, despite the fact that there is no other country there that speaks its language—literally and figuratively—we still believe in the United Nations. We do so because we are the ones who first conceived the idea that all humanity will someday be one. We got the idea not from Dumbarton Oaks and not from Geneva, but from Isaiah and Micah and from the opening pages of Genesis.

Those prophets lived in the eighth century BCE, and here is the amazing thing: some fifteen hundred years later, despite wars with Rome, despite another exile, and despite persecution under the church, an anonymous writer of prayers still dreamed the same dream: that someday, all the nations of the world would form an *agudah achat*, one single united group of peoples, intent on serving God. And the miracle continues: over a millennium later still, despite continuing medieval persecution, despite pogroms in modern-day Russia, and even despite Hitler, we still recite his words over and over again, in every *Amidah* of Rosh Hashanah and Yom Kippur.

It is hard, sometimes very hard, for Jews to believe in the possibility of a united humankind, but if this author—whoever he was—who lived in a world that was so insular and so small, if he who lived in a world where very few people traveled more than a few hundred miles from where they were born, if he who lived surrounded by so much hatred and who endured so much abuse—if he could believe in the concept of a united humankind, then so can we. *Let it be!*

The Second *Uv'khen*

The second dream that this writer envisions is that his much maligned people may someday have a little bit of honor, that those who have stayed loyal to God despite all they have endured may finally have a little bit of appreciation, that those who have sought to live by God's teachings may have a little bit of hope, and that those who have put their trust in God may finally be able to respond to those who have demeaned them for so long. The author dreams that there will come a day when there will be happiness in the Land of Israel and joy in Jerusalem. He dreams that there will yet be a day when the horn with which David, God's servant, was anointed will be manifest once again and when the light that was lit for the son of Jesse will shine brightly once again. May that day come soon, he says, soon, soon—in our lifetimes—soon!

I read these words in the light of the Jewish People's age-old promise that the Jewish homeland of Israel would be reborn with light enough to illumine the world, and I wince again. For the real State of Israel is no shining light. The real city of Jerusalem has sewage problems, and pollution problems, and prostitution problems, and garbage collection problems, and religious conflict beyond the wildest imagination of its founders. Where is the divine light that this prayer talks about in a city whose partisan politics and cultural conflict divide rich from poor and *charedi* (ultra-Orthodox) from secular? Where is the light that we pray for in the city that is so often darkened by disputes among its citizens and whose fate seems to be tied up more with the oil of its neighbors than with the anointing oil of David? How far away does the real Israel seem from the ideal that this prayer describes!

The answer, I believe, is found in a line by the Israeli poet and novelist Amos Oz: "Israel is a dream come true—and therefore it is bound to be flawed and imperfect. The only way to keep a dream pure is not to fulfill it. Israel is flawed and imperfect, precisely because it is a dream come true."[1]

Our prayer *Uv'khen* is likewise a vision, a goal, a dream, a standard toward which we must continually aspire. The reality of Israel is necessarily flawed—an imperfect version of the ideal that the liturgy here presents. We are to measure the reality of Israel on the ground against the ideal of Israel in our prayers, so as not to be satisfied with the reality that we have. The High Holy Days remind us always that there has to be more: more within us individually, more in our collective future, more that we personally can do, and more that Israel must become as well. *Let it be; let it be.*

The Third *Uv'khen*

The third *Uv'khen* is a promise that a time will come when "the righteous will … rejoice, the upright will celebrate, and the pious will jubilantly delight." It follows that the opposite, the way the world is now, must be set right. But here we find an amazing change of language. The first half of the vision (the victory of the righteous, the upright, and the pious) is in the plural, the normal Hebrew way of referencing individuals: "the righteous *people*, the upright *people*, the pious *people*." We expect the second half of the vision too to be in the plural—that is, we are braced to read about the eradication of "evil *people*, wicked *people*." But that is not what it says. Instead, we are promised that "injustice" (*olatah*) and "all wickedness" (*kol harishah*) "will vanish like smoke."

Do you see the difference between the phrasing of the first half of this vision and the second?

We do not pray that evil *people* be destroyed or silenced. We pray that *wickedness* disappear from within the wicked people, who will then become good. The idea goes back to the story of Beruriah, the wife of Rabbi Meir (Talmud, Berakhot 10a). When her husband expressed the wish that certain evil people be killed, Beruriah urged him to pray instead that they overcome their evil inclination, which was moving them toward sin. So here, we do not pray that sinners be destroyed, but that sin be destroyed from within the hearts of the wicked people—so that they can become good.

I find that such a moving insight. A people that suffered so much, a people that endured what the Jewish People did in the Middle Ages, somehow transcended the brutal treatment that it went through and was able to pray not for revenge, not for retribution, not for the annihilation of its persecutors, but for wickedness to be removed from the hearts of the wicked so that they could become good people instead. And that is the wonder of this prayer!

What an extraordinary three-part vision this is: that all the world unite to serve God in love, that the Jewish People be restored to the dignity it deserves, and that wickedness disappear so that the wicked can become good.

We are still a long, long way from achieving these three goals—that is for sure—but we reaffirm them over and over again on Rosh Hashanah and on Yom Kippur. *Let it be! Let it be! Let it be!*

☙❧

What We Can All Believe

Rabbi Jeffrey K. Salkin, DMin

I represent one of the most significant support groups in contemporary American Jewish life: recovering classical Reform Jews.

Like many Reform rabbis of my generation, I rebelled against services that overdosed on decorum; sermons that invoked vague, humanistic generalities; a Hebraically challenged liturgy; and a general attitude that it was the role of the Jewish People to fit in.

Any additional criticisms of classical Reform would just be unfair piling on and, frankly, discourteous to my Reform ancestors. We might generously say that they did what they did, and taught what they taught, with the best of intentions and following the spirit of their times.

But, at this moment in American Jewish history, it is time for us to reclaim one of the greatest gifts of classical Reform Judaism, and to celebrate it, and to put it back at the center of our Jewish worldview. In fact, it may well be crucial if the Jewish People is to survive.

I am speaking of that hoary notion that the role of the Jewish People is to be a "light to the nations," to bring the world a message of

---

Rabbi Jeffrey K. Salkin, DMin, is a noted author whose work has appeared in many publications, including the *Wall Street Journal, Reader's Digest*, and the *Forward*. He is editor of *The Modern Men's Torah Commentary: New Insights from Jewish Men on the 54 Weekly Torah Portions* and *Text Messages: A Torah Commentary for Teens*; and author of *Being God's Partner: How to Find the Hidden Link Between Spirituality and Your Work*, the bestseller *Putting God on the Guest List: How to Reclaim the Spiritual Meaning of Your Child's Bar or Bat Mitzvah*, and *Righteous Gentiles in the Hebrew Bible: Ancient Role Models for Sacred Relationships* (all Jewish Lights), among other books. He contributed to *We Have Sinned: Sin and Confession in Judaism*—Ashamnu *and* Al Chet (Jewish Lights).

a better time to come: a "messianic era" (as these Reform Jews called it). An alternative metaphor they used to describe the Jewish People was the biblical image "a kingdom of priests."

But what could that possibly mean? At the time when the Israelites heard that instruction, at the foot of Mount Sinai, what did they know about priests? The only priest with whom they had any experience was Jethro, *kohen Midian* ("a Midianite priest"; Exodus 18:1), Moses's father-in-law. Jethro was Moses's teacher, guide, and consultant.

And so, using SAT-analogy thinking, this is what we wind up with. Jethro:Moses::Jews:world. As Jethro influenced, taught, and guided Moses, using persuasion and not coercion, the Jews would ultimately influence, teach, and guide the world, using our powers of persuasion and of personal and communal example.

Over the past year, I have developed a close relationship with various Sikh leaders. One evening, over a delicious home-cooked Indian meal, they added a spiritual spice to the conversation that had not been present in the cuisine at the table.

"Jeff," they said, "we admire you Jews for how well you have been able to educate your young people and to successfully transmit your traditions and values to the next generation." (Was I going to burst their bubble? Not a chance. We might grouse about our failures, but to the outside world, our efforts look like enviable successes.) "Do you think that we could get prominent Jewish teachers and thought leaders to teach us how to do that with our young people?" (Shades of the Dalai Lama, more than twenty years ago, turning to Jewish activists and asking them, essentially, the same question!)

All of which brings us to a *piyyut* from the liturgy of the Days of Awe—"Everyone Believes" (*V'khol Ma'aminim*), a *piyyut* that is part of the traditional *Musaf* service for Rosh Hashanah. Along with various other liturgical pieces, not to mention *Musaf* itself, this *piyyut* wound up (in Reform synagogues) on God's cutting-room floor. The first time I encountered this poem was in a Conservative synagogue that had welcomed my family for services.

And, frankly, I was stunned—at its apparent arrogance.

The poem lists various theological affirmations about God:

- God is a faithful judge.
- God searches our conscience.

- God is omnipotent.
- God answers "silent prayers," that is, prayer delivered *b'lachash*, "in a whisper"; and, we must suppose (by a Talmudic process of *kal vachomer*), if whispered prayers are heard, certainly full-throated prayers make it through on high.

V'khol ma'aminim, the prayer assures us, from the word *emunah*, "faith"— "*Everyone believes on faith*" that all of this is true.

But do we? This comprehensive liturgical catechism, however impressive, is more likely to be challenging for most Jews, who would have to admit that the whole realm of *emunah* ("believing on faith") is not exactly our strong suit. Even for those who are of the believing sort, at least some of the prayer's assertions are more than controversial. Is God really omnipotent? If so, why do the good suffer? Why does evil prosper? Why do prayers go unanswered?

And yet, here we are, proclaiming that not just Jews believe this— chutzpah in and of itself—but that the whole world (*kol*, "everyone") does so. Let the record note the all-important verbal tense: not *ya'aminu* (the future) = "the whole world *will* believe," but *ma'aminim* (the present) = "the whole world *already believes*"—as in now, already, a done deal; as in "self-evident truths" that any rational person, and not just Jews, would readily understand and accept.

A little presumptuous, if you ask me.

I remain skeptical that Jews can subject the nations of the world to a theology seminar, beyond (perhaps) the simplistic "God is one," the meaning of which would be open to spirited debate in any case, especially now, as various non-Western faiths become increasingly part of the religious and ethnic fabric of American life. We are far beyond the 1950s, when theologian Will Herberg could write *Protestant, Catholic, Jew*, to describe an America composed solely of Jews and Christians in happy celebration of their country's destiny.

But we are global Jethros, remember: charged to be priests to all humanity. That, too, may sound like chutzpah, but take it as a metaphor, an image of Jewish purpose, designed to remind us that we can, in fact, be teachers to the nations.

The contents of *V'khol Ma'aminim* may no longer be our curriculum of choice. But what, then, are the teachings we might truly offer the world—teachings that we might readily invite *kol* ("everyone") *ma'aminim* ("to believe on faith"), teachings that might truly bring that messianic age a little closer?

Here would be my list.

1. *The image of God.* Trumping other theological assertions, because it is at the very core of our ethical teachings, is the idea that each of us carries within ourselves the spark of God. Or, even more tantalizing, that all of us, together, constitute the face of God—pixels in the photo of the *Shekhinah*, as the contemporary scholar of mysticism Melilah Helner-Eshed once suggested. Frankly, a world where everyone is treated as made in the divine image would be a world that has already greeted the messiah (or the messianic age).

2. *Pluralism.* In an environment where opposing sides in public debates are often demonized, we Jews have something to teach about the nature of truth. We might point to the Rabbinic notion of *shivim panim latorah* ("seventy faces of the Torah"). Or we might point to the mishnah from Bava Metzia that speaks of two people fighting over a cloak, and ultimately dividing it, as a metaphor for discerning the kind of truth that is shared in mutually complementary ways. The very word *emet* ("truth") is composed of the first, middle, and last letters of the Hebrew alphabet—as if to say that truth is all-encompassing and dialectical. The world, we would caution, is not either/or, but both/and, so that the most invigorating and redemptive exercise possible may be befriending someone with whom we profoundly disagree and asking, "How did you arrive at your position?"

3. *Responsibilities, not rights.* There is no good Hebrew term for "rights." *Z'khut* (plural: *z'khuyot*), which comes closest, doesn't quite make it. But there are many words for "responsibilities": *chiyuv*, *mitzvah*, and so on. America is overdosing on the rhetoric of rights. We need a slightly more communitarian view of shared obligation to each other. Yes, there is a right to health care, but more than that, there is an obligation to provide it. Jews and Judaism have a lot to teach here.

4. *Shabbat.* This is the only ritual item on the list. I include it to remind the world that time has a sacred dimension to it. Abraham Joshua Heschel understood the subtle nature of the sacred. Writing, as he did, at the beginning of American Jewry's postwar period of prosperity, he realized the spiritual dangers of the all-out quest for wealth. Therefore, he taught that the essence of the Sabbath was its potential to liberate people from their "things":

The seventh day is the armistice in man's cruel struggle for existence, a truce in all conflicts, personal and social, peace between man and man, man and nature, peace within man; a day on which handling money is a desecration, on which man avows his independence of that which is the world's chief idol.[1]

It is precisely this aspect of the Sabbath that contemporary Christian observers covet. As the Christian preacher Barbara Brown Taylor writes:

There is no talking about the loss of the Sabbath, then, without also talking about the rise of consumerism. There is no talking about Sabbath rest without also talking about Sabbath resistance. Since I am technically a Lord's Day Christian, I have no authority to speak of the Jewish Sabbath, but I freely indulge in what I call "holy envy." When I find something in another religious tradition that sets my heart on fire, I do not admonish myself for wishing it were mine....

By interrupting our economically sanctioned social order every week, Sabbath practice suspends our subtle and not so subtle ways of dominating one another on a regular basis. Because our work is so often how we both rank and rule over one another, resting from it gives us a rest from our own pecking orders as well. When the Wal-Mart cashier and the bank president are both lying on picnic blankets at the park, it is hard to tell them apart.[2]

This, then, is my short list of what we might indeed already believe and what we might invite the rest of the world to believe along with us. Like Jethro of Midian, we might assume our roles as teachers/advisors/consultants. And in that way, we might actualize that moment, when, to quote that liturgical masterpiece, "All the world shall come to serve Thee."

☙

The Dance of the One and the Many

Rabbi Sandy Eisenberg Sasso, DMin,
and Rabbi Dennis C. Sasso, DMin

There is often a tension between universal accounts of the world's creation and the more particular ways of reckoning time that a given people ascribes to its own origins. Judaism affirms both, the universal and the particular. While the Torah readings for Rosh Hashanah, for example, tell of our spiritual progenitors Abraham and Sarah, we do not count calendric time from their story. Rather, the Jewish New Year observance of the High Holy Days celebrates the creation

---

Rabbi Sandy Eisenberg Sasso, DMin, is rabbi emerita of Congregation Beth-El Zedeck in Indianapolis, where she has served for thirty-six years, and director of the Religion, Spirituality, and Arts Initiative at Butler University in partnership with Christian Theological Seminary. She is the author of award-winning children's books, including *God's Paintbrush* and *Shema in the Mezuzah: Listening to Each Other*, winner of the National Jewish Book Award (both Jewish Lights); and *Creation's First Light*, a finalist for the National Jewish Book Award. Her book for adults is *Midrash: Reading the Bible with Question Marks*. She contributed to *Who by Fire, Who by Water—Un'taneh Tokef*, *All These Vows—Kol Nidre*, and *May God Remember: Memory and Memorializing in Judaism—Yizkor* (all Jewish Lights).

Rabbi Dennis C. Sasso, DMin, has been senior rabbi of Congregation Beth-El Zedeck since 1977. He lectures worldwide on Caribbean and Central American Sephardic Jewry and teaches about Reconstructionism and on interfaith relations. He serves on the board of directors for the United Way of Central Indiana, the Greater Indianapolis Progress Committee, and the Lake Family Institute for Faith and Giving of the IUPUI Center on Philanthropy. He is affiliate professor of Jewish studies at Christian Theological Seminary (Disciples of Christ).

of the world. In this regard, Jews differ from Christians and Muslims. Christianity counts time from the birth of Jesus, and Islam from the year of Muhammad's Hegira. Judaism, by contrast, offers a date that belongs to all humanity: the birthing of the universe.

To be sure, Jews understand their origins from a particular family, Abraham's, and we read on Rosh Hashanah that from Abraham and Sarah will grow a great nation. On Yom Kippur, however, we return to the universal, as the prophet Isaiah reminds us that no nation can endure without a universal ethic of justice and compassion (Isaiah 57–58).

Thus, we walk a tightrope, balancing concern for the world with concern for ourselves; universal ethics on one hand and national promise on the other. Such is the tension contained in the three paragraphs called *Uv'khen*, included in the *K'dushah* ("Sanctification"), the third blessing of the High Holy Day *Amidah*. The *Uv'khen* passages are a sequel to the blessing's proclamation of holiness: "Holy are You and holy is your name. Holy are those who praise You daily." The triple holiness of the *K'dushah* invites a triple affirmation in *Uv'khen*, each one a distinct yet overlapping dimension of the sacred: (1) the fullness of creation; (2) the sacred community; (3) the righteous individual. Read backward, they remind us that without individual commitment to living justly and kindly (3), without solidarity that binds us as a people (2), there can be no universalism (1). Universal love is empty if it does not address the individual whom we encounter daily and the neighborhood in which we live. We cannot love everyone in general and no one in particular.

Individualism without responsibility to others dissolves into selfishness. Nationalism morphs easily into chauvinism. Therefore, we need all three poles: the universal, the communal, and the personal. They sustain one another. If one of them fails, the tent cannot stand. *Uv'khen* speaks of those poles, those overlapping spheres.

Regina Jonas, the first woman to become a rabbi, captured the significance of these interdependent spheres during her last sermon (Terezin, October 12, 1944):

> To be blessed by God means that no matter where we go, we must always spread goodness, blessing and perseverance in all of life's situations. It is humility toward God, unselfish dedicated love toward all His creations which uphold the world. It is and has always been Israel's task to sustain these basic pillars of the world.[1]

Other High Holy Day prayers proclaim a similar message, notably, *V'ye'etayu*, a medieval *piyyut* (liturgical poem) that forms part of this volume. Although absent from many modern versions of the *machzor*, which tend to omit complex medieval Hebrew poetry, it is a staple in the traditional services, where it immediately follows *Uv'khen*. *V'ye'etayu* captures the same themes in its especially majestic hymnic translation by Israel Zangwill, which appears even in some modern liturgies that omit the Hebrew original: "All the world shall come to serve Thee and bless Thy glorious Name, and Thy righteousness triumphant the islands shall acclaim." Solomon Schechter called it "the Marseillaise of the people of the Lord of Hosts."[2]

Both *Uv'khen* and *V'ye'etayu* are inserts into the third blessing of the *Amidah*, the *K'dushah*. Its full name, *K'dushat Hashem* ("Sanctification of [God's] Name"), indicates that it celebrates the holiness of the God, not just of Israel, but of all humanity. By contrast, the blessing that follows it is fully particularistic: *K'dushat Hayom*. It is a celebration of the "sanctity of the holy day" that Israel alone celebrates as sacred. Its wording clearly conflicts with the earlier universal message when it insists, "You have chosen us from among all peoples."

We must pause and wonder what this affirmation is doing here. Didn't we just exclaim the obligation to stand in awe at life's totality, its oneness, and its interconnectedness? Didn't we just speak of God's sovereignty over *all* people? Didn't we just recite, "*All* creation will burst into song, and hills and islands will rejoice"? Why are we now asked to affirm that we *alone* are chosen? Having spoken words of inclusivity and righteousness, do we now slide into exclusivity and self-righteousness?

In truth, the very presence of the proclamation of chosenness clarifies the constrained nature of the universalism being described here, which turns out to be different than the kind that most modern people would affirm. This is not a pluralistic or multicultural universalism celebrating the coexistence of differing religious and national identities in a setting of peace. It is, rather, the sovereignty of Israel's God alone who will rule all from Jerusalem. The vision of Micah, "All the nations shall walk in the name of their gods, even as we walk in the name of Adonai our God, forever" (Micah 4:5), had not yet come to fruition.

Mordecai Kaplan taught us that the culprit here is the exclusivity of chosenness, a concept he wanted to replace with the universal notion of vocation. His hope of expressing uniqueness in the language of vocation rather than chosenness was ahead of its time; it could not flourish in a world and time that still saw truth as exclusive and allied with dominion. What is *behind* this Jewish romance with chosenness?[3]

Perhaps the historical context of late antiquity explains why "chosenness" became such a prominent Jewish dogma. Our liturgy begins to crystallize during the period of Roman persecution that followed the destruction of the Temple and the capture of Jerusalem. In the face of this imperial power and situated, as they were, in the very heart of the empire, the Jews could have capitulated spiritually to the overwhelming Roman might. Some indeed did, leaving Judaism for any number of alternative religious options that the Roman imperial cults offered. Those who retained their Judaism, however, responded with the claim that the empire would not prove lasting; only the kingdom of God would continue forever. Jews felt chosen to represent and further that eternal divine realm.

The affirmations of *Uv'khen* thus oscillate between the particularism of Israelite chosenness and the universalism of a God whose realm exceeds Rome's. They call for the rule of the one God of Israel over the conquerors of Israel (*memshelet zadon*, "the empire of arrogance"). This is the triumphalism of the disempowered yearning for power. The downtrodden are at least elected to proclaim the sovereignty of justice and righteousness in the face of iniquity and oppression. However much the nations may hate us, the God of Israel claims us. We affirm *our* God's sovereignty and feel designated to proclaim it.

As Israel, a people born in redemption from bondage, we are reminded that we live in a world where all do not share equally in blessings, where some are more victimized than others. We dare ask God the simple question, "What about us? Throughout history we have been reviled, exiled, persecuted, and murdered. If despite all this You want us to love the world, You must show us that we are loved. Others may reject us, overlook us, oppress us, but You will not. In the Shabbat *Amidah* You remind us, 'Moses rejoiced in his portion because You called him your faithful servant.' Call us, who are faithful to the Torah of Moses, your faithful servants, and we too will rejoice and proclaim your sovereignty over all the world."

But then we must take a step further. Knowing that we are loved in all our distinctiveness, so must we love others in theirs. It is not enough to say that "everyone will arrive to serve You.... You alone, Adonai, will reign over all your creatures from Mount Zion." Adonai is *our* God, Mount Zion *our* sacred place, but other nations call God by different names from different places. Only when we all learn to honor this diversity, will "one nation not lift up sword against another nation and every person shall sit undisturbed under his/her own fig tree" (Micah 4:3–4; Isaiah 2:4).

In the best of all worlds, it is like the tidal dance of the ocean. At low tide, the beach along the shoreline fills with thousands of grains of sand. But when the tide is high, all those single particles of sand are covered by the ocean and difference disappears from sight.

We fluctuate between the receding tide that reveals the many ways in which we differ and the high tide that washes the shores with oceanic oneness. We know that there is beauty in multiplicity, richness in diversity. Meaning and purpose may be everywhere, but we can best find it in that one place called home. Its doors are open to welcome others. We also know that there are other homes and that it is good to visit there. We enjoy each other's hospitality. We know that we cannot survive alone, isolated from one another.

We choose where we would like to be at any one time—on the beach or in the ocean. The High Holy Days teach us to live in both. For the steadfast universalist, we pray, "Come out of the ocean, rest in the warm sand, collect your shells, and build your castles." To the staunch particularist, we plead, "The sands can be hot, come into the cool of the ocean. Enjoy the waves. But resist the pull of the undertow; to stand and to build, you must return to the shore again."

⚬〰〰〰⚬

In God, Even the Infinite Becomes One

Rabbi Jonathan P. Slater, DMin

O n Rosh Hashanah we declare, "Today the world was conceived, born into existence." It is that mythical idea that leads us to identify this day as the beginning of the New Year: if this day was the first day of all existence, then its return annually celebrates the New Year of creation, which is to say, a new beginning, all over again. But there is another mythic theme at play on this holy day: the renewal of God's sovereignty, our reaffirmation of God as our king.

Think of this in terms of the opening stanza of *Adon Olam*:

> Master of the world who ruled
> before any creature was created;
> Only when, by your loving desire, all came into being,
> could you truly be called "king."

While God was surely God before anything else came into being, it was only after a conscious being came into existence that God's power, authority, or sovereignty could be acknowledged. The midrash *Pirkei D'rabbi Eliezer* reads, "If there is no people to praise the king, where is

---

Rabbi Jonathan P. Slater, DMin, was ordained at The Jewish Theological Seminary of America and has a doctor of ministry degree from the Pacific School of Religion. He is the author of *Mindful Jewish Living: Compassionate Practice* and *A Partner in Holiness: Deepening Mindfulness, Practicing Compassion and Enriching Our Lives through the Wisdom of R. Levi Yitzhak of Berdichev's* Kedushat Levi. He is also codirector of programs at the Institute for Jewish Spirituality as well as an instructor in meditation at the JCC in Manhattan and other venues. He contributed to *Who by Fire, Who by Water*—Un'taneh Tokef, *All These Vows*—Kol Nidre, and *We Have Sinned: Sin and Confession in Judaism*—Ashamnu *and* Al Chet (all Jewish Lights).

the king's honor?" and Hasidic teachers regularly paraphrase even more emphatically, "There is no king without a people." This is given an even more radical turn in the early Rabbinic midrash *Sifrei*, on Deuteronomy 33:5, "Then He became king in Jeshurun, when the heads of the people assembled, the tribes of Israel together":

> When is it that "He became king in Jeshurun"? When "the tribes of Israel are together": This applies when you make yourselves one group bound together, and not when you scatter into many groups.... In a similar vein we read (Isaiah 43:12), "You are my witnesses—declares Adonai— and I am God"—"When you testify to Me, then I am God; but it is as if when you do not testify to Me, then I am not God."

Our awareness affects God. Our willingness to recognize God's sovereignty, to proclaim God "king," changes God's relationship with the world. Without us, without people to acknowledge God in the world, it is as if God has no power.

But, of course, all this is just "as if." In reality, God was surely God before anything else came into being, and all of God's creative powers would have been in effect even without anyone to notice them: God's loving desire for life, for love, for just communities—these flow through all existence with or without creatures to recognize them. That we exist at all is testimony to God's love; our consciousness witnesses to God's living presence within each of us.

In fact, we can go farther. God who was all there was before creation came into being is still all there is; all existence takes place within God, unfolding as God, testifying to the infinite forms that God can take to offer blessing to the world.

This life force is so pervasive, so transparent, that it is difficult to perceive. We cannot easily imagine that we are part of a much larger, even infinite whole called God and that what we perceive of our own personal power is not actually existent in and of itself. Taking for granted that life is a given, a blessing, a patrimony, we live as if we were independent masters of fate and fortune. We expect that our efforts should rule the day, that our power should define the parameters of our dominion. And we suffer, therefore, when this self-centeredness turns out to be an illusion, when our self-important efforts are frustrated, when our power is thwarted, when the limits of our mortality are thrown in our face. This suffering is universal, our shared human experience.

There are forces at work in the world that affect all people equally: the frailty of the body, its propensity to illness and its drift to decay; the power of natural forces over our vaunted strength; the web of interconnection into which we are inextricably woven. These are all aspects of God's sovereignty to which we must bow.

If we are prepared to concede these universal truths, we will find ourselves with all others in the unity of God's universal dominion. We may suffer loss, disaster, frustration, and death—but we will never be ashamed. There is no shame in living fully, consciously, before God. We, with all other beings, strive with full dignity before God and receive our full reward: life in this moment, vitality and awareness here and now. Inspired by the felt sense of God's presence in our lives—the vital force of life coursing through our bodies, the web of interconnectedness with all existence—we can meet whatever comes with grace, willingness, and courage.

Accepting God's sovereignty, then, demands consciousness in both circumstances: in moments of ease, when we sense the divine vital force coursing through us; in moments of loss, when we sense the truth of our limits, the force majeure of mortal existence. We neither overreach in hubris nor give up in futility. We receive our lives with gratitude in all instances and direct our efforts to bring ease to suffering, justice to the oppressed, and peace to all hearts.

This is a universal effort. All conscious beings participate in this drama. We Jews respond with our own particular voice, as others do with theirs. For us, that means the prayers of the High Holy Days, when we seek to wake up to the truth of our creatureliness—to witness and accept God's sovereignty. In similar manner, we meet for prayer on Shabbat and festivals, engage in the rituals of daily life and the cycle of life, and work to repair the world and care for others. There is no other way. Each of us as individuals will bring our own experience to these practices and prayers, hoping to find our way to consciousness, to meeting the universal truth of our existence. So do all people, in their own ways, through their own practices.

On the High Holy Days, we recite *V'khol Ma'aminim*, a double acrostic testifying to what "everyone believes." There are forty-four different expressions of what it is that we believe—because there can be no one way. We need to find our own way in, knowing that others are doing the same, but the goal is the same for all. That *piyyut* is followed by a transitional prayer: "You alone will be exalted and You will rule over all in unity." Each of our particular testimonies, the witness of each person and each people, declares God sovereign. Those multiple and varied voices—particular, but testifying to the universal—express the oneness of God and all existence. To this we can be faithful.

ᏓᎳᎦ

Yoga Poses for the Mind

WRAPPING OUR MINDS AROUND IT ALL

Rabbi Margaret Moers Wenig, DD

When a typhoon hits the Philippines, an earthquake devastates Haiti, a tsunami wipes out villages half a globe away from us, we pray for the survivors, the injured, the mourners, the homeless, and the orphaned. We contribute funds toward recovery efforts, and we send relief workers.

When a suicide bomber blows a building to smithereens or leaves a bomb-filled backpack in the midst of a marathon, we are shaken.

When a shooter mows down children and teachers in their classrooms, we reach out to the mourners, lobby for tighter gun-control laws, and increase security in our institutions.

When a neighbor's child is killed by a speeding car or fallen tree, we pray for the mourners, we sit with them and bring them food, and we advocate for safer streets.

When our own loved ones are ill, we pray that they be healed; we visit them and try to alleviate their suffering. And when we ourselves are suffering, we may cry out to God in pain or express our belief that no matter what, we remain always in God's hands.

Rabbi Margaret Moers Wenig, DD, teaches liturgy and homiletics at Hebrew Union College–Jewish Institute of Religion in New York and is rabbi emerita of Beth Am, The People's Temple. She contributed to *Who by Fire, Who by Water*—Un'taneh Tokef, *All These Vows*—Kol Nidre, *We Have Sinned: Sin and Confession in Judaism*—Ashamnu *and* Al Chet, and *May God Remember: Memory and Memorializing in Judaism*—Yizkor (all Jewish Lights).

We can't imagine the many who suffer in our own city or who ride the same trains we ride, let alone the lives of the whole house of Israel living thousands of miles away—not to mention the whole world of humanity! Here and everywhere, there are more people suffering than anyone can count! More natural and human disasters than are reported, more children shot dead than make the news, more refugees, more orphans, more homeless, more victims of war. We never see them all. We don't even know their numbers. We couldn't even name all the countries in which they suffer.

Our perspective is contained by the limited news that is reported, by the limited news we chance to encounter, by the limited time we have to notice the world beyond our work and family, by our limited capacity to take in, recall, and act on behalf of others. We can't possibly contribute *tz'dakah* even to all those worthy causes that come across our radar screens, let alone to those that have not yet discovered us. "All the world?" I can't possibly imagine the whole house of Israel let alone all the world.

And yet, in every Rosh Hashanah *Amidah* we pray that God's sovereignty, a divine realm of justice and compassion, extend over "the entire world" (*kol ha'olam kulo*), "all the earth" (*kol ha'aretz*), "all the inhabitants of your universe" (*kol yoshvei tevel artzekha*). And we look forward to a time when "everything made [*kol pa'ul*] will know that You made it, and every fashioned thing [*kol yatzur*] will understand that You fashioned it, and everything that has breath [*kol asher n'shamah b'apo*] will say: Sovereign God ... will rule over all."[1] In every *Amidah* on Rosh Hashanah and Yom Kippur we imagine a time when "all of your creatures" (*kol ma'asekha*) and "all that You have made" (*kol mah shebarata*) will feel reverence and awe for God and will unite to do God's will.[2]

"The entire world ... all the earth ... all the inhabitants of your universe ... everything made ... every fashioned thing ... everything that has breath ... all of your creatures ... all that You have made"—these are unimaginable categories for us but not, we imagine, for God.

To the God of our *machzor*, "All secrets and countless mysteries from the beginning of time are open ... there is nothing hidden from your eyes. You remember every deed, and nobody is kept out of your sight. All things are well known to You."[3] The God Jews imagine doesn't need our reminders to keep the whole world in mind. The God Jews imagine isn't dependent on NPR, the *New York Times*, the *Forward*, Pro Publica, Jon Stewart, or the blogosphere for news of us. We humans, by contrast, cannot share that perspective. We are dependent on sources such as those for our knowledge of the world beyond our immediate sight, and we choose each day which sources to follow, which to like, which to bookmark, which feeds to subscribe to. Our awareness is by necessity finite, for we are finite.

How, then, do we even begin to take in worlds beyond our very own? To comprehend even dimly what is meant by God's knowing "it all"?

On Rosh Hashanah, Yom Kippur, and all the days in between, four brief insertions in every *Amidah* serve, in effect, as four yoga poses.[4] They stretch the muscles of mind and heart to extend our concerns from the very personal to the national (easier for some), international (easier for others), and universal, that we might play at least some small role in the establishment of a divine dominion that extends "over all the earth" (*al kol ha'aretz*).

The first mind pose, "Remember *us* unto life, sovereign who delights in life, and inscribe *us* in the book of life, for your sake, God of life" (*Zokhrenu l'chayim, melekh chafetz bachayim v'khotvenu b'sefer hachayim l'ma'ankha elohim chayim*), is the easiest, for it asks only that we be mindful of "us." Ourselves and our partner who is sick. Ourselves and our partner who is barely speaking to us. Our household in financial straits. Ourselves and our adult children struggling to find their way. Ourselves and a friend, undergoing treatment for cancer. We need only be mindful of ourselves and one other person to say: *Zokhrenu*, "Remember *us*." First pose: as private and personal as that.

The second mind pose, "Who is like You, merciful parent, lovingly remembering *his/her creations* for life?" (*Mi khamokha av harachamim, zokher y'tzurav l'chayim b'rachamim*), is the most open, challenging us to be mindful of all that God fashioned, not a subset of it—all of it, not a particular couple, family, congregation, neighborhood, or nation, not even a particular species, but all that God fashioned, including mammals, birds, fish, plants, trees, air, lakes, rivers, oceans, ozone layer, polar ice caps, and all. This pose directs our consciousness out of the world of *us* into the wider world of all creation in whose viability we have a stake and a role to play. Can we be mindful of God who is "the one who remembers his/her creation" (*zokher y'tzurav*) without at the same time remembering our role as stewards of that creation?

The third mind pose, "Inscribe for a good life, *all the children of your covenant*" (*Ukh'tov l'chayim tovim kol b'nei v'ritekha*), stretches different muscles. It stipulates the covenant, which we should read as the covenant with Noah, the one God made with all humankind. Any *Mi Sheberakh*, any prayer for the sick that we might recite, could go on for hours and we still would be unable to wrap our minds around all those in need of a good life. But we can be mindful *of the concept* that it's not only *our* people who deserve a good life, but *all* people: children in Gaza and in Syrian refugee camps; political prisoners in Egypt and in Russia; Brooklyn six-year-olds whose fathers are in jail and whose teenage mothers don't make sure they get adequate sleep; boy soldiers in war-torn African countries; those incarcerated in U.S. prisons for decades for nonviolent crimes; those whose life savings were lost as a result of white-collar crimes; not only our nation but the nations of Djibouti and Burundi, Bahrain and Botswana, Mauritania and Mali, Kyrgyzstan and Kenya, Myanmar and Madagascar. We hardly know the names of all the members within this covenant, but we can be open to imagining them all as a group.

The fourth mind pose, "Remember and inscribe *us and your entire people, the house of Israel,* in the book of life, blessing, and honest livelihood" (*B'sefer chayim b'rakhah v'shalom, ufarnasah tovah, nizakher v'nikatev l'fanekha, anachnu v'khol amkha bet yisra'el, l'chayim tovim ul'shalom*), focuses our mindfulness on ourselves and all the people of Israel. Why is "us" mentioned again here when it was the focus of our first pose as well? Because here "us" does not stand alone. The following conjunction, "and," connects us with the whole house of Israel—which sociologists tell us is waning. For many North American Jews it is frankly easier to be mindful of tornado victims in the Philippines than of Jews in France or in Jerusalem. "Us and your entire people, the house of Israel" connects me to the Jews of Israel who support the establishment of a Palestinian state, as well as to those who don't, because they fear for their safety when Palestine becomes the twenty-third Arab state and the fifty-eighth Muslim state. It connects me to the children and grandchildren of those who left Europe for Palestine but who now face international boycotts, divestment, and sanctions for the "imperialism" they manifest by being there. "When my father was a young man in Vilna," writes Amos Oz, "every wall in Europe said 'Jews go home to Palestine.' Fifty years later, when he went back to Europe on a visit, the walls all screamed, 'Jews get out of Palestine.'"[5]

God who is "sovereign over all the earth" (*melekh al kol ha'aretz*) is also "the sanctifier of Israel" (*m'kadesh yisra'el*).[6] How can we even begin to wrap our minds around such difficult and abstract notions? Gradually, bit by bit, day after day, for ten whole days, these four mind poses stretch us into postures that open us up, moving from the personal to the national, the international, and the universal.

Universal in Vision, Particular by Necessity

Rabbi Daniel G. Zemel

I am regularly drawn to that great statement of Ben Bag Bag, "Turn it and turn it because everything is in it" (*Pirkei Avot* 5:22). I like to think that when Ben Bag Bag said "everything," he meant "everything": wisdom and ignorance, love and hate, good and evil, joy and sadness; in short, everything. The Hebrew Bible gives us all of it—the nobility of Abraham arguing for the lives of strangers in Sodom and Gomorrah, but also Cain killing his brother Abel. Isn't every reader of the Bible shocked to discover that we go from paradise to fratricide in a mere eight verses? We have the ironic wisdom of Ecclesiastes and the buffoonery of Ahasuerus; the devotion of Ruth for Naomi and the rebellion of Absalom against his father David.

So, of course these High Holy Days have both particularism and universalism, which is to say that no less than the Bible, they have "everything." And it has them both positively and negatively. Particularism is admirable when we hold ourselves responsible to live up to what God commanded us on Sinai. It is questionable when we pray for Jewish well-being as if the destiny of others is unimportant. Proper universalism locates our own best interests among the family of nations; improper universalism loses sight of the particular vantage point on those interests that Judaism alone provides.

I like to think that the Jewish instinct is universal; the Jewish method is particular. Avishai Margalit cites critic G. K. Chesterton in

Rabbi Daniel G. Zemel is the senior rabbi of Temple Micah in Washington, D.C. He contributed to *Who by Fire, Who by Water*—Un'taneh Tokef, *All These Vows*—Kol Nidre, *We Have Sinned: Sin and Confession in Judaism*—Ashamnu and Al Chet, and *May God Remember: Memory and Memorializing in Judaism*—Yizkor (all Jewish Lights).

saying, "The trouble with the Christian project of transforming humanity into a community of love is not that it has been tried and found wanting but that it has been left untried."[1] Margalit's point is that caring requires a sense of belonging, and belonging to the family of man is simply not "thick" enough to induce a motivation capable of compelling serious obligation to others.

In other words, the Christian project is undoable, contrary to human nature. Human beings are incapable of carrying it out because our human sense of "caring" dissipates the farther removed we are from the genuine experience of belonging to a "something" rather than an "everything."

Judaism offers a different approach. To be sure, our God created the whole universe and obliges us to care for it all. But we care for it all as Jews. We inhabit the universe from the perspective of concentric circles: our family, our tribe or people, then the entire human family. The first comes so naturally that it is hard to generalize from it directly to the world as a whole; the second can follow easily enough, however, because peoplehood is experienced as extended family; only then does the third one follow—and not just as a mental construct, a hypothetical case (as it were), but a visceral demand because of the emotional pull we experience from being part of a particular people.

Rosh Hashanah and Yom Kippur, therefore, provide a universal message, but only from within a strong sense of particularism.

Rosh Hashanah is spectacularly universal, celebrating, as it does, the creation of the universe and the birth of humanity. Its concerns are the possibility and potential of life—all life. The scriptural readings give us Abraham, "the father of a multitude of nations." They introduce Sarah and Hagar, Isaac and Ishmael. The primary liturgical texts celebrate "the day of the world's conception" and God who is "passionate for life." The dominant sound is the blast of the shofar—no knowledge of a particular language is required to understand the call of the horn.

Yom Kippur, too, evokes a powerful universal disposition. The uniform is all white. The diet is fasting. The universal God is judge, and the ultimate aim is universal human redemption—"All the world shall come to serve Thee."

When seen through this lens, Rosh Hashanah and Yom Kippur recall the earlier intent of the biblical authors. The universal God creates humanity in his/her image to be his/her partner in the adventure called "creation." The plan goes wrong when the first partners, Adam and Eve, trash the partnership by disobeying its terms. Their exile serves to reveal even greater shortcomings in God's chosen partners: Cain kills Abel, failing to realize that he is supposed to be "his brother's keeper." By the time of Noah, things are so out of hand—the evil and corruption so great—that God decides to begin again. The Flood proves to be successful in destroying all of humankind except Noah and his family, but their descendants are easily as corrupt as their ancestors.

With Abraham, God takes a different approach. Rather than working in partnership with the entire human race, God enters into a covenant with one man and his family to pursue what is "good and just" but to do so for "all the families of the earth." God's design is still universal—it is just being pursued one family at a time. Margalit would say that the Torah promotes the belonging, connection, and "thickness" that were missing before.

The High Holy Days contain this side of the equation as well—not just hypothetical universalism, but universalism from the perspective of the Jewish covenant. It is not just our obligation, but our *Jewish* obligation to remember that humanity is created in the image of God, that we are each part of a greater whole, and that Genesis signals a universal covenant with all humankind. It is the particularistic *Jewish* celebration of a particularistic *Jewish* New Year that heralds the birth of the universal family of humankind.

This same intermingling of the universal and the particular is inherent in *Uv'khen*. We first hear the call for God to be recognized by all creation. This is the God of the garden with Adam and Eve; the God who hears Cain's cry "Am I my brother's keeper?"; the God of the rainbow covenant after the Flood wherein humanity is reminded of God's constant presence and promise. God seeks the entire human family to "form one group to do your will with complete dedication." God needs no particulars. God's triumph will come with eventual human enlightenment, not as the result of the "strength of your hand, the might of your grasp." The first *Uv'khen* is the call to an endlessly patient God awaiting the evolution of universal human consciousness.

The second *Uv'khen* is the call for God to recognize the Jewish People, who, in all their particularity, have carried God's universal message to the world. It pleads the case of those who have committed themselves to the universal human brotherhood by virtue of Torah. This is acknowledgment of the Jewish experience in history, too often marginalized and defeated, but by virtue of their own experience, able to empathize with others and pursue the universal mandate to care for all the world. If Israel is to continue its task, it needs constant "good hope" that it is not forgotten.

This is the call of those to whom Yehuda Bauer refers when he writes:

> European culture has two pillars: Athens and Rome on the one hand and Jerusalem on the other.... When the Nazis wanted to carry out their rebellion against Western culture, was it not the Jews, those still living reminders of one of the sources of that culture, that they had to annihilate?[2]

This is the particularism of a long-suffering minority who seek out their God for the support and the confidence to continue speaking at all.

The last *Uv'khen* longs for the triumphal day when we will know that the wait has been worth it. With the universal mandate proclaimed and the particularistic suffering recognized, the poet turns to the guarantee that in the longest run possible God's word will prevail and God's triumph will be final. This is Isaiah's messianic vision of the lion and the lamb. This is the psalmist recognizing that "all the nations will come to ascend the mountain of Adonai" and in the end of days, God's house will be "a house for all people." This is the glory of "All the world shall come to serve Thee."

Uv'khen becomes a marvelous encapsulation of Jewish history and theology, people and faith. The Bible, the most universal of books, is preserved by a people who know that redemption is earned by one family caring for its own, then one clan caring for its own, and only eventually, one group forging a bond with another.

The universal vision of the Bible is at one and the same time the story of a particular people in history, whose task it is to proclaim the message of the universal God in the first place. The final *Uv'khen* signals a confidence in both: there will be sustenance for Israel and reward for all the suffering, because it is Israel's task to transform evil into goodness and bring redemption for all.

ᘒᙏᙏᘙ

Notes

Why Be Jewish? The Universalist Message of the High Holy Days, by Rabbi Lawrence A. Hoffman, PhD

1. A threefold dichotomy drawn from ritual theory; see, especially, Tom F. Driver, *The Magic of Ritual* (New York: Harper San Francisco, 1991). Later editions renamed *Liberating Rites*.
2. For the term "moral space," see Charles Taylor, *Sources of the Self* (Cambridge, MA: Harvard University Press, 1989), 25–52.
3. Found in Menachem Zulay, *The Poems of Yannai Collected from Genizah Fragments and Other Sources* [in Hebrew] (Berlin: Schocken, 1938), 335–36.
4. Rabbi Lawrence A. Hoffman, PhD, ed., *Who by Fire, Who by Water:* Un'taneh Tokef, Prayers of Awe (Woodstock, VT: Jewish Lights, 2010), 13–28.
5. Menahem Zulay, *Piyyutei Yannai* (Berlin: Schocken, 1938), 336–37.
6. See Ismar Elbogen, *Jewish Liturgy: A Comprehensive History*, trans. Raymond Scheindlin (original German, 1913; Philadelphia: Jewish Publication Society, 1993), 118.

Monotheism, Mission, and Multiculturalism: Universalism Then and Now, by Dr. Annette M. Boeckler

1. Other examples from various times can be found in Isaiah 49:7, 55:5–13, 60; Jeremiah 3:17; Micah 4; Zechariah 2:15, 6:15, 8:20–22; Psalms 96, 100, 102:23.
2. An overview of the history of the debate that was virulent throughout the nineteenth century can be found in Reinhold Bernhardt, *Der Absolutheitsanspruch des Christentums: Von der Aufklärung bis zur Pluralistischen Religionstheologie*, 2nd ed. (Gütersloh, Germany: Gütersloher Verlagshaus, 1993).
3. Louis Lewandowski, *Todah W'simrah: Vierstimmige Chöre und Soli für den israelitischen Gottesdienst. Zweiter Teil: Festgesänge* (Berlin: Ed. Bote & G. Bock, 1882), no. 193 (pp. 202–5).
4. A collection of three tunes can be found in *Songs of Repentance: Music for Rosh Hashanah and Yom Kippur* (New York: Transcontinental Music Publication, 2000), 244ff. For Michael Isaacson, pp. 246–48; for Max Janowski, p. 249, to the Hebrew text by Mary Feinsinger. For the tune by A. W. Binder, see *Union Hymnal, Songs and Prayers for Jewish Worship*, 3rd ed. (New York: Central Conference of American Rabbis, 1948), no. 63. For the tune by Leon M. Kramer, see *The Army and Navy Hymnal* (1921), no. 14, p. 385.
5. Abraham Geiger, *Plan zu einem neuem Gebetbuche nebst Begründungen* (Breslau, 1870), 6.

6. Claude Montefiore, *The Synoptic Gospels*, vol. II (London: Macmillan, 1909), 594.

7. For an overview on Jewish understandings of a missionary task, see Reuven Silverman, "Jewish Mission," in *Jewish and Christians: Perspectives on Mission; The Lambeth-Jewish Forum*, ed. Reuven Silverman, Patrick Morrow, and Daniel Langton (Cambridge: Woolf Institute, 2011), 3–21; see also Deborah Prinz, "The Convert among Us" (paper for UAHC Outreach Commission), huc.edu/gerecht/images/sermonsarticles/r.%20prinz%20article; Sue Fishkoff, "The More Jews the Better?" *Moment Magazine* (July/August 2002), www.beliefnet.com/Faiths/Judaism/2002/07/The-More-Jews-The-Better.aspx?p=1.

8. Israel I. Mattuck, "The Missionary Idea," in *Aspects of Progressive Jewish Thought*, ed. I. I. Mattuck (London: Victor Gollancz, 1954), 49.

9. Samuel Holdheim, "This Is Our Task" (1853), translation quoted in W. Gunther Plaut, *The Rise of Reform Judaism: A Sourcebook of Its European Origins* (New York: World Union for Progressive Judaism, 1963), 138.

10. Leo Baeck, *Das Wesen des Judentums* (1905), 77.

11. Leo Baeck, "The Mission of Judaism: Its Later Development and Its Significance for World Judaism Today," in *Report of the 6th International WUPJ Conference*, London, July 14–19, 1949, 72–77.

12. Leo Baeck, 1946 Presidential Address to the Fifth International Conference of the World Union for Progressive Judaism.

13. Abraham Joshua Heschel, "No Religion Is an Island," *Union Theological Seminary Quarterly Review* 21, no. 2, pt. 1 (January 1966): 14.

A Sage among the Gentiles? A Halakhic Lesson on Moral Universalism, by Rabbi Daniel Landes

1. Mossad Harav Kook edition of the *Mishneh Torah, Rambam Le'Am*, vol. 14, p. 398, n. 69.

The Prayer for the State of Israel: Universalism and Particularism, by Rabbi Dalia Marx, PhD

1. For example, the blessing recited in the morning service "Blessed ... who did not create me a gentile," a blessing that was changed in liberal liturgy to a positive language: "Blessed ... who created me a Jew." See Joel Kahn, *The Three Blessings: Boundaries, Censorship, and Identity in Jewish Liturgy* (New York: Oxford University Press, 2011).

2. Jonathan Sarna, "Jewish Prayers for the U.S. Government," in *Moral Problems in American Life*, ed. K. Halttunen and L. Perry (Ithaca, NY: Cornell University Press, 1998), 202.

3. See Joseph Tabory, "The Piety of Politics: Jewish Prayers for the State of Israel," in *Liturgy in the Life of the Synagogue: Studies in the History of Jewish Prayer*, ed. Ruth Langer and Steven Fine (Winona Lake, IN: Eisenbrauns, 2005), esp. 229–31. For examples of such prayers, see David Golinkin, "Prayers for the Government and the State of Israel," 2006, Schechter Institute website, www.schechter.edu/insightIsrael.aspx?ID=35.

4. *Sefer Abudraham Hashalem* (Jerusalem: T'khiyah, 1963), 136.

5. Barry Schwartz, "'*Hanoten Teshua*': The Origin of the Traditional Jewish Prayer for the Government," *Hebrew Union College Annual* 57 (1986): 113–20.

6. Regarding the leadership of the founder of Chabad, see, e.g., Samuel Heilman and Menachem Friedman, *The Rebbe: The Life and Afterlife of Menachem Mendel Schneerson* (Princeton, NJ: Princeton University Press, 2010).

7. *Siddur Hashalom* (Moscow 1956, 1968) contains special prayers for the leaders of the USSR, "the defenders of peace in the entire world."

8. See Sarna, "Jewish Prayers," 204–5.

9. See Aharon Arend, *Pirkey Mechkar L'yom Ha'atsma'ut* (Ramat Gan, Israel: Bar Ilan University, 1998), 176–200; Rabbi Dalia Marx, "Liturgical Responses to the Disengagement Process in Summer 2005" [in Hebrew], *Akdamot* 18 (2007): 119–39; Joel Rappel, *The Prayer for the State of Israel* (forthcoming).

10. Regarding the Prayer for the State of Israel, see Joel Rappel, *The Convergence of Politics and Prayer: Jewish Prayers for the Government and the State of Israel* (Boston: Academic Studies Press, 2008); Tabory, "The Piety of Politics."

11. See Rappel, *Prayer for the State of Israel*.

12. Ibid.

13. References to the Arab countries do appear in the different versions of *Al Hanissim*, another Israeli-Zionist liturgical innovation. (See Rabbi Dalia Marx, "*Al Hanissim for Yom Ha'atsma'ut*," forthcoming.)

14. Rappel, *Prayer for the State of Israel*.

15. In some cases one may say that *Ha'avodah Shebalev* reflects a hyper-Zionist perspective, much more accented than in traditional prayer books. See Rabbi Dalia Marx, "Ideology, Theology, and Style in Israeli Reform Liturgy," *CCAR Journal* (Winter 2010): 52–62.

16. See Uriel Tal, "Contemporary Hermeneutics and Self-Views on the Relationship between State and Land," in *The Land of Israel: Jewish Perspectives*, ed. Rabbi Lawrence A. Hoffman (Notre Dame, IN: University of Notre Dame Press, 1986), 316–38.

17. See Michael Meyer, *Response to Modernity: A History of the Reform Movement in Judaism* (New York: Oxford University Press, 1988), esp. 326–34.

18. *Gates of Prayer* also contains a "meditation," titled "Land of Hope and Prayer" (p. 240), composed by Rabbi Stephan O. Parnes. It appears as a personal text, not as part of the communal service. This text, slightly revised, is printed also in the U.S. military siddur from 1984.

19. "Fathers" became, in the 2008 edition, "[God of the] generations"; "all mankind" was changed to "all." I thank Rabbi Jonathan Magonet, for the information regarding the creation of this text and its evolvement.

20. *Daily Prayer Book of the United Hebrew Congregations of the British Empire*, 1890. It had been issued by the office of Chief Rabbi Nathan Marcus Adler and provided with an English translation by Rabbi Simon Singer, whence it received its name.

21. The prayer appears originally in Hebrew and German; I translated it into English. In some circles, both liberal and more traditional, this change to the jussive is currently made in the way the words are spoken aloud, even if the written version does not already contain it.

22. After fierce discussions on this question, the editing committee of the Israeli Reform Passover Haggadah, *Haggadah Lazman Hazeh*, decided to keep the traditional text but to add the jussive form in parentheses (Jerusalem, 2009, p. 88).

23. Aryeh Cohen, quoted in Ruth Andrew Ellenson, "Avant-Garde L.A. Minyan Adopts Prayer for Zion," *Forward*, June 28, 2002.

24. Cohen, ibid.

25. Translation by Ariella Radwin and Aryeh Cohen.

26. For a discussion of the references of the Holocaust in modern prayer books, see Rabbi Dalia Marx, "Memorializing the Holocaust," in *May God Remember: Memory and Memorializing in Judaism—Yizkov, Prayers of Awe*, ed. Rabbi Lawrence A. Hoffman (Woodstock, VT: Jewish Lights, 2012), 39–62.

27. See above, note 10.

28. It is hard to collect data reflecting this phenomenon; sometimes it seems that the press exaggerates its proportions.

29. Cf., in general, Lawrence A. Hoffman, "The Liturgical Message," in *Gates of Understanding*, ed. Rabbi Lawrence A. Hoffman (New York: Union of American Hebrew Congregations, 1977), 1:117–31; Rabbi Lawrence A. Hoffman "Jewish Liturgy and American Experience," *Religion and Intellectual Life* 5, no. 1 (Fall 1987): 71–80; Rabbi Lawrence A. Hoffman, *Beyond the Text: A Holistic Approach to Liturgy* (Bloomington: Indiana University Press), 1987.

30. This chart, albeit general and schematic, may show the evolvement of the tension between particularism and universalism in liberal liturgy:

	Particularism	Universalism
Traditional prayer	+	(-)
Classic Reform prayer	-	+
Contemporary Liberal prayer	+	+

31. A conspicuous exception to this rule is a prayer composed by Rabbi Shmuel Avidor Hakohen, who was ordained by Rabbi Herzog, the composer of the official PSI. The last paragraph of his PSI begins with the following words:

Our Heavenly Father, bless us, our neighbors and all the nations of the world, and fulfill the words of the prophet, "Nation shall not lift up sword against nation, neither shall they learn war any more" (Isa. 2:4).

אבינו שבשמים, ברך אותנו, את
שכנינו ואת כל עמי תבל, למען
יקוימו בנו דברי הנביא: 'לֹא יִשָּׂא
גוֹי אֶל גּוֹי חֶרֶב וְלֹא יִלְמְדוּ עוֹד
מִלְחָמָה' (ישעיהו ב, ד).

I thank Rabbi Lawrence A. Hoffman, the editor of this book, and Rabbi Shelton Donnell for their abundant help, as well as Dr. Joel M. Hoffman for his translation of some of the Hebrew prayers into English. I also thank the people who helped me collect the prayers for the State of Israel and those who allowed me to use the prayers they composed: Rabbi Aryeh Cohen, Professor Aharon Loewenschuss, Rabbi Jonathan Magonet, Rabbi Yehoram Mazor, Orna Meir-Stacey, Paul Piwnicki, and Dr. Joel Rappel. Every effort has been made to trace and acknowledge the copyright holders for the material included in this chapter. The contributor apologizes for any errors or omissions that may remain and asks that any omissions be brought to her attention so that they may be corrected in future editions.

The Music of *V'ye'etayu*—"All the World," by Dr. Mark L. Kligman

1. Jeffrey Shiovitz, ed., *Zamru Lo: The Next Generation*, vol. 2 (New York: Cantors Assembly, 2006), 148–49.

For a Judaism of Human Concerns, by Rabbi Walter Homolka, PhD, DHL

1. Bradley Shavit Artson, "Building a Future Worthy of Our Past," blog on the *Times of Israel*, December 1, 2013.
2. Hermann Cohen, *Religion of Reason Out of the Sources of Judaism* (Oxford, UK: Oxford University Press, 1995), 452.
3. Artson, "Building a Future."

Is Judaism Too Important to Be Left Just to Jews? The *Sh'ma* and the *Alenu*, by Rabbi Reuven Kimelman, PhD

1. See *Sifrei Deuteronomy* 32, ed. Finkelstein, p. 54.

2. עלינו: הוא אלהינו אין עוד אמת מלכנו אפס זולתו

שמע של ערבית: אמת...הוא יי אלהינו ואין זולתו

שמע של שחרית: אמת אלהי עולם מלכנו

Alenu:	hu eloheinu ein od **emet** malkeinu efes zulato		
Shema shel arvit:	**emet** hu adonai eloheinu		v'ein zulato
Shema shel shaharit: **emet**	elohei olam	malkeinu	

Alenu:	He is our God, there is no other; **truly** our king,		none besides Him
Evening Sh'ma: **Truly**, He is Adonai our God			there is no one besides Him
Morning Sh'ma: **Truly**	the eternal God	is our king	

3. *Esther Rabbah* 1:4 (end).

4. See Reuven Kimelman, "The Rabbinic Theology of the Physical: Blessings, Body and Soul, Resurrection, Covenant and Election," in *The Cambridge History of Judaism*, vol. 4, *The Late Roman-Rabbinic Period*, ed. Steven Katz (Cambridge, UK: Cambridge University Press, 2006), 946–76.

5. See Reuven Kimelman, "Blessing Formulae and Divine Sovereignty in Rabbinic Liturgy," in *Liturgy in the Life of the Synagogue: Studies in the History of Jewish Prayer*, ed. Ruth Langer and Steven Fine (Winona Lake, IN: Eisenbrauns, 2005), 1–39.

6. Mitchell First, "Aleinu: Obligation to Fix the World or the Text?," *Hakirah* 11 (2011): 187–97, points out that the Rabbinic expression is *tikkun ha'olam*, not *tikkun olam* as here, and is more likely to be followed by *et* rather than a *bet* as here; see Isaiah 40:12, Job 28:25, Psalm 89:3b.

7. For the debate on this, see Reuven Kimelman, *The Mystical Meaning of Lekhah Dodi and Kabbalat Shabbat* [in Hebrew] (Jerusalem: Magnes Press and Cherub Press, 2003), 97–103, 175–76. The biblical precedents are Jethro, Rahab, and Naaman.

8. I am indebted to the editor of this volume, Lawrence Hoffman, and to Emily Wichland, vice president of Editorial at Jewish Lights, for their substantive and stylistic improvements.

"We" and "They" in Jewish Liturgy, by Rabbi Jonathan Magonet, PhD

1. I am grateful to Lawrence A. Hoffman for drawing my attention to this pattern.

2. The form appears twice in the *Tanakh*: Ecclesiastes 8:10 and Esther 4:16. The latter may be the source of the term here, Esther having fasted in preparation for risking her life in approaching King Ahasuerus. However, fasting is not relevant to Rosh Hashanah, and in Esther the term refers back to pre-existing conditions, whereas here it refers forward as an imperative to God to establish the divine reign.

3. Either etymologically related to the root *kun*, "to establish," or simply as a wordplay. So if it is linked to Genesis, *uv'khen* would mean "because the world is established by God...."

4. The same theme is addressed indirectly in the choice of the Torah reading for the first day of Rosh Hashanah. The birth of Isaac leads to the sending away of Ishmael (Genesis 21), thus creating the "other" who will himself become a twelvefold nation as the child, like Isaac, of God's blessing to Abraham.

5. *Denkschrift*, 1869, as cited in Jakob J. Petuchowski, *Prayerbook Reform in Europe* (New York: World Union for Progressive Judaism, 1968), 299.

6. For the terminology, see Henri Atlan, "Chosen People," in *Contemporary Jewish Religious Thought*, ed. Arthur A Cohen and Paul Mendes-Flohr (London: Collier Macmillan, 1987), 55–59.

All Shall Come to Serve (My Version of) Thee, by Dr. Wendy Zierler

1. Edna Nahshon, ed., *From the Ghetto to the Melting Pot: Israel Zangwill's Jewish Plays* (Detroit: Wayne State University Press, 2006), 29.
2. Ibid., 33.
3. Meri-Jane Rochelson, *A Jew in the Public Arena: The Career of Israel Zangwill* (Detroit: Wayne State University Press, 2008), 4.
4. "Israel Zangwill at the Judaeans," *American Hebrew*, October 28, 1898, 771. Quoted in Nahshon, *From the Ghetto to the Melting Pot*, 42.
5. Arthur Davis and Herbert M. Adler, eds. *Synagogue Service for New Year*, (London: George Routledge & Sons, 1906), 99–100, 105–6, 145–46, 151–52. Zangwill also contributed translations of such standard yearlong prayers as *Adon Olam* and *Yigdal* (see pp. 23, 26). The other three are *Aderet Mamlakhah* ("Ah, Why Is the Kingdom"), *Adirei Ayumah* ("The Terrible Sons"), and *Melekh Elyon* ("Highest Divinity").
6. See www.bartleby.com/98/411.html, www.hymnary.org/text/all_the_world_shall_come_to_serve_thee, and www.hymntime.com/tch/htm/a/l/l/w/all-worsc.htm.
7. Rochelson, *Jew in the Public Arena*, 19.
8. Israel Zangwill, *The Melting Pot*, in Nahshon, *From the Ghetto*, 288.
9. Email correspondence with Meri-Jane Rochelson, August 23, 2013.
10. Zangwill, *Melting Pot*, 362–63; emphasis added.
11. Nahshon, *From the Ghetto*, 249.
12. Israel Zangwill, "The Mission of Israel," *Jewish Quarterly Review* 9 (1897): 222.
13. David Biale, "The Melting Pot and Beyond: Jews and the Politics of American Identity" in *Insider/Outsider*, ed. David Biale, Michael Galchinsky, and Susannah Heschel (Berkeley: University of California Press, 1998), 19.
14. Ibid., 21–22.
15. S. Y. Agnon, "*Han'shikah Harishonah*," *Keshet* 20 (Summer 1963): 5–8.
16. S. Y Agnon, "First Kiss," trans. Neal Kozodoy, in *Twenty-One Stories*, ed. Nahum Glatzer (Philadelphia: Jewish Publication Society, 1970), 273.
17. Deuteronomy 7:1–2.
18. Agnon, "First Kiss," 274.
19. Ibid., 275–76.
20. Ibid., 276.
21. S. Y. Agnon, "*Zikaron Lasefer*," in *Yamim Noar'im*, 3rd ed. (Jerusalem and New York: Schocken Books, 1946), 3–4.

Two Kinds of Universalism, by Rabbi Marc Saperstein, PhD

1. *UPB* II NR, 79; *UPB* II R, 76; cf. *UPB* II, 71. In quotations from various editions of the *UPB*, references to "man," "men," "brothers," and so forth should *not* be understood as excluding women. Liturgical abbreviations: *UPB* I = *Union Prayer Book* Part I (1895); *UPB* I R = *Union Prayer Book*

Part I Revised (1930); *UPB* I NR = *Union Prayer Book* Part I Newly Revised (1960); *UPB* II = *Union Prayer Book* Part II (1894); *UPB* R II = *Union Prayer Book* Part II Revised (1942); *UPB* II NR = *Union Prayer Book* Part II Newly Revised (1953); *MT* = *Mishkan T'filah* (CCAR, 2007); *FOP* I = *Forms of Prayer* I (UK Movement for Reform Judaism, 2008).

2. *UPB* II NR, 84.

3. Some contemporary prayer books have reinserted this line; cf. *ArtScroll Siddur* series and even the *Koren Siddur* (2009), edited by the former chief rabbi of the United Hebrew Congregations of the Commonwealth, Jonathan Sacks.

4. See Marc Saperstein, "Universalism versus Martyrdom: *Un'taneh Tokef* and Its Frame Narrative," in *Who by Fire, Who by Water:* Un'taneh Tokef, Prayers of Awe, ed. Lawrence A. Hoffman (Woodstock, VT: Jewish Lights, 2010), 73–74.

5. *UPB* I NR, 39.

6. *UPB* I NR, 45.

7. *UPB* I NR, 34; cf. *UPB* I R, 32; *UPB* I, 39.

8. *MT*, 70.

9. *FOP* I, 226.

Worshiping in Technicolor; Seeing Others in Black and White, by Rabbi Tony Bayfield, CBE, DD

1. Tom Holland, *In the Shadow of the Sword: The Battle for Global Empire and the End of the Ancient World* (London: Little, Brown, 2012).

2. These are genuine references but carefully chosen from a vast sea of literature. The discussion on penis size is in the Babylonian Talmud, Bava Metzia 84a.

3. It is so regarded by the British scholar Hyam Maccoby in *The Day God Laughed* (London: Robson Books, 1978).

4. The covenant with Noah, Genesis 9:9.

5. The origins of the book of Jonah probably go back to 500 BCE.

6. *Service of the Heart* was published by the Union of Liberal and Progressive Synagogues, London, in 1967.

7. *Forms of Prayer for Jewish Worship*, vol. 3 (London: Reform Synagogues of Great Britain, 1985), 589.

8. Jonathan Sacks, *The House We Build Together* (London: Continuum, 2007), 26. It is fascinating that Rabbi Sacks includes racial difference as a Jewish characteristic to be retained.

9. One of the challenges involved in liturgical change and innovation is that so few new prayers stand the test of time. But each generation today has to take the risk that involves. In any event, the Yom Kippur *Vidui* is *the* place where we can rebalance our particularism and universalism in terms that resonate both communally and individually.

An Open Door, by Dr. Erica Brown

1. In a funeral speech for Black Buffalo, heroic Indian leader, delivered June 14, 1815, at a great council at Portage des Sioux.

Our Jewish Golden Rule,
by Rabbi Lawrence A. Englander, CM, DHL, DD

1. Talmud, Shabbat 31a.
2. See, e.g., Carl Sagan's essay "Venus and Dr. Velikovsky," in *Broca's Brain* (New York: Random House, 1979), chap. 7.
3. *Iliad* 18:356–57.
4. Immanuel Velikovsky, *Worlds in Collision* (London: Abacus, 1972), 285.

A "Light unto the Nations" or a "People Who Dwell Alone"?,
by Rabbi Shoshana Boyd Gelfand

1. Thomas L. Friedman, *The Lexus and the Olive Tree* (New York: Anchor Books, 2000), 31.

Laughing Islands, Dancing Prayer Books,
by Rabbi Edwin Goldberg, DHL

1. Jonathan Sacks, ed., *The Koren Rosh Hashana Mahzor* (Jerusalem: Koren, 2011), 587.

Crowning "the Un-king" King, by Rabbi Elie Kaunfer, DHL

1. *Pirkei D'rabbi Eliezer* 3. Cf. *Midrash T'hillim* 13:1, ed. Buber, 55a.
2. Talmud, Rosh Hashanah 31a. Cf. Solomon Schechter, *Some Aspects of Rabbinic Theology* (New York: Macmillan, 1910), 82.
3. Schechter, *Aspects*, 82.

Word and World: From Faith to Action,
by Ruth Messinger and Lisa Exler

1. While previously in Genesis God speaks to Abraham, this is notably the first time that Abraham responds and speaks to God. At this point in the narrative, Abram's name has not yet been changed to Abraham, but we will refer to him as Abraham in the interest of consistency.
2. Nahum Sarna, *JPS Torah Commentary: Genesis* (Philadelphia: Jewish Publication Society, 1989), 112–3.
3. Ibid., 113.
4. Jonathan Sacks, *The Koren Rosh Hashana Mahzor* (Jerusalem: Koren, 2011), 581.
5. In his commentary on the *machzor*, Rabbi Yosef Tzvi Rimon cites Rabbi Samson Raphael Hirsch's commentary on Genesis 15:6 in which Hirsch asserts that belief is not only an intellectual affirmation but that it implies action as well. See Yosef Tzvi Rimon, *Machzor Koren L'yom Hakippurim* (Jerusalem: Koren, 2012), 355.
6. Martin Luther King Jr., "Nobel Peace Prize Acceptance Speech," 1964, www.nobelprize.org/nobel_prizes/peace/laureates/1964/king-acceptance_en.html.
7. Joseph B. Soloveitchik, *Halakhic Man* (Philadelphia: Jewish Publication Society, 1984), 105.

"So Loud Your Praise Shall Sing," by Rabbi Charles H. Middleburgh, PhD

1. R. Loewe, *Hebrew Poems and Translations* (Israel: Haberman Institute, 2010), 327–35.
2. Unpublished.
3. Precedent for preferring *shilton* actually goes back to pioneering progressive liturgies such as David Einhorn's *Olat Tamid* (1856) and Marcus Jastrow's *Avodat Yisrael* (1872).
4. Kohelet (Ecclesiastes) is now viewed as a post-exilic work, due to the high frequency of Aramaisms, the latest date to which it can be assigned being 180 BCE, when Ben Sirach, who quotes Kohelet, was living and writing in Jerusalem.
5. *Iolanthe, The Mikado,* and *The Pirates of Penzance,* to name but three.
6. The tune called "Noel" was adapted by Sir Arthur Sullivan for a carol, "It Came Upon the Midnight Clear," written in 1849 by Edmund Hamilton Sears.
7. F. Brown, S. R. Driver, and C. A. Briggs, *Hebrew and English Lexicon of the Old Testament* (Oxford: Oxford University Press, 1972).

Let It Be! Let It Be! Let It Be!, by Rabbi Jack Riemer

1. Amos Oz, *In the Land of Israel,* trans. Maurice Goldberg-Bartura (San Diego, CA: Harcourt, 1983), 259.

What We Can All Believe, by Rabbi Jeffrey K. Salkin, DMin

1. Abraham Joshua Heschel, *The Sabbath: Its Meaning for Modern Man* (New York: Farrar, Straus, and Young, 1951), 28–29.
2. Barbara Brown Taylor, *An Altar in the World: A Geography of Faith* (New York: HarperOne, 2009), Kindle Edition.

The Dance of the One and the Many, by Rabbi Sandy Eisenberg Sasso, DMin, and Rabbi Dennis C. Sasso, DMin

1. From the film *Regina,* a poetic documentary by Diana Groó (Katapult Film).
2. Ed Feld, ed., *Mahzor Lev Shalem: Rosh Hashanah and Yom Kippur* (New York: Rabbinical Assembly, 2010), 150.
3. The Reconstructionist *machzor* does not use the language of chosenness. The prayer that sanctifies the day's holiness (the *K'dushat Hayom*) reads, "You have loved us, and have taken pleasure in us, and have made us holy with your mitzvoth, and you have brought us, Sovereign One, near to your service, and have called us to the shelter of your great and holy name." *Kol Haneshama: Prayerbook for the Days of Awe* (Philadelphia: Reconstructionist Press, 1999), 367.

Yoga Poses for the Mind: Wrapping Our Minds around It All, by Rabbi Margaret Moers Wenig, DD

1. From the *K'dushat Hayom*, the central blessing of the *Amidah*. See Philip Birnbaum, trans. and ed., *High Holiday Prayer Book* (New York: Hebrew Publishing Company, 1951), 35, 205, 265, 337, 383, etc.
2. *Uv'khen ten pachd'kha*, a focus of this volume.
3. Birnbaum, *High Holiday Prayer Book*, 386, for example. I have changed "Thee" and "Thy" to "You" and "your."
4. These four single sentence insertions, *Zokhrenu, Mi khamokha av harachamim, Ukh'tov l'chayim tovim,* and *B'sefer chayim,* called "Little *Zikhronot,*" form bookends within each *Amidah*, as they appear in the first two and the last two blessings. They all are appeals for life, but each insertion is unique in two ways: each is linguistically connected to the blessing in which it is inserted, and each appeals for life on behalf of a different constituency.
5. Amos Oz, *A Tale of Love and Darkness*, trans. Nicholas de Lange (New York: Houghton Mifflin Harcourt, 2004), 60.
6. Part of the *chatimah*, the seal on Rosh Hashanah and on Yom Kippur, of the central blessing *K'dushat Hayom*.

Universal in Vision, Particular by Necessity, by Rabbi Daniel G. Zemel

1. Avishai Margalit, *The Ethics of Memory* (Cambridge, MA: Harvard University Press, 2002), 74.
2. Yehuda Bauer, *Rethinking the Holocaust* (New Haven, CT: Yale University Press, 2001), 270.

Glossary

The glossary presents names and Hebrew words used regularly throughout this volume and provides the way they are pronounced. Sometimes two pronunciations are common, in which case the first is the way the word is sounded in Hebrew, and the second is the way it is sometimes heard in common speech, under the influence of English or, sometimes, of Yiddish, the folk language of Jews in northern and eastern Europe (a combination, mostly, of Hebrew and German). Our goal is to provide the way that many Jews actually use these words, not just the technically correct version.

The pronunciations are divided into syllables by dashes.

The accented syllable is written in capital letters.

"Kh" represents a guttural sound, similar to the German (as in "sprach").

The most common vowel is "a" as in "father," which appears here as "ah."

The short "e" (as in "get") is written as either "e" (when it is in the middle of a syllable) or "eh" (when it ends a syllable).

Similarly, the short "i" (as in "tin") is written as either "i" (when it is in the middle of a syllable) or "ih" (when it ends a syllable).

A long "o" (as in "Moses") is written as "oe" (as in the word "toe") or "oh" (as in the word "Oh!")

Alenu: See **Great** *Alenu*.

Amidah (pronounced ah-mee-DAH or, commonly, ah-MEE-dah): One of three titles for the second of two central units in the worship service, the first being the *Sh'ma* and Its Blessings. It is composed of a series of blessings, many of which are petitionary, except on Sabbaths and holidays, when the petitions are removed out of deference to the holiness of the day. Also called *T'fillah* (pronounced t'-fee-LAH or, commonly, t'-FEE-lah) and *Sh'moneh Esreh* (pronounced sh'-moh-NEH ehs-RAY or, commonly, sh'-MOH-neh EHS-ray). *Amidah* means "standing" and refers to the fact that the prayer is said standing up.

Apikorsim (pronounced ah-pee-kohr-SEEM; sing, *apikoros*, pronounced ah-pee-koh-ROHS or, commonly ah-pee-KOH-r's): Literally, "Epicurean"; hence, a group despised by the Rabbis for its denial of a God who

263

is engaged or even interested in human behavior, and which, therefore, denied also any objective morality other than the ethic of maximizing pleasure and minimizing pain. By extension, *apikoros* came to be a general term for "heretic," and, eventually, a Yiddish phrase also, with the playful implication of being a "mischief maker."

Ashkenazi (pronounced ahsh-k'-nah-ZEE or, commonly, ahsh-k'-NAH-zee): From the Hebrew word *Ashkenaz*, denoting the geographic area of northern and eastern Europe. Ashkenazi is the adjective, describing not just the inhabitants but also the liturgical rituals and customs practiced in Ashkenaz, as opposed to Sephardi (pronounced s'-fahr-DEE, or, commonly, s'-FAHR-dee), meaning rituals and customs derived from Sefarad, modern-day Spain and Portugal (see **Sephardi**).

Bar'khu (pronounced bah-r'-KHOO or, commonly, BAHR-khoo): Literally, the imperative verb "Praise!" and, therefore, the first word (and hence the name) of the official call to prayer in the morning and evening service. ("Praise [Adonai, who is to be praised].")

B'nei No'ach (pronounced b'NAY NOH-akh): Literally, "the children of Noah," or "Noahides," the term used to refer to all non-Jews, people descended from Noah who are not Jewish. The term is used particularly to describe the Noahide Covenant, the divine covenant made with humanity as a whole rather than the specifically Jewish covenant made with Abraham alone.

Bris (pronounced BRIS): Yiddish for Hebrew *brit* (pronounced BREET), "covenant"; hence, the word for circumcision, the ritual that admits baby boys into the covenant established by Abraham when he circumcised himself and his family (Genesis 17:23–27).

Challah (pronounced khah-LAH or, commonly, KHAH-lah): Originally, a loaf of bread (e.g., Leviticus 24:5, II Samuel 6:19) but also a portion of dough set aside for the priests (Numbers 15:19–20) and, nowadays, taken from the dough before baking and burned; also a kind of grain sacrifice (Leviticus 6:13). Commonly used (as in this book) simply as the name for the braided egg bread baked for Sabbath and festival meals.

Gehinnom (pronounced gay-hee-NAHM or, popularly, g'-HIH-nuhm): Originally the biblical name for a valley south of Jerusalem. It was associated with a cult involving the burning of children, against which the prophets inveighed; and from that negative association, *Gehinnom* came to be used as a metaphoric term for hell, the place where evil people would receive punishment after death.

Goyish (pronounced GOY-ish): An anglicized adjective of the Hebrew *goy*, "nation," a term yiddishized in modern times to mean "Gentile." Generally used disparagingly, however ("like a gentile"), to indicate something that seems to resemble Gentile rather than Jewish practice and should not, therefore, by adopted by Jews as if it were authentically Jewish.

Great *Alenu* (pronounced ah-LAY-noo). *Alenu* is the first word, and, therefore, the name, of a major prayer compiled in the second or third century as part of the New Year (Rosh Hashanah) service, but from about the fourteenth century on, used also as part of the concluding section of every daily service. *Alenu* means "it is incumbent upon us" and introduces the prayer's theme, our duty to praise God. On Rosh Hashanah, it still occurs also in its original position: as an introduction to the blowing of the shofar, at which time it is known as "the Great *Alenu*," and accompanied by a special melody for the occasion.

Haftarah (pronounced hahf-tah-RAH or, commonly, hahf-TOH-rah): The section of Scripture taken from Prophets and read publicly as part of Shabbat and holiday worship services. From a word meaning "to conclude," because it is the "concluding reading," that is, it follows a reading of Torah (the Five Books of Moses).

Halakhah (pronounced hah-lah-KHAH or, commonly, hah-LAH-khah): The Hebrew word for Jewish law. Used adjectivally in the anglicized form, "halakhic" (pronounced hah-LAH-khic), meaning "legal." From the Hebrew root *h.l.kh*, meaning "to walk" or "to go," denoting the way one should walk or go through life.

Havdalah (hahv-dah-LAH or, commonly, hahv-DAH-lah): Literally, "separation"; hence, the name of the ritual prayers said at the end of Sabbaths and holy days, marking the conclusion of sacred time and the onset of regular workday time.

Kabbalah (pronounced kah-bah-LAH or, popularly, kah-BAH-lah): A general term for Jewish mysticism, but used properly for a specific set of mystical doctrines that began in western Europe in the eleventh and twelfth centuries, was recorded in the *Zohar* (pronounced ZOH-hahr) in the thirteenth century, and then was further elaborated, especially in the Land of Israel (in Safed), in the sixteenth century. From a Hebrew word meaning "to receive" or to "welcome," it means also "tradition," implying the receiving of tradition from one's past.

Kashrut (pronounced kahsh-ROOT): The laws of keeping kosher (pronounced kah-SHEHR but, commonly, KOH-sh'r), that is, the Jewish dietary laws.

K'dushat Hayom (pronounced k'-doo-SHAHT hah-YOHM): Literally, "sanctification of the day"; hence, a prayer that concludes by acknowledging the sanctification of Shabbat or holy days. It occurs three times in the service: the middle blessing of the Shabbat and holy-day *Amidah* (see *Amidah*); the final blessing after reciting the Haftarah (see **Haftarah**); and the *Kiddush* (see **Kiddush**). Recited in the synagogue as part of the *Amidah* (see *Amidah*) for Shabbat and holy days. Also, refers to the *Kiddush* said at home, prior to eating the evening meal that inaugurates the onset of Shabbat and holy days.

Kiddush (pronounced kee-DOOSH but, commonly, KIH-dihsh): Literally, "sanctification," and shorthand for *K'dushat Hayom,* but used only for the version that is said at the conclusion of the evening service that inaugurates Shabbat and holy days; or at the home meal that similarly inaugurates those times. See *K'dushat Hayom.*

Klal Yisrael (pronounced K'LAL yis'rah-AYL): Literally, "the entirety of Israel," a term denoting the theological unity of all Jews, no matter what their denomination or ideological preference.

Kohelet (pronounced koh-HEH-leht): The Hebrew title for the biblical book of Ecclesiastes; from the first verse there, "The words of Kohelet, son of David, king in Jerusalem."

Kol Nidre (pronounced KOHL nee-DRAY or, commonly, kohl NIH-dray): Literally, "All these vows," the first words and, therefore, the name of an introductory prayer on the eve of Yom Kippur; the topic of Volume 2, *All These Vows*—Kol Nidre, in the Prayers of Awe series. Also used by extension to refer to the entire evening service in which *Kol Nidre* appears.

Limmud (pronounced lee-MOOD): Literally, "learning"; hence, a learning session or the act of learning itself. But used here as the title of an annual conference for Jewish learning that began in England and now has been replicated in many other countries worldwide.

Lubavitch (pronounced loo-BAH-vitch or, commonly, LOO-bah-vitch): The name of a Hasidic sect founded in 1796 by Shneur Zalman of Liadi, known also as CHaBaD (pronounced khah-BAHD), an acronym of the initials for *CHochmah, Binah,* and *Da'at* ("wisdom, understanding, and knowledge"), the first three *sefirot* (pronounced s'-fee-ROHT) or divine emanations, in kabbalistic theology.

Luftmensch (pronounced LOOFT-mehnsh): Yiddish for a person (*mensch*) who seems to live on air (*luft*) alone; that is, someone without noticeable means of employment, a common type in eastern nineteenth-century European Jewish settlements, where economic scarcity forced many to eke out a living by any means possible.

Machzor (pronounced mahkh-ZOHR or, commonly, MAHKH-zohr; pl. *machzorim*, pronounced mahkh-zoh-REEM): Literally, "cycle," as in "the annual cycle" of time; hence, the name given to the prayer book for holy days that occur once annually and that mark the passing of the year. Separate *machzorim* exist for Rosh Hashanah and Yom Kippur.

Malkhuyot (pronounced mahl-khoo-YOHT): Literally, "kingships," the name given to the first of three parts in the service of blowing the shofar on Rosh Hashanah, the part that emphasizes God's rule over all of creation. Preceded by the Great *Alenu* (see **Great *Alenu***).

Megillah (pronounced m'-gee-LAH or, commonly, m'-GIH-lah): Literally, "scroll," hence, the name for each of the "five scrolls" in the Hebrew canon (Ecclesiastes, Esther, Lamentations, Ruth, and Song of Songs); more specifically, when supplied with the definite article "the" (The *Megillah*), the designation of Esther alone.

Mezuzot (pronounced m'zoo-ZOHT, sing. *mezuzah*, pronounced m'zoo-ZAH or, commonly, m'-ZOO-zah): A tiny parchment scroll and its container, affixed to the doorposts of Jewish homes, from a biblical word meaning "doorpost" (Deuteronomy 6:9, 11:20). On the parchment are written Deuteronomy 6:4–9, and 11:13–21 (the relevant biblical instructions) with the name of God, *Shaddai*, on the reverse side; *Shaddai* is also taken here as an acronym (SH[a]D[a]Y) for the initials of the three Hebrew words *SHomer D'latot Yisra'el,* "Guardian of Israel's doors."

Mishnah (pronounced mihsh-NAH or, commonly, MIHSH-nah): The name of the first rabbinic code of Jewish law, c. 200 CE.

Mitzvah (pronounced meetz-VAH or, commonly, MITZ-vah; pl. *mitzvot*, pronounced meetz-VOHT): A Hebrew word used commonly to mean "good deed," but in the more technical sense, a commandment from God; from the Hebrew root *tz.v.h*, meaning "command."

Musaf (pronounced moo-SAHF or, commonly, MOO-sahf): Literally, "additional"; hence, the additional offering made in the ancient Temple cult on Sabbaths and holidays and, from there, the name given to the additional synagogue service for those days (following the morning service, *Shacharit* [pronounced shah-khah-REET]).

N'ilah (pronounced n'-ee-LAH or, commonly, n'-EE-lah): Literally, "locking," hence (1) the time at night when the gates to the sacrificial Temple of late antiquity were closed; and (2) additional worship services that developed then just for fast days, one of which, the final service for Yom Kippur, is still the norm today.

Noahide (pronounced NOH-ah-hide): See *B'nei No'ach*.

Pirkei D'rabbi Eliezer (pronounced peer-KAY d'RAH-bee e-lee-EH-zehr): An eighth-century rabbinic work summarizing and elaborating on tales and legends from many earlier rabbinic sources.

Piyyut (pronounced pee-YOOT, pl. *piyyutim*, pronounced pee-yoo-TEEM): Poem; more specifically, a term for a type of liturgical poetry common from late antiquity to the Middle Ages.

Prozdor (pronounced prohz-DOHR or, commonly, PROHZ-dohr): Anteroom to the dining room in a Roman villa, but used theologically to describe the life of this world, seen as a preparatory stage for life after death.

Rimon (pronounced ree-MOHN; pl. *rimonim*, pronounced ree-moh-NEEM): Literally, "pomegranate" (and in modern Hebrew, also "grenade"), but used traditionally as the name for decorative coverings, often made out of silver, for the wooden handles on a Torah scroll.

Satmar (pronounced SAHT-mahr): The name of a conservative Hasidic sect founded in 1928 by Yoel Teitelbaum (1887–1979) and named after its city of origin, Szatmar in Hungary (now Satu Mare in Romania).

Sephardi (pronounced s'-fahr-DEE or, commonly, s'-FAHR-dee): From the Hebrew word *Sefarad* (pronounced s'-fah-RAHD), meaning the geographic area of modern-day Spain and Portugal. Sephardi is the adjective, describing the liturgical rituals and customs that are derived from *Sefarad* prior to the expulsion of Jews from there at the end of the fifteenth century; as opposed to Ashkenazi (see **Ashkenazi**), meaning the liturgical rituals and customs common to northern and eastern Europe. Nowadays, Sephardi refers also to customs of Jews from North Africa and Arab lands whose ancestors came from Spain.

Sheol (pronounced sh'-OHL): The biblical name for the netherworld to which one descends after death.

Shiksah (pronounced SHIHK-sah): Somewhat old and deprecatory Yiddish word for a woman who is not Jewish.

Shofar (pronounced shoh-FAHR or, commonly, SHOH-fahr): Literally, "ram's horn," the instrument customarily sounded on Rosh Hashanah (the New Year), following rabbinic interpretation of Leviticus 23:24 ("a sacred occasion, commemorated with loud blasts,") and Numbers 29:1 ("a day when the horn is sounded").

Shofarot (pronounced shoh-fah-ROHT): Literally, "Shofar [verses]," the name given to the third of three parts in the service of blowing the shofar on Rosh Hashanah, the part that emphasizes the role played by the shofar in the Bible and, by implication, its role rabbinically in heralding the end of time.

Siddur (pronounced see-DOOR or, commonly, SIH-d'r): From the Hebrew word *seder,* meaning "order," and by extension, the name given to the order of daily and Sabbath prayers or prayer book. See also *Machzor.*

S'lichah (pronounced s'-lee-KHAH; pl. *s'lichot* pronounced s'-lee-KHOHT): From the root *s.l.ch,* "to forgive"; hence, a liturgical poem requesting divine forgiveness. The singular, *s'lichah,* is also the name given to a blessing in the daily *Amidah* requesting forgiveness. The plural, *s'lichot,* is also, by extension, the title given to penitential services held on Saturday night prior to Rosh Hashanah (or, if Rosh Hashanah falls in the first half of the week following, the Saturday before that).

Tanakh (pronounced tah-NAKH): The Hebrew word for Bible, an acronym T[a]N[a]KH, from the initials of the three Hebrew titles of the sections comprising it: T[orah] (the Five Books of Moses);

N[-'vi'im] (Prophets); and Kh [=K of K'tuvim] (the rest of the Bible, known as writings).

T'fillah (pronounced t'-fee-LAH or, commonly, t'-FEE-lah): A Hebrew word meaning "prayer," but used technically to denote a specific prayer, namely, the second of the two main units in the worship service; known also as the *Amidah* or the *Sh'moneh Esreh* (see *Amidah*). Also the title of the sixteenth blessing of the *Amidah*, a petition for God to accept our prayer.

Tikkun olam (pronounced tee-KOON oh-LAHM or, commonly, TEE-koon oh-LAHM): Literally, "repair of the world," a term taken today to denote social action, but originally a kabbalistic reference to the impact our actions have upon the world.

T'shuvah (pronounced t'-shoo-VAH or, commonly, t'-SHOO-vah): Literally "repentance"; also the title of the fifth blessing in the daily *Amidah*, a petition by worshipers that they successfully turn to God in heartfelt repentance.

Tzaddik (pronounced tsah-DEEK or, commonly, TSAH-deek): Literally, a "righteous" or saintly person. See *Tz'dakah*.

Tz'dakah (pronounced tz'-dah-KAH but, commonly, ts'-DAH-kah): Literally, "[acts of] righteousness," hence, the normative rabbinic word for charity.

Un'taneh Tokef (pronounced oo-n'-TAH-neh TOH-kehf): A *piyyut* (liturgical poem; see *piyyut*) for the High Holy Days emphasizing the awesome nature of these days when we stand before God for judgment; but originally, the climactic part of a longer poem for the *Amidah* called *k'dushta* (pronounced k'-doosh-TAH or, commonly, k'-DOOSH-tah). Although widely connected with a legend of Jewish martyrdom in medieval Germany, the poem more likely derives from a Byzantine poet, circa sixth century. It is known for its conclusion: "Penitence, prayer, and charity help the misfortune of the decree pass." See full treatment in Rabbi Lawrence A. Hoffman, PhD, ed., *Who by Fire, Who by Water*—Un'taneh Tokef (Woodstock, VT: Jewish Lights, 2010).

Yizkor (pronounced yihz-KOHR or, commonly, YIHZ-k'r): Literally, "May he remember," and hence, the first word (and title) of the main memorial prayer, titled "May God Remember" (*Yizkor Elohim*, pronounced yihz-KOHR eh-loh-HEEM).

Zikhronot (pronounced zikh-roh-NOHT): Literally, "Remembrances," the name given to the second of three parts in the service of blowing the shofar on Rosh Hashanah, the part that emphasizes God's acts of remembering.

Bible Study / Midrash

Passing Life's Tests: Spiritual Reflections on the Trial of Abraham, the Binding of Isaac *By Rabbi Bradley Shavit Artson, DHL*
Invites us to use this powerful tale as a tool for our own soul wrestling, to confront our existential sacrifices and enable us to face—and surmount—life's tests.
6 x 9, 176 pp, Quality PB, 978-1-58023-631-7 **$18.99**

The Messiah and the Jews: Three Thousand Years of Tradition, Belief and Hope *By Rabbi Elaine Rose Glickman; Foreword by Rabbi Neil Gillman, PhD; Preface by Rabbi Judith Z. Abrams, PhD*
Explores and explains an astonishing range of primary and secondary sources, infusing them with new meaning for the modern reader.
6 x 9, 192 pp, Quality PB, 978-1-58023-690-4 **$16.99**

Speaking Torah: Spiritual Teachings from around the Maggid's Table—in Two Volumes *By Arthur Green, with Ebn Leader, Ariel Evan Mayse and Or N. Rose*
The most powerful Hasidic teachings made accessible—from some of the world's preeminent authorities on Jewish thought and spirituality.
Volume 1—6 x 9, 512 pp, Hardcover, 978-1-58023-668-3 **$34.99**
Volume 2—6 x 9, 448 pp, Hardcover, 978-1-58023-694-2 **$34.99**

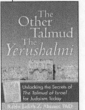

Masking and Unmasking Ourselves: Interpreting Biblical Texts on Clothing & Identity *By Dr. Norman J. Cohen*
Presents ten Bible stories that involve clothing in an essential way, as a means of learning about the text, its characters and their interactions.
6 x 9, 224 pp, HC, 978-1-58023-461-0 **$24.99**

The Genesis of Leadership: What the Bible Teaches Us about Vision, Values and Leading Change *By Rabbi Nathan Laufer; Foreword by Senator Joseph I. Lieberman*
6 x 9, 288 pp, Quality PB, 978-1-58023-352-1 **$18.99**

Hineini in Our Lives: Learning How to Respond to Others through 14 Biblical Texts and Personal Stories *By Rabbi Norman J. Cohen, PhD*
6 x 9, 240 pp, Quality PB, 978-1-58023-274-6 **$18.99**

The Modern Men's Torah Commentary: New Insights from Jewish Men on the 54 Weekly Torah Portions *Edited by Rabbi Jeffrey K. Salkin*
6 x 9, 368 pp, HC, 978-1-58023-395-8 **$24.99**

Moses and the Journey to Leadership: Timeless Lessons of Effective Management from the Bible and Today's Leaders *By Rabbi Norman J. Cohen, PhD*
6 x 9, 240 pp, Quality PB, 978-1-58023-351-4 **$18.99**; HC, 978-1-58023-227-2 **$21.99**

The Other Talmud—The *Yerushalmi*: Unlocking the Secrets of *The Talmud of Israel* for Judaism Today *By Rabbi Judith Z. Abrams, PhD*
6 x 9, 256 pp, HC, 978-1-58023-463-4 **$24.99**

Sage Tales: Wisdom and Wonder from the Rabbis of the Talmud
By Rabbi Burton L. Visotzky
6 x 9, 256 pp, Quality PB, 978-1-58023-791-8 **$19.99**; HC, 978-1-58023-456-6 **$24.99**

The Torah Revolution: Fourteen Truths That Changed the World
By Rabbi Reuven Hammer, PhD 6 x 9, 240 pp, HC, 978-1-58023-457-3 **$24.99**

The Wisdom of Judaism: An Introduction to the Values of the Talmud
By Rabbi Dov Peretz Elkins 6 x 9, 192 pp, Quality PB, 978-1-58023-327-9 **$16.99**

Theology / Philosophy

Believing and Its Tensions: A Personal Conversation about God, Torah, Suffering and Death in Jewish Thought
By Rabbi Neil Gillman, PhD
Explores the changing nature of belief and the complexities of reconciling the intellectual, emotional and moral questions of Gillman's own searching mind and soul.
5½ x 8½, 144 pp, HC, 978-1-58023-669-0 **$19.99**

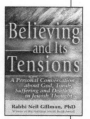

God of Becoming and Relationship: The Dynamic Nature of Process Theology   *By Rabbi Bradley Shavit Artson, DHL*
Explains how Process Theology breaks us free from the strictures of ancient Greek and medieval European philosophy, allowing us to see all creation as related patterns of energy through which we connect to everything.
6 x 9, 208 pp, HC, 978-1-58023-713-0 **$24.99**

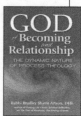

The Other Talmud—The *Yerushalmi*: Unlocking the Secrets of *The Talmud of Israel* for Judaism Today   *By Rabbi Judith Z. Abrams, PhD*
A fascinating—and stimulating—look at "the other Talmud" and the possibilities for Jewish life reflected there.   6 x 9, 256 pp, HC, 978-1-58023-463-4 **$24.99**

The Way of Man: According to Hasidic Teaching
By Martin Buber; New Translation and Introduction by Rabbi Bernard H. Mehlman and Dr. Gabriel E. Padawer; Foreword by Paul Mendes-Flohr
An accessible and engaging new translation of Buber's classic work—*available as an e-book only.*   eBook, 978-1-58023-601-0 Digital List Price **$14.99**

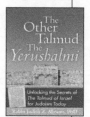

The Death of Death: Resurrection and Immortality in Jewish Thought
By Rabbi Neil Gillman, PhD   6 x 9, 336 pp, Quality PB, 978-1-58023-081-0 **$19.99**

Doing Jewish Theology: God, Torah & Israel in Modern Judaism   *By Rabbi Neil Gillman, PhD*
6 x 9, 304 pp, Quality PB, 978-1-58023-439-9 **$18.99**; HC, 978-1-58023-322-4 **$24.99**

From Defender to Critic: The Search for a New Jewish Self
By Dr. David Hartman   6 x 9, 336 pp, HC, 978-1-58023-515-0 **$35.00**

The God Who Hates Lies: Confronting & Rethinking Jewish Tradition
By Dr. David Hartman with Charlie Buckholtz   6 x 9, 208 pp, Quality PB, 978-1-58023-790-1 **$19.99**

A Heart of Many Rooms: Celebrating the Many Voices within Judaism
By Dr. David Hartman   6 x 9, 352 pp, Quality PB, 978-1-58023-156-5 **$19.95**

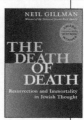

Jewish Theology in Our Time: A New Generation Explores the Foundations and Future of Jewish Belief   *Edited by Rabbi Elliot J. Cosgrove, PhD; Foreword by Rabbi David J. Wolpe; Preface by Rabbi Carole B. Balin, PhD*   6 x 9, 240 pp, Quality PB, 978-1-58023-630-0 **$19.99**; HC, 978-1-58023-413-9 **$24.99**

Maimonides—Essential Teachings on Jewish Faith & Ethics: The Book of Knowledge & the Thirteen Principles of Faith—Annotated & Explained
Translation and Annotation by Rabbi Marc D. Angel, PhD
5½ x 8½, 224 pp, Quality PB Original, 978-1-59473-311-6 **$18.99***

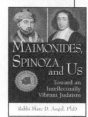

Maimonides, Spinoza and Us: Toward an Intellectually Vibrant Judaism
By Rabbi Marc D. Angel, PhD   6 x 9, 224 pp, HC, 978-1-58023-411-5 **$24.99**

Our Religious Brains: What Cognitive Science Reveals about Belief, Morality, Community and Our Relationship with God
By Rabbi Ralph D. Mecklenburger; Foreword by Dr. Howard Kelfer; Preface by Dr. Neil Gillman
6 x 9, 224 pp, HC, 978-1-58023-508-2 **$24.99**

Your Word Is Fire: The Hasidic Masters on Contemplative Prayer
Edited and translated by Rabbi Arthur Green, PhD, and Barry W. Holtz
6 x 9, 160 pp, Quality PB, 978-1-879045-25-5 **$16.99**

I Am Jewish
Personal Reflections Inspired by the Last Words of Daniel Pearl
Almost 150 Jews—both famous and not—from all walks of life, from all around the world, write about many aspects of their Judaism.
Edited by Judea and Ruth Pearl   6 x 9, 304 pp, Deluxe PB w/ flaps, 978-1-58023-259-3 **$19.99**
Download a free copy of the *I Am Jewish Teacher's Guide* at www.jewishlights.com.

**A book from SkyLight Paths, Jewish Lights' sister imprint*

Inspiration

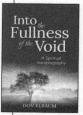

Into the Fullness of the Void: A Spiritual Autobiography *By Dov Elbaum*
The spiritual autobiography of one of Israel's leading cultural figures that provides insights and guidance for all of us. 6 x 9, 304 pp, Quality PB Original, 978-1-58023-715-4 **$18.99**

Saying No and Letting Go: Jewish Wisdom on Making Room for What Matters Most *By Rabbi Edwin Goldberg, DHL; Foreword by Rabbi Naomi Levy*
Taps into timeless Jewish wisdom that teaches how to "hold on tightly" to the things that matter most while learning to "let go lightly" of the demands and worries that do not ultimately matter. 6 x 9, 192 pp, Quality PB, 978-1-58023-670-6 **$16.99**

The Bridge to Forgiveness: Stories and Prayers for Finding God and Restoring Wholeness *By Rabbi Karyn D. Kedar* 6 x 9, 176 pp, Quality PB, 978-1-58023-451-1 **$16.99**

The Empty Chair: Finding Hope and Joy—Timeless Wisdom from a Hasidic Master, Rebbe Nachman of Breslov *Adapted by Moshe Mykoff and the Breslov Research Institute* 4 x 6, 128 pp, Deluxe PB w/ flaps, 978-1-879045-67-5 **$9.99**

A Formula for Proper Living: Practical Lessons from Life and Torah *By Rabbi Abraham J. Twerski, MD* 6 x 9, 144 pp, HC, 978-1-58023-402-3 **$19.99**

The Gentle Weapon: Prayers for Everyday and Not-So-Everyday Moments—Timeless Wisdom from the Teachings of the Hasidic Master, Rebbe Nachman of Breslov *Adapted by Moshe Mykoff and S. C. Mizrahi, together with the Breslov Research Institute* 4 x 6, 144 pp, Deluxe PB w/ flaps, 978-1-58023-022-3 **$9.99**

The God Upgrade: Finding Your 21st-Century Spirituality in Judaism's 5,000-Year-Old Tradition *By Rabbi Jamie Korngold; Foreword by Rabbi Harold M. Schulweis* 6 x 9, 176 pp, Quality PB, 978-1-58023-443-6 **$15.99**

God Whispers: Stories of the Soul, Lessons of the Heart *By Rabbi Karyn D. Kedar* 6 x 9, 176 pp, Quality PB, 978-1-58023-088-9 **$16.99**

God's To-Do List: 103 Ways to Be an Angel and Do God's Work on Earth *By Dr. Ron Wolfson* 6 x 9, 144 pp, Quality PB, 978-1-58023-301-9 **$16.99**

Happiness and the Human Spirit: The Spirituality of Becoming the Best You Can Be *By Rabbi Abraham J. Twerski, MD* 6 x 9, 176 pp, Quality PB, 978-1-58023-404-7 **$16.99**; HC, 978-1-58023-343-9 **$19.99**

Life's Daily Blessings: Inspiring Reflections on Gratitude and Joy for Every Day, Based on Jewish Wisdom *By Rabbi Kerry M. Olitzky* 4½ x 6½, 368 pp, Quality PB, 978-1-58023-396-5 **$16.99**

The Magic of Hebrew Chant: Healing the Spirit, Transforming the Mind, Deepening Love *By Rabbi Shefa Gold; Foreword by Sylvia Boorstein* 6 x 9, 352 pp, Quality PB, 978-1-58023-671-3 **$24.99**

Restful Reflections: Nighttime Inspiration to Calm the Soul, Based on Jewish Wisdom *By Rabbi Kerry M. Olitzky and Rabbi Lori Forman-Jacobi* 4½ x 6½, 448 pp, Quality PB, 978-1-58023-091-9 **$16.99**

Sacred Intentions: Morning Inspiration to Strengthen the Spirit, Based on Jewish Wisdom *By Rabbi Kerry M. Olitzky and Rabbi Lori Forman-Jacobi* 4½ x 6½, 448 pp, Quality PB, 978-1-58023-061-2 **$16.99**

The Seven Questions You're Asked in Heaven: Reviewing and Renewing Your Life on Earth *By Dr. Ron Wolfson* 6 x 9, 176 pp, Quality PB, 978-1-58023-407-8 **$16.99**

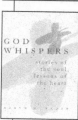

Kabbalah / Mysticism

Ehyeh: A Kabbalah for Tomorrow *By Rabbi Arthur Green, PhD* 6 x 9, 224 pp, Quality PB, 978-1-58023-213-5 **$18.99**

The Gift of Kabbalah: Discovering the Secrets of Heaven, Renewing Your Life on Earth *By Tamar Frankiel, PhD* 6 x 9, 256 pp, Quality PB, 978-1-58023-141-1 **$16.95**

Jewish Mysticism and the Spiritual Life: Classical Texts, Contemporary Reflections *Edited by Dr. Lawrence Fine, Dr. Eitan Fishbane and Rabbi Or N. Rose* 6 x 9, 256 pp, HC, 978-1-58023-434-4 **$24.99**; Quality PB, 978-1-58023-719-2 **$18.99**

Seek My Face: A Jewish Mystical Theology *By Rabbi Arthur Green, PhD* 6 x 9, 304 pp, Quality PB, 978-1-58023-130-5 **$19.95**

Zohar: Annotated & Explained *Translation & Annotation by Dr. Daniel C. Matt; Foreword by Andrew Harvey* 5½ x 8½, 176 pp, Quality PB, 978-1-893361-51-5 **$16.99**
(A book from SkyLight Paths, Jewish Lights' sister imprint)

See also *The Way Into Jewish Mystical Tradition* in The Way Into... Series.

Spirituality

Amazing Chesed: Living a Grace-Filled Judaism
By Rabbi Rami Shapiro Drawing from ancient and contemporary, traditional and non-traditional Jewish wisdom, reclaims the idea of grace in Judaism.
6 x 9, 176 pp, Quality PB, 978-1-58023-624-9 **$16.99**

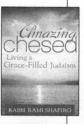

Jewish with Feeling: A Guide to Meaningful Jewish Practice
By Rabbi Zalman Schachter-Shalomi with Joel Segel
Takes off from basic questions like "Why be Jewish?" and whether the word God still speaks to us today and lays out a vision for a whole-person Judaism.
5½ x 8½, 288 pp, Quality PB, 978-1-58023-691-1 **$19.99**

Perennial Wisdom for the Spiritually Independent: Sacred Teachings— Annotated & Explained   *Annotation by Rami Shapiro; Foreword by Richard Rohr*
Weaves sacred texts and teachings from the world's major religions into a coherent exploration of the five core questions at the heart of every religion's search.
5½ x 8½, 336 pp, Quality PB Original, 978-1-59473-515-8 **$16.99**

Aleph-Bet Yoga: Embodying the Hebrew Letters for Physical and Spiritual Well-Being
By Steven A. Rapp; Foreword by Tamar Frankiel, PhD, and Judy Greenfeld; Preface by Hart Lazer
7 x 10, 128 pp, b/w photos, Quality PB, Lay-flat binding, 978-1-58023-162-6 **$16.95**

A Book of Life: Embracing Judaism as a Spiritual Practice
By Rabbi Michael Strassfeld 6 x 9, 544 pp, Quality PB, 978-1-58023-247-0 **$24.99**

Bringing the Psalms to Life: How to Understand and Use the Book of Psalms
By Rabbi Daniel F. Polish, PhD 6 x 9, 208 pp, Quality PB, 978-1-58023-157-2 **$18.99**

Does the Soul Survive? A Jewish Journey to Belief in Afterlife, Past Lives & Living with Purpose *By Rabbi Elie Kaplan Spitz; Foreword by Brian L. Weiss, MD*
6 x 9, 288 pp, Quality PB, 978-1-58023-165-7 **$18.99**

Entering the Temple of Dreams: Jewish Prayers, Movements and Meditations for the End of the Day *By Tamar Frankiel, PhD, and Judy Greenfeld*
7 x 10, 192 pp, illus., Quality PB, 978-1-58023-079-7 **$16.95**

First Steps to a New Jewish Spirit: Reb Zalman's Guide to Recapturing the Intimacy & Ecstasy in Your Relationship with God *By Rabbi Zalman M. Schachter-Shalomi with Donald Gropman* 6 x 9, 144 pp, Quality PB, 978-1-58023-182-4 **$16.95**

Foundations of Sephardic Spirituality: The Inner Life of Jews of the Ottoman Empire
By Rabbi Marc D. Angel, PhD 6 x 9, 224 pp, Quality PB, 978-1-58023-341-5 **$18.99**

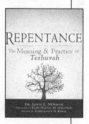

God & the Big Bang: Discovering Harmony between Science & Spirituality
By Dr. Daniel C. Matt 6 x 9, 216 pp, Quality PB, 978-1-879045-89-7 **$18.99**

God in Our Relationships: Spirituality between People from the Teachings of Martin Buber *By Rabbi Dennis S. Ross* 5½ x 8½, 160 pp, Quality PB, 978-1-58023-147-3 **$16.95**

The Jewish Lights Spirituality Handbook: A Guide to Understanding, Exploring & Living a Spiritual Life *Edited by Stuart M. Matlins*
6 x 9, 456 pp, Quality PB, 978-1-58023-093-3 **$19.99**

Judaism, Physics and God: Searching for Sacred Metaphors in a Post-Einstein World
By Rabbi David W. Nelson 6 x 9, 352 pp, Quality PB, inc. reader's discussion guide, 978-1-58023-306-4 **$18.99**; HC, 352 pp, 978-1-58023-252-4 **$24.99**

Meaning & Mitzvah: Daily Practices for Reclaiming Judaism through Prayer, God, Torah, Hebrew, Mitzvot and Peoplehood *By Rabbi Goldie Milgram*
7 x 9, 336 pp, Quality PB, 978-1-58023-256-2 **$19.99**

Repentance: The Meaning and Practice of Teshuvah
By Dr. Louis E. Newman; Foreword by Rabbi Harold M. Schulweis; Preface by Rabbi Karyn D. Kedar
6 x 9, 256 pp, HC, 978-1-58023-426-9 **$24.99** Quality PB, 978-1-58023-718-5 **$18.99**

The Sabbath Soul: Mystical Reflections on the Transformative Power of Holy Time
Selection, Translation and Commentary by Eitan Fishbane, PhD
6 x 9, 208 pp, Quality PB, 978-1-58023-459-7 **$18.99**

Tanya, the Masterpiece of Hasidic Wisdom: Selections Annotated & Explained
Translation & Annotation by Rabbi Rami Shapiro; Foreword by Rabbi Zalman M. Schachter-Shalomi
5½ x 8½, 240 pp, Quality PB, 978-1-59473-275-1 **$16.99**

These Are the Words, 2nd Edition: A Vocabulary of Jewish Spiritual Life
By Rabbi Arthur Green, PhD 6 x 9, 320 pp, Quality PB, 978-1-58023-494-8 **$19.99**

Spirituality / Prayer

Davening: A Guide to Meaningful Jewish Prayer
By Rabbi Zalman Schachter-Shalomi with Joel Segel; Foreword by Rabbi Lawrence Kushner
A fresh approach to prayer for all who wish to appreciate the power of prayer's poetry, song and ritual, and to join the age-old conversation that Jews have had with God.   6 x 9, 240 pp, Quality PB, 978-1-58023-627-0 **$18.99**

Jewish Men Pray: Words of Yearning, Praise, Petition, Gratitude and Wonder from Traditional and Contemporary Sources
Edited by Rabbi Kerry M. Olitzky and Stuart M. Matlins; Foreword by Rabbi Bradley Shavit Artson, DHL
A celebration of Jewish men's voices in prayer—to strengthen, heal, comfort, and inspire—from the ancient world up to our own day.
5 x 7¼, 400 pp, HC, 978-1-58023-628-7 **$19.99**

Making Prayer Real: Leading Jewish Spiritual Voices on Why Prayer Is Difficult and What to Do about It *By Rabbi Mike Comins* 6 x 9, 320 pp, Quality PB, 978-1-58023-417-7 **$18.99**

Witnesses to the One: The Spiritual History of the *Sh'ma*
By Rabbi Joseph B. Meszler; Foreword by Rabbi Elyse Goldstein
6 x 9, 176 pp, Quality PB, 978-1-58023-400-9 **$16.99**; HC, 978-1-58023-309-5 **$19.99**

My People's Prayer Book Series: Traditional Prayers, Modern Commentaries *Edited by Rabbi Lawrence A. Hoffman, PhD*
Provides diverse and exciting commentary to the traditional liturgy. Will help you find new wisdom in Jewish prayer, and bring liturgy into your life. Each book includes Hebrew text, modern translations and commentaries from all perspectives of the Jewish world.

Vol. 1—The *Sh'ma* and Its Blessings
7 x 10, 168 pp, HC, 978-1-879045-79-8 **$29.99**
Vol. 2—The *Amidah* 7 x 10, 240 pp, HC, 978-1-879045-80-4 **$24.95**
Vol. 3—*P'sukei D'zimrah* (Morning Psalms)
7 x 10, 240 pp, HC, 978-1-879045-81-1 **$29.99**
Vol. 4—*Seder K'riat Hatorah* (The Torah Service)
7 x 10, 264 pp, HC, 978-1-879045-82-8 **$29.99**
Vol. 5—*Birkhot Hashachar* (Morning Blessings)
7 x 10, 240 pp, HC, 978-1-879045-83-5 **$24.95**
Vol. 6—*Tachanun* and Concluding Prayers
7 x 10, 240 pp, HC, 978-1-879045-84-2 **$24.95**
Vol. 7—Shabbat at Home 7 x 10, 240 pp, HC, 978-1-879045-85-9 **$24.95**
Vol. 8—*Kabbalat Shabbat* (Welcoming Shabbat in the Synagogue)
7 x 10, 240 pp, HC, 978-1-58023-121-3 **$24.99**
Vol. 9—Welcoming the Night: *Minchah* and *Ma'ariv* (Afternoon and Evening Prayer) 7 x 10, 272 pp, HC, 978-1-58023-262-3 **$24.99**
Vol. 10—Shabbat Morning: *Shacharit* and *Musaf* (Morning and Additional Services) 7 x 10, 240 pp, HC, 978-1-58023-240-1 **$29.99**

Spirituality / Lawrence Kushner

I'm God; You're Not: Observations on Organized Religion & Other Disguises of the Ego
6 x 9, 256 pp, Quality PB, 978-1-58023-513-6 **$18.99**; HC, 978-1-58023-441-2 **$21.99**

The Book of Letters: A Mystical Hebrew Alphabet
Popular HC Edition, 6 x 9, 80 pp, 2-color text, 978-1-879045-00-2 **$24.95**
Collector's Limited Edition, 9 x 12, 80 pp, gold-foil-embossed pages, w/ limited-edition silkscreened print, 978-1-879045-04-0 **$349.00**

The Book of Miracles: A Young Person's Guide to Jewish Spiritual Awareness
6 x 9, 96 pp, 2-color illus., HC, 978-1-879045-78-1 **$16.95** *For ages 9–13*

God Was in This Place & I, i Did Not Know: Finding Self, Spirituality and Ultimate Meaning 6 x 9, 192 pp, Quality PB, 978-1-879045-33-0 **$16.95**

Honey from the Rock: An Introduction to Jewish Mysticism
6 x 9, 176 pp, Quality PB, 978-1-58023-073-5 **$18.99**

Invisible Lines of Connection: Sacred Stories of the Ordinary
5½ x 8½, 160 pp, Quality PB, 978-1-879045-98-9 **$16.99**

The Way Into Jewish Mystical Tradition
6 x 9, 224 pp, Quality PB, 978-1-58023-200-5 **$18.99**; HC, 978-1-58023-029-2 **$21.95**

Holidays / Holy Days

Prayers of Awe Series

An exciting new series that examines the High Holy Day liturgy to enrich the praying experience of everyone—whether experienced worshipers or guests who encounter Jewish prayer for the very first time.

May God Remember: Memory and Memorializing in Judaism—*Yizkor*
Edited by Rabbi Lawrence A. Hoffman, PhD
Examines the history and ideas behind *Yizkor*, the Jewish memorial service, and this fascinating chapter in Jewish piety.
6 x 9, 304 pp, HC, 978-1-58023-689-8 **$24.99**

We Have Sinned—Sin and Confession in Judaism: *Ashamnu* and *Al Chet*
Edited by Rabbi Lawrence A. Hoffman, PhD 6 x 9, 304 pp, HC, 978-1-58023-612-6 **$24.99**

Who by Fire, Who by Water—*Un'taneh Tokef*
Edited by Rabbi Lawrence A. Hoffman, PhD
6 x 9, 272 pp, Quality PB, 978-1-58023-672-0 **$19.99**; HC, 978-1-58023-424-5 **$24.99**

All These Vows—*Kol Nidre*
Edited by Rabbi Lawrence A. Hoffman, PhD 6 x 9, 288 pp, HC, 978-1-58023-430-6 **$24.99**

Rosh Hashanah Readings: Inspiration, Information and Contemplation
Yom Kippur Readings: Inspiration, Information and Contemplation
Edited by Rabbi Dov Peretz Elkins; Section Introductions from Arthur Green's These Are the Words
Rosh Hashanah: 6 x 9, 400 pp, Quality PB, 978-1-58023-437-5 **$19.99**
Yom Kippur: 6 x 9, 368 pp, Quality PB, 978-1-58023-438-2 **$19.99**; HC, 978-1-58023-271-5 **$24.99**

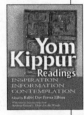

Reclaiming Judaism as a Spiritual Practice: Holy Days and Shabbat
By Rabbi Goldie Milgram 7 x 9, 272 pp, Quality PB, 978-1-58023-205-0 **$19.99**

The Sabbath Soul: Mystical Reflections on the Transformative Power of Holy Time
Selection, Translation and Commentary by Eitan Fishbane, PhD
6 x 9, 208 pp, Quality PB, 978-1-58023-459-7 **$18.99**

Shabbat, 2nd Edition: The Family Guide to Preparing for and Celebrating the Sabbath
By Dr. Ron Wolfson 7 x 9, 320 pp, Illus., Quality PB, 978-1-58023-164-0 **$21.99**

Hanukkah, 2nd Edition: The Family Guide to Spiritual Celebration
By Dr. Ron Wolfson 7 x 9, 240 pp, Illus., Quality PB, 978-1-58023-122-0 **$18.95**

Passover

My People's Passover Haggadah
Traditional Texts, Modern Commentaries
Edited by Rabbi Lawrence A. Hoffman, PhD, and David Arnow, PhD
A diverse and exciting collection of commentaries on the traditional Passover Haggadah—in two volumes!
Vol. 1: 7 x 10, 304 pp, HC, 978-1-58023-354-5 **$24.99**
Vol. 2: 7 x 10, 320 pp, HC, 978-1-58023-346-0 **$24.99**

Creating Lively Passover Seders, 2nd Edition: A Sourcebook of Engaging Tales,
Texts & Activities *By David Arnow, PhD* 7 x 9, 464 pp, Quality PB, 978-1-58023-444-3 **$24.99**

Freedom Journeys: The Tale of Exodus and Wilderness across Millennia
By Rabbi Arthur O. Waskow and Rabbi Phyllis O. Berman
6 x 9, 288 pp, HC, 978-1-58023-445-0 **$24.99**

Leading the Passover Journey: The Seder's Meaning Revealed, the Haggadah's
Story Retold *By Rabbi Nathan Laufer*
6 x 9, 224 pp, Quality PB, 978-1-58023-399-6 **$18.99**

Passover, 2nd Edition: The Family Guide to Spiritual Celebration
By Dr. Ron Wolfson with Joel Lurie Grishaver 7 x 9, 416 pp, Quality PB, 978-1-58023-174-9 **$19.95**

The Women's Passover Companion: Women's Reflections on the Festival of Freedom
Edited by Rabbi Sharon Cohen Anisfeld, Tara Mohr and Catherine Spector; Foreword by Paula E. Hyman
6 x 9, 352 pp, Quality PB, 978-1-58023-231-9 **$19.99**; HC, 978-1-58023-128-2 **$24.95**

The Women's Seder Sourcebook: Rituals & Readings for Use at the Passover Seder
Edited by Rabbi Sharon Cohen Anisfeld, Tara Mohr and Catherine Spector
6 x 9, 384 pp, Quality PB, 978-1-58023-232-6 **$19.99**

About Jewish Lights

People of all faiths and backgrounds yearn for books that attract, engage, educate, and spiritually inspire.

Our principal goal is to stimulate thought and help all people learn about who the Jewish People are, where they come from, and what the future can be made to hold. While people of our diverse Jewish heritage are the primary audience, our books speak to people in the Christian world as well and will broaden their understanding of Judaism and the roots of their own faith.

We bring to you authors who are at the forefront of spiritual thought and experience. While each has something different to say, they all say it in a voice that you can hear.

Our books are designed to welcome you and then to engage, stimulate, and inspire. We judge our success not only by whether or not our books are beautiful and commercially successful, but by whether or not they make a difference in your life.

For your information and convenience, at the back of this book we have provided a list of other Jewish Lights books you might find interesting and useful. They cover all the categories of your life:

Bar/Bat Mitzvah	Life Cycle
Bible Study / Midrash	Meditation
Children's Books	Men's Interest
Congregation Resources	Parenting
Current Events / History	Prayer / Ritual / Sacred Practice
Ecology / Environment	Social Justice
Fiction: Mystery, Science Fiction	Spirituality
Grief / Healing	Theology / Philosophy
Holidays / Holy Days	Travel
Inspiration	Twelve Steps
Kabbalah / Mysticism / Enneagram	Women's Interest

Stuart M. Matlins, Publisher

Printed in the USA
CPSIA information can be obtained
at www.ICGtesting.com
JSHW022213140824
68134JS00018B/1028